CIPS Study Matters

Level 6

Graduate Diploma in Purchasing and Supply

COURSE BOOK

Legal Aspects

in

Purchasing and Supply

Printed and distributed by the Chartered Institute of Purchasing & Supply

Easton House, Easton on the Hill, Stamford, Lincolnshire PE9 3NZ

Tel: +44 (0) 1780 756 777

Fax: +44 (0) 1780 751 610

Email: info@cips.org

Website: www.cips.org

First edition July 2006
Second edition April 2009
Third edition April 2010
Reprinted with minor amendments October 2010

Contents

Preface

Welcome to your new Study Pack.

For each subject you have to study, your Study Pack consists of three elements.

- A **Course Book** (the current volume). This provides detailed coverage of all topics specified in the unit content.

- A small-format volume of **Passnotes**. For each learning objective, these highlight and summarise the key points of knowledge and understanding that should underpin an exam answer. Use your Passnotes in the days and weeks leading up to the exam.

- An extensive range of **online resources**. These include a **Quick Start Guide** (a rapid 40-page overview of the subject), practice questions of exam standard (with full suggested solutions), notes on recent technical developments in the subject area, and recent news items (ideal for enhancing your solutions in the exam). These can all be downloaded from the study resources area at www.cips.org. You will need to log in with your membership details to access this information.

For a full explanation of how to use your new Study Pack, turn now to page xiii. And good luck in your exams!

A note on style

Throughout your Study Packs you will find that we use the masculine form of personal pronouns. This convention is adopted purely for the sake of stylistic convenience – we just don't like saying 'he/she' all the time. Please don't think this reflects any kind of bias or prejudice.

October 2010

The Exam

The format of the paper

The time allowed is three hours. The examination is in two sections.

Section A – case study scenario, with two application questions based on the case study, each worth 25 marks.

Section B – questions to test knowledge and understanding. Candidates will be required to answer two questions from a choice of four. As with Section A, questions will be worth 25 marks each.

The unit content

The unit content is reproduced below, together with reference to the chapter in this Course Book where each topic is covered.

Unit characteristics

This unit seeks to familiarise students with the law that regulates the purchasing function.

The purchasing and supply manager needs to understand where legal issues may impact on the organisation and when to take action to avoid risk. They should also be able to recognise situations when the appropriate action would be to seek legal expertise.

The content provides an essential overview of different legal issues with particular emphasis on contractual issues and sale of goods legislation. Other areas covered include the legal aspects of outsourcing, competition law, intellectual property law, electronic trading and international trade*. It is designed to assist professionals who work in either the public or private sector.

Statements of Practice

On completion of this unit, students will be able to:

*   Analyse the process of contract formation and assess the validity of a range of contract clauses

*   Assess the legal rules governing the sale of goods and services, third party rights and agency arrangements

*   Diagnose the impact of specific UK and EU regulations on the purchasing and supply function

*   Analyse the statutory provisions applicable to a range of intellectual property rights (IPRs)

*   *When the syllabus was first published in 2006 it included coverage of legal aspects of international trade. At that point, the detail of coverage was specified in the final two syllabus headings, numbers 4.3 and 4.4. In the revised syllabus, effective from the November 2009 exam onwards, these two syllabus headings have been removed and no coverage of international trade is now required. The reference to international trade above (under Unit Characteristics) is presumably just an oversight – it should have been removed from the revised syllabus.*

Learning objectives and indicative content

1.0 Contract law
(Weighting 35%)

Chapter

1.1 Analyse the legal problems that may arise from the process of contract formation and the problems of reconciling the buyer's terms and conditions with those of the seller when faced with the battle of the forms. — **2**

- Offer and acceptance — **3**
- Consideration — **4**
- Battle of the forms — **3**
- Letters of intent — **5**
- Letters of comfort — **18**
- Electronic contracting — **5**

1.2 Distinguish between different types of contractual terms and assess the legal validity of specific types of contractual clauses. — **6**

- Expressed and implied terms — **6**
- Conditions, warranties and innominate terms — **6**
- Exclusion and limitation clauses — **6**
- Indemnity clauses — **6**
- *Force majeure* clauses — **6**
- Penalty and liquidated damages clauses — **9**
- Retention of title clauses — **13**

1.3 Determine the factors that may vitiate consent to a contract. — **7**

- Duress — **7**
- Misrepresentation — **7**
- Mistake — **7**
- Undue influence — **7**

1.4 Evaluate the different common law methods by which a contract is terminated and the remedies available should a contract be breached. — **8, 13**

- Performance — **8**
- Frustration — **8**
- Agreement including variation of a contract — **8**
- Breach — **8, 13**
- Assessment of unliquidated damages — **9**
- Equitable remedies — **9**

How to Use Your Study Pack

Familiarisation

At this point you should begin to familiarise yourself with the package of benefits you have purchased.

- Go to www.cips.org and log on. Then go to Study and Qualify/Study Resources. Browse through the free content relating to this subject.

- Download the Quick Start Guide and print it out. Open up a ring binder and make the Quick Start Guide your first item in there.

- Now glance briefly through the Course Book (the text you're reading right now!) and the Passnotes.

Organising your study

'Organising' is the key word: unless you are a very exceptional student, you will find a haphazard approach is insufficient, particularly if you are having to combine study with the demands of a full-time job.

A good starting point is to timetable your studies, in broad terms, between now and the date of the examination. How many subjects are you attempting? How many chapters are there in the Course Book for each subject? Now do the sums: how many days/weeks do you have for each chapter to be studied?

Remember:

- Not every week can be regarded as a study week – you may be going on holiday, for example, or there may be weeks when the demands of your job are particularly heavy. If these can be foreseen, you should allow for them in your timetabling.

- You also need a period leading up to the exam in which you will revise and practise what you have learned.

Once you have done the calculations, make a week-by-week timetable for yourself for each paper, allowing for study and revision of the entire unit content between now and the date of the exams.

Getting started

Aim to find a quiet and undisturbed location for your study, and plan as far as possible to use the same period each day. Getting into a routine helps avoid wasting time. Make sure you have all the materials you need before you begin – keep interruptions to a minimum.

Begin by reading through your Quick Start Guide. This should take no more than a couple of hours, even reading slowly. By the time you have finished this you will have a reasonable grounding in the subject area. You will build on this by working through the Course Book.

Using the Course Book

You should refer to the Course Book to the extent that you need it.

- If you are a newcomer to the subject, you will probably need to read through the Course Book quite thoroughly. This will be the case for most students.

- If some areas are already familiar to you – either through earlier studies or through your practical work experience – you may choose to skip sections of the Course Book.

The content of the Course Book

This Course Book has been designed to give detailed coverage of every topic in the unit content. As you will see from pages vii–xi, each topic mentioned in the unit content is dealt with in a chapter of the Course Book. For the most part the order of the Course Book follows the order of the unit content closely, though departures from this principle have occasionally been made in the interest of a logical learning order.

Each chapter begins with a reference to the learning objectives and unit content to be covered in the chapter. Each chapter is divided into sections, listed in the introduction to the chapter, and for the most part being actual captions from the unit content.

All of this enables you to monitor your progress through the unit content very easily and provides reassurance that you are tackling every subject that is examinable.

Each chapter contains the following features.

- Introduction, setting out the main topics to be covered
- Clear coverage of each topic in a concise and approachable format
- A chapter summary
- Self-test questions

The study phase

For each chapter you should begin by glancing at the main headings (listed at the start of the chapter). Then read fairly rapidly through the body of the text to absorb the main points. If it's there in the text, you can be sure it's there for a reason, so try not to skip unless the topic is one you are familiar with already.

Then return to the beginning of the chapter to start a more careful reading. You may want to take brief notes as you go along, but bear in mind that you already have your Quick Start Guide and Passnotes – there is no point in duplicating what you can find there.

Test your recall and understanding of the material by attempting the self-test questions. These are accompanied by cross-references to paragraphs where you can check your answers and refresh your memory.

Practising what you have learned

Once you think you have learned enough about the subject, or about a particular topic within the overall subject area, it's good to practise. Access the study resources at www.cips.org, and download a practice question on the relevant area. Alternatively, download a past exam question. Attempt a solution yourself before looking at our suggested solution or the Senior Assessor's comments.

Make notes of any mistakes you made, or any areas where your answer could be improved. If there is anything you can't understand, you are welcome to email us for clarification (course.books@cips.org).

The revision phase

Your approach to revision should be methodical and you should aim to tackle each main area of the unit content in turn. Begin by re-reading your Quick Start Guide. This gives an overview that will help to focus your more detailed study. Then re-read your notes and/or the separate Passnotes accompanying this Course Book. Then return to question practice. Review your own solutions to the practice questions you have had time to attempt. If there are gaps, try to find time to attempt some more questions, or at least to review the suggested solutions.

Additional reading

Your Study Pack provides you with the key information needed for each module but CIPS strongly advocates reading as widely as possible to augment and reinforce your understanding. CIPS produces an official reading list of books, which can be downloaded from the bookshop area of the CIPS website.

To help you, we have identified one essential textbook for each subject. We recommend that you read this for additional information.

The essential textbook for this unit is *Law for Purchasing and Supply* by Ivor and Margaret Griffiths, published by Pearson (ISBN: 0–273–64679–6).

CHAPTER 1

Elements of English Law

Chapter headings

1   The exam syllabus

2   The meaning of law

3   The sources of law

4   The doctrine of judicial precedent

Introduction

In this chapter we provide a brief overview of the Legal Aspects syllabus and look at some of the basic elements in the English legal system: the way in which law is created, the procedures for applying it, the structure of the courts and so on.

1   The exam syllabus

1.1   The Legal Aspects syllabus is divided into four sections. You are required to study the law of contract and the law relating to sale and supply of goods and services. You also study manufacturers' and subcontractors' liability, legal aspects of tendering and outsourcing, competition law, intellectual property and confidentiality.

1.2   The importance of this material to purchasing professionals should be fairly obvious. Much of your professional work will be concerned with buying from suppliers, and every time you do so you are entering into a contract – a legally binding agreement. The law gives rise to rights and obligations for both buyer and seller and it is clearly important that you understand these clearly.

1.3   To do so you first need a sound grasp of the general principles governing contracts of all kinds. These have grown up over the centuries as legal principles and procedures have developed. However, Parliament has also played a part by codifying many of these principles in the form of legal statutes. This applies for example to the law relating to sale of goods.

1.4   Sale of goods is an area of crucial concern in your professional work. It involves a knowledge of general contract principles, because purchasing goods from a supplier is just one special type of contract. But it also involves knowledge of rules laid down by Parliament in the Sale of Goods Act 1979 (and its later amendments).

1.5   Manufacturers' and subcontractors' liability, the rights of third parties, and legal aspects of tendering and outsourcing are all topics related to contract and the sale of goods.

1.6 Competition is partly concerned with regulations designed to restrict the growth of monopoly. In general, governments regard it as unhealthy in economic terms if a single organisation controls the supply of a particular commodity or service. A measure of competition is regarded as essential in order to raise standards and keep prices at a reasonable level. To promote these objectives the UK government, and the European Union, have made regulations that restrict an organisation's ability to secure a monopoly position.

1.7 Competition law also deals with abuses of an organisation's market position. For example, there are regulations against practices such as price collusion between different organisations.

1.8 The law of intellectual property recognises the right of an organisation (or an individual) to profit from intellectual breakthroughs: new product designs, improved manufacturing processes and so on. The law provides a range of measures to prevent other organisations from 'stealing' such ideas.

2   *The meaning of law*

The development of English law

2.1 The English legal system incorporates the law of England and Wales. Within the United Kingdom both Scotland and Northern Ireland have different legal systems.

2.2 In any community laws are essential in order to be able to police the actions of its citizens. Law consists of a body of rules laid down by society to regulate human conduct. If these rules are broken penalties and other sanctions can be imposed.

2.3 Parts of the English law have been **codified**. This means to set down the decisions made in a formal way; by Act of Parliament, or statute. Judges may then have the job of interpreting the statutes if the words of Parliament are not clear.

2.4 The initial purpose of the law was to lay down codes to protect property and control public order. More recently, as society has reformed, there has been an increasing amount of law passed to deal with social problems, such as the Sex Discrimination Acts of 1975 and 1986 and the Race Relations Act of 1976. It is often suggested that law reflects the social conscience.

Civil and criminal law

2.5 It is important to understand the terminology used to classify the various areas of English law. One important distinction is between civil and criminal law.

2.6 **Civil law** assists individuals to recover property or enforce obligations owed to them. **Criminal law** is designed to suppress crime and punish offenders, and is largely enforced by the state.

2.7 Civil law aims to provide the individual with compensation for any loss he has suffered. It is a fundamental principle of civil law that the person bringing the claim to court cannot recover more than he has lost. Criminal law, by contrast, rarely has anything to do with compensation: its aims are to deter or punish wrongdoers, and in principle to correct and reform them.

2.8   Criminal proceedings are usually instigated by the Crown (ie the state) in respect of wrongs which are considered injurious to society generally. This is known as a prosecution. It may result in conviction or sentence if the accused is found guilty, or in acquittal if the case against him is not proved. The parties involved in the case are known as the **prosecution** (ie the state) and the **accused** or **defendant**. The court hearing is called a trial.

2.9   A civil action is brought by a private individual (the **claimant**). The term 'individual' in this context is interpreted widely; for example, a company or other organisation may be the claimant. The claimant sues another 'individual' (the **defendant**) to obtain redress, usually in the form of financial compensation (called damages). The court hearing is called **litigation**. Legal cases are usually referred to in the form **Smith v Jones** (1999), where the first named person (Smith) is the claimant, and the second individual is the defendant. The date of the case is given in brackets.

2.10   To prove a criminal wrong, the prosecution must prove it **beyond reasonable doubt**. In a civil case, the claimant must prove his case on a **balance of probabilities**. This difference may be summarised by stating that the **standard of proof** is higher in a criminal case.

2.11   Certain acts may be both civil and criminal wrongs. The Legal Aspects syllabus is concerned mostly with civil wrongs.

3   *The sources of law*

Common law and equity

3.1   The law relating to England and Wales derives from four main sources.

- •   Common law
- •   Equity
- •   Statute law (Acts of Parliament)
- •   European Community (EC) law

3.2   The common law is that which applies throughout England and Wales, declared by judges as the basis of fundamental legal principles. This is the very centre of English law. It is judge-made, in the sense that principles have been laid down by judges in the process of determining legal disputes that came before them.

3.3   The common law rests on the doctrine of **judicial precedent**. This doctrine states that where a decision has been made it must be followed, where possible, in later cases. There are records of judicial decisions made from the fourteenth century onwards and these are the forerunners of today's law reports which contain the principles of contemporary decisions.

3.4   Early application of the common law was beset by problems, particularly the fact that the new system of justice was cumbersome, and completely inaccessible to most ordinary people. In response to such problems the body of law known as **equity** developed. Equity is the body of discretionary rules and remedies devised by the courts on the basis of fairness and good conscience to remedy the defects of the common law.

3.5   The main distinguishing features of common law and equity are summarised in Table 1.1.

Table 1.1 *Common law and equity*

Common law	Equity
The common law is rigid and inflexible. It is bound by rules of bureaucracy.	Equity is based on fairness, conscience and a moral code. It is flexible.
The common law is a complete system. It was first in time and was intended to be all encompassing.	Equity supplements the common law. It is often regarded as adding a 'gloss' to the common law by imposing fairness.
The only remedy available under the common law is damages.	Equity has several different remedies, each appropriate to the given situation.
There are time limits under which an action must be brought under the common law. The Limitation Acts impose limits on the commencement of proceedings.	There are no strict time limits for bringing an action in equity, although the principle 'delay defeats equity' applies to impose the overall burden of reasonableness on the claimant.

3.6   The Judicature Acts 1873–1875 amalgamated common law and equity. They created the Supreme Court of Judicature with capacity to dispense both forms of justice. This Court consists of two parts: the Court of Appeal and the High Court of Justice. The Court will always have a discretion as to whether to grant an equitable remedy rather than damages under the common law. However, if there is a conflict between the two sources of law equity will always prevail.

Statute law

3.7   Statute is the law created by parliament and its delegated bodies. There are two main forms of statute law: Acts of Parliament and delegated legislation.

3.8   An **Act of Parliament**, or **statute**, is binding on everyone in the jurisdiction. It is the highest source of law and will supersede both the common law and equity.

3.9   An Act may be passed for a variety of reasons.

- To create new law. An example of this is the Sex Discrimination Act 1975. This Act made it illegal, for the first time, to discriminate on the grounds of sex in certain circumstances.

- To authorise taxation. A Finance Act is passed each year after the Chancellor of the Exchequer has published the Government's budget. This Act will then authorise the levying of taxes.

- To codify existing law derived from cases.

- To consolidate existing statutes. This is where an Act brings together in a single statute all of the provisions, codes and rules previously contained in several statutes.

3.10   The process of enacting a statute can be an arduous one. Parliamentary time is very precious and it would not be possible to debate and consider in full all of the minute details required, for example, for welfare and finance legislation.

3.11 **Delegated legislation** is used to save Parliamentary time. It means that Parliament is given the time and the opportunity to do the job that it was elected to do while the detail can be delegated to another body. Powers to make legislation are quite literally delegated to bodies outside Parliament.

3.12 This legislation is sometimes called subordinate or indirect legislation. It means that certain types of legislation can become part of the body of laws in the United Kingdom without having to endure the lengthy procedure necessary to enact an Act of Parliament.

3.13 The main type of indirect legislation is effected through **statutory instruments** – these are the detailed appendices to an Act of Parliament effected by the relevant Minister in charge of the Department concerned.

3.14 Statutory instruments are subjected to the scrutiny of Parliament either before or after coming into force. The more important statutory instruments will not become operative at all unless they have been approved by both Houses of Parliament.

EC legislation

3.15 The United Kingdom became a member state of the European Community (EC) on 1 January 1973 when the European Communities Act 1972 was enacted. Section 2 of the Act provides that the UK will be bound by Community legislation relating to social, economic and industrial matters. As a consequence certain types of EC law are given direct legal effect within the UK's legal system, without the need for further enactment by Parliament. Although the UK is now a member of the European Union, it is still common to refer to EC law, rather than EU law, because most law emanates from the EC (one of the three 'pillars' of the EU).

3.16 The treaties are the primary source of EC law. The foundations of the EU legal system were laid in the original treaties of Paris and Rome, and have been added to by further treaties, such as the Treaty of Accession. Some treaty provisions are so specific that they take direct effect in member states and give rise to enforceable EC rights. Other treaty provisions are less explicit and therefore not directly applicable. Member states are expected to give effect to such provisions by enacting specific legislation in their own parliaments.

3.17 The Council of the EU and the European Commission exercise law-making powers that have an effect on the English legal system. The treaties empower the Council and Commission to make three types of legislation.

- **Regulations** – These are designed to achieve uniformity of law among the member states. They are of general application and have direct force of law in all member states without the need for further legislation. Regulations must be applied even if the member state has already passed legislation which conflicts with them.

- **Directives** – These seek to harmonise the law of member states. They are instructions to member states to bring their laws into line with EU law by a certain date. The member states are free to choose the methods by which the changes are implemented, such as by Act of Parliament or statutory instrument (eg the Directive on Unfair Terms in Consumer Contract Regulations 1999).

- **Decisions** – These may be addressed to a member state, a company or an individual, and are binding on the addressee.

Summary of sources of law

3.18   The primary source of law in the English legal system is statute. Statute comes from two sources.

- Parliament (either directly via the process for enacting Acts of Parliament or by delegated legislation).
- EC law.

3.19   Delegated legislation is essential where the detailed processes of Parliament make it impossible to pass every prospective item of legislation through the elective body.

3.20   EC legislation is the most recently introduced source of English law. New EC law is created by:

- Regulations – equivalent to Acts of Parliament. They are self-executing and directly applicable to the member states.
- Directives – not self-executing but a way of bringing member states into line.
- Decisions – addressed to a particular member state or its citizens.

4   The doctrine of judicial precedent

Introduction

4.1   Common law and equity developed through a series of judge-made decisions. These decisions were recorded and a huge amount of rules and regulations evolved. Judges created law in this way and it became essential to provide consistency. If the legal system is to be just and is to be seen as being just it must be fair and consistent. Members of society can live by way of a code of conduct based on certainty. If case decisions are recorded and judges in later cases follow these decisions a code of conduct can be built up.

4.2   The doctrine of judicial precedent in the English legal system states that if the facts of a previous case are similar to the present situation, then in most circumstances the decision of the first court should not just be persuasive but binding on the later court.

4.3   Three definitions are important.

- **Ratio decidendi** – this is a statement of the law as it applies in the case. It is the legal reasoning behind the decision. This is the vital element of the case that will bind future judges.
- **Obiter dictum** – this is either a statement of law based on facts other than those that exist in the case at hand, or a part of the decision that does not agree with the judgement and so which is not part of the *ratio decidendi*. As a result *obiter dicta* (the plural form of *obiter dictum*) do not form part of the law and are not binding on future judges. However such statements may assist judges in the future if they are relevant and based on good sense. As such they are persuasive authority.
- **Stare decisis** – this means to stand by a decision. This is the whole concept upon which the doctrine of judicial precedent is based. It reflects the view that it is not the function of the judge to make the law but to decide cases in accordance with existing rules and earlier precedents.

The hierarchy of the Courts

4.4   The *ratio decidendi* of a case must be applied in any similar case heard in a court, which is on the same level, or below the level in the hierarchy, of the court originally making the decision. The hierarchy of courts is described below.

Figure 1.1 *The Court system (civil courts)*

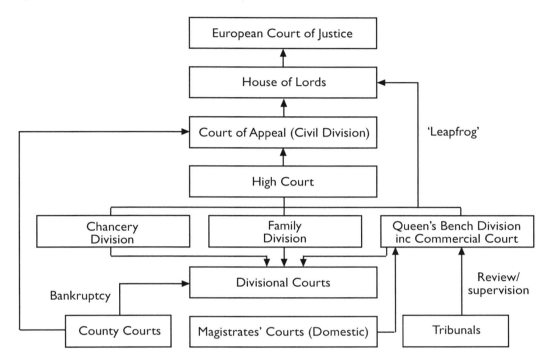

Figure 1.2 *The Court system (criminal courts)*

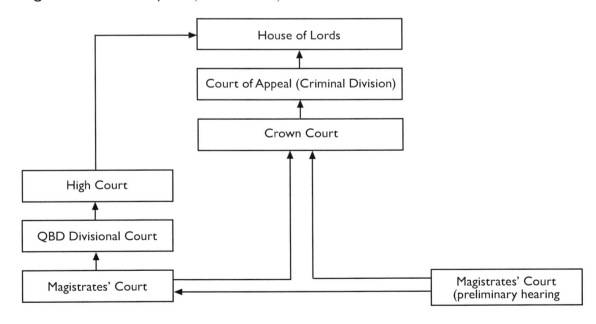

4.5   At the top of the hierarchy is the House of Lords. This is the highest court in England and Wales and its decisions are binding on all other courts. However, since 1966 the Lords are not bound by their own decisions if they consider, in exceptional circumstances, that they do not want to follow the *ratio decidendi* laid down. Following the decision in **Bulmer v Bollinger** (1974), which is based on an interpretation of Article 177 of the Treaty of Rome, the House of Lords is bound to refer any appeal to the European Court of Justice at Luxembourg, should either party request it.

4.6   The House of Lords is an appellate court, hearing appeals either from the Court of Appeal or, with leave, direct from the High Court on a matter of law by way of the 'leap-frog' procedure.

4.7   Next in the hierarchy comes the Court of Appeal. The Court of Appeal's decisions are binding on all courts except for the House of Lords. It is bound by its own previous decisions.

4.8   Next comes the High Court of Justice. A single High Court judge is bound by the decisions of higher courts (eg the House of Lords and the Court of Appeal). However, a single High Court judge is not bound by the decision of another single High Court judge. When two or more High Court judges are sitting together (as a Divisional Court) their decisions are binding on any other Divisional Court and upon a single High Court judge. The High Court is split into three Divisions: the Queen's Bench (which includes a specialist Commercial Court); the Chancery Division, and the Family Division. Only the Family Division has no jurisdiction to hear litigation (civil business cases).

4.9   Other courts include the Crown Courts, County Courts and Magistrates Courts. Decisions of these courts are not usually reported (so they are not part of the system of precedent). They are bound by the decisions of higher courts. The Crown Court deals predominantly with criminal matters, the County Court deals with civil matters of all types (subject to financial or complexity limits), and the Magistrates Court deals with a wide range of criminal matters and some private matters.

The nature of precedent

4.10   A precedent will not be binding if:

- it has been overruled by a higher court. This will not reverse the previous decision but it will change the law for future cases

- it has been overruled by statute. An Act of Parliament is the highest legal authority

- it was made *per incuriam* (through lack of care)

- the facts of the earlier case can be materially distinguished from the fact of the case presently before the court. This will not apply just because the facts are not identical. A case will only be distinguished from one previously decided if the differences appear so significant that it would not be just and fair to apply the *ratio decidendi* in the later case;

- the *ratio decidendi* is obscure and so cannot be clearly followed. This may apply where the judges in the same case reach the same conclusion but for different reasons, so that no single *ratio* emerges.

Chapter summary

- Civil law assists individuals to recover property or enforce obligations owed to them. Criminal law is designed to suppress crime and punish offenders, and is largely enforced by the state.

- The main sources of UK law are common law and equity (both based on case law), statute, and EC law.

- Statute law takes the form of Acts of Parliament and delegated legislation, such as statutory instruments.

- EC law includes regulations (immediately applicable in member states), directives (requiring legislation by member states) and decisions (addressed to particular member states or individuals).

- Case law is founded on the doctrine of judicial precedent: decisions arrived at in earlier cases are usually binding in relation to later cases.

Self-test questions

Numbers in brackets refer to the paragraphs above where your answers can be checked.

1   Who is the defendant in the (fictional) case of *Black v White*? (2.9)

2   What is meant by the doctrine of judicial precedent? (3.3)

3   What are the main features distinguishing common law from equity? (Table 1.1)

4   For what reasons may a new Act of Parliament be passed? (3.9)

5   What is a statutory instrument? (3.13)

6   Distinguish between regulations, directives and decisions as sources of EC law. (3.17)

7   Distinguish between *ratio decidendi* and *obiter dictum*. (4.3)

8   Outline the hierarchy of courts in England and Wales. (4.4–4.9)

9   In what circumstances is a precedent not binding? (4.10)

CHAPTER 2

The Formation of a Contract

Learning objectives and indicative content

1.1   Analyse the legal problems that may arise from the process of contract formation and the problems of reconciling the buyer's terms and conditions with those of the seller when faced with the battle of the forms.

Chapter headings

1   The nature of a contract

2   Essential elements in a binding contract

3   The form of a contract

Introduction

In this chapter we begin our coverage of the central topic in the examination syllabus: contract law. Later chapters will deal with detailed rules relating to contracts, but here we will simply examine what a contract is, what features must be present to make a contract valid and binding on the parties, and what form a contract takes.

1   The nature of a contract

Contracts in everyday life

1.1   Contracts are a central feature of modern life. Not only do they affect entire nations (treaties are effectively contracts) they also feature in ordinary daily life: the purchase of a book in a bookshop; the boarding of a bus; the ordering of goods; the booking of a course of study – all constitute contracts.

1.2   A contract is an agreement between two or more parties which is intended to be enforceable by the law. It is very important to distinguish this from a social agreement, such as arranging a meeting between two friends. In a 'contract' between two friends if one of the persons involved does not carry out his side of the agreement he will not be taken to court by the other person in order to enforce the agreement.

1.3   In such a case it is said that the parties had no intention to create legal relations and so a contract does not exist. However, if the agreement is between two commercial enterprises it is presumed that there is an intention to enforce the agreement if one of the parties does not act in accordance with it.

An outline of contract law

1.4   The law of contract is concerned with four basic questions.

- Is there a contract in existence? The answer depends on the presence or absence of five essential elements; these are discussed in the next section of this chapter.

- Is the agreement one which the law should recognise and enforce? Some contracts will be wholly or partly invalid at law because of a vitiating factor, such as a mistake or misrepresentation. These issues will be discussed in Chapter 7.

- When do the obligations of the parties come to an end? The most common method of termination of a contract is when each party performs his contractual obligations and this necessarily requires knowledge of exactly what each party undertook to do, ie the terms of the contract. Termination of a contract is discussed in Chapter 8.

- What remedies are available if either party is in breach of his contractual obligations? Possible remedies include damages (monetary compensation), an action for the price, and the court orders of specific performance and injunction. Remedies for breach are discussed in Chapter 9.

General principles relating to contracts

1.5   Two important general principles are referred to as **freedom of contract** and **sanctity of contract**.

1.6   Freedom of contract means that the parties are at liberty to make their own bargain, and the courts will not interfere with the terms they agree upon. There are some limitations to this principle.

- Some contracts are made on **standard terms**. A person faced with a standard form contract may find difficulty in altering the terms; he must either take it or leave it. This happens in such common cases as the purchase of a train ticket. The traveller has no practical choice in the matter – he must travel on the terms set out by the train operator.

- In some cases there will be **implied terms**. Where the parties have failed to express all the terms of their contract, the court may imply terms into the agreement based on the presumed but unexpressed intention of the parties. Sometimes, such terms are implied automatically because statute requires it. For example, when we study contracts relating to the sale of goods we will see that the Sale of Goods Act 1979 lays down certain implied terms which will apply to all such contracts unless specifically excluded.

- Clauses limiting the liability of a party (**exclusion clauses**) may not be allowable under the Unfair Contract Terms Act 1977. For example, it would not be allowable for a fairground operator to disclaim liability for personal injury caused to customers on a fairground ride.

1.7   Despite these restrictions, the principle of freedom of contract remains important, especially in commercial transactions where the parties who negotiate are on an equal footing.

1.8 The principle of sanctity of contract means that the agreement cannot be interfered with either by the parties themselves, or by the courts, or by third parties. Once he has made an agreement, a party must abide by it unless he is released from his obligations by the other party. This remains true even if circumstances change so as to affect his expectations; and it is still true even if he is in no way at fault. He must still perform his obligations.

1.9 Again, there are some limitations on the general principle. For example, we will see in Chapter 8 that both parties may be released from their obligations if the agreement is 'frustrated', but the courts are reluctant to accept that frustration has occurred other than in exceptional circumstances.

Types of contract

1.10 We end this section by explaining some terminology that is used in classifying contracts: bilateral and unilateral contracts, and void, voidable and unenforceable contracts.

1.11 A contract whereby both parties make promises and are bound is a **bilateral contract**. This of course is the usual type of contract. For example, a seller promises to transfer ownership of goods to a buyer, and in return the buyer promises to pay an agreed sum of money.

1.12 In contrast to this is the case where one party (the promisor) makes a promise and is bound, while the other person is free to perform or not as he chooses. This is called a **unilateral contract**. A classic example is the case of **Carlill v Carbolic Smokeball Company** (1893). The company, in an advertisement, promised to pay £100 to anyone who bought their smokeball and still caught influenza. Mrs Carlill bought and used the smokeball, but caught influenza. She successfully claimed the £100. In such cases, the promisor is bound if the promisee performs the act which the promisor promised to reward.

1.13 A contract may be vitiated (ie flawed) by a number of factors, such as mistake, misrepresentation, duress, undue influence, or illegality. In such cases the contract is either void or voidable.

1.14 A **void contract** has no legal effect on either party – it is just as though no contract exists at all. Any property which is transferred under a void contract must be handed back to the transferor, as he remains the owner of it. If the transferee keeps the goods, he could be sued by the real owner for wrongfully detaining the goods (called **conversion**).

1.15 A **voidable contract** exists unless and until it is brought to an end (avoided) at the option of one of the parties, usually at the option of the innocent party. The act by which the innocent party avoids a voidable contract is called **rescission**.

1.16 An **unenforceable contract** is a valid contract even though its terms cannot be enforced. If property is transferred under it, it cannot be recovered even from the other party to the contract. However, if either party refuses to carry out its part of the contract the court will not compel him to do so. For example, contracts of guarantee are unenforceable unless evidenced in writing.

2 Essential elements in a binding contract

2.1 In order for a contract to exist and to be legally binding five essential elements must be present.

- Agreement (ie offer and acceptance)
- Consideration
- Intention to create legal relations
- Contractual capacity
- Correct form

2.2 **Agreement** arises when an offer and an acceptance of the offer take effect.

- One party, called the 'offeror', must make a definite promise to be legally bound on specific terms. This is the offer.
- The other party, called the 'offeree', must accept the offer. This acceptance must be clear and unconditional. It must also be freely given, and not extorted by duress or undue influence.

2.3 **Consideration** must be exchanged between the parties. This means that each party must suffer some kind of loss or 'detriment' in return for the benefit received (eg the payment of money in exchange for goods).

2.4 The parties must have an **intention to create legal relations**. This means that if a dispute arises between the parties over the terms of the contract (for example, if one party refuses to pay the agreed price) they will go to a court of law to decide the matter.

2.5 **Contractual capacity** must exist. This means that each of the parties must be legally able to be bound by the contract. In simple terms, the parties should usually be 18 or over and of sound mind.

2.6 Finally, the contract must be made in the **correct form**. This is discussed below.

3 The form of a contract

The common law rule

3.1 For most contracts, there is no problem in the form of contract to be adopted; in general, no particular form is prescribed. For example, it is not necessary in principle for most contracts to be in writing. Oral agreements are binding. However, it is preferable to put agreements in writing to avoid later disputes about exactly what was agreed. And there are some contracts that **must** be in written form.

Statutory exceptions to the common law rule

3.2 Statutes lay down certain exceptions to the general rule described above. In particular, statute insists that certain contracts (**specialty contracts**) must be made in the form of a deed – which is a written, signed and witnessed document – while certain others must at least be in writing even if not in the form of a deed.

3.3 Contracts which must be made by deed include a conveyance of land, an assignment of a lease (where the lease is for three years or more), and the transfer of a ship.

3.4 Several types of contract must be made in writing. These include:

- bills of exchange, such as cheques
- contracts of marine insurance
- regulated consumer credit agreements, eg hire purchase agreements
- transfers of shares in registered companies
- legal assignment of debts
- contracts for the sale or other disposition of land.

3.5 Under the Electronic Communications Act 2000, which followed the EC Electronic Signatures Directive 1999, the government took statutory powers to amend existing legislation, to allow for the use of electronic communications to make the contracts listed above, where necessary and desirable. The Act also makes provision for the recognition of electronic signatures as legally valid. Contracts formed by electronic means and the associated legislation are discussed in more detail in Chapter 6.

3.6 In addition, contracts of guarantee must be **evidenced** in writing, even though the contract itself may be oral. We discuss contracts of guarantee in Chapter 6.

Chapter summary

- Four basic questions provide a framework for contract law. Is there a contract? Is it enforceable? When does it terminate? What are the remedies for breach?

- Freedom of contract means that, with some limitations, parties are free to contract on whatever terms they prefer. Sanctity of contract means that the agreed terms may not be interfered with.

- Most contracts are bilateral: each party contracts to do something. Some are unilateral: one party promises to do something, whereas the other is free to act or not, as he chooses.

- A void contract is no contract. A voidable contract exists unless and until it is avoided. An unenforceable contract is valid, but its terms cannot be enforced.

- There are five essential elements in a legally binding contract: agreement (ie offer and acceptance), consideration, intention to create legal relations, contractual capacity, and correct form.

Self-test questions

Numbers in brackets refer to the paragraphs above where your answers can be checked.

1   Distinguish between a contract and a social agreement. (1.2, 1.3)

2   What is the usual means by which a contract is terminated? (1.4)

3   Explain the principle of freedom of contract. What exceptions are there to the general principle? (1.6)

4   Which case is a classic example of a unilateral contract? (1.12)

5   What is meant by conversion? (1.14)

6   What is meant by consideration in the context of contract law? (2.3)

7   Which types of contract must be made in writing? (3.4)

CHAPTER 3

Offer and Acceptance

Learning objectives and indicative content

1.1   Analyse the legal problems that may arise from the process of contract formation and the problems of reconciling the buyer's terms and conditions with those of the seller when faced with the battle of the forms.

- •   Offer and acceptance
- •   Battle of the forms

Chapter headings

1   The offer

2   Situations where there is no offer

3   Acceptance

4   Tenders

5   Reconciliation of buyer's and seller's terms

Introduction

In the previous chapter we listed the five essential elements that must be present in a binding contract. First on the list was agreement: there must be an offer and an acceptance of that offer.

In this chapter we look at this requirement in more detail and examine what constitutes an offer, and an acceptance, and what situations fall short of full offer and acceptance.

We also look at two particular situations relating to offer and acceptance that are of particular importance to purchasing professionals: the law relating to tenders, and the problem of dealing on standard contract terms.

1   The offer

The form of the offer

1.1   An offer is a proposal or promise to be bound on specified terms. An offer is made by an offeror to an offeree. It should be clear and definite and the offeree must intend to be legally bound by it. The terms of the offer must include all the terms of the proposed contract (expressly or by implication).

- •   The offeror can make the offer expressly. This is where a person makes the offer by spoken words or in writing.
- •   The offeror can make the offer by implication. This is where a person's behaviour implies the offer. An example of this would be a person filling his tank with petrol, at a petrol station. It is implicit in his behaviour that he is offering to buy the petrol.

1.2   In order to be valid the offer must have certain elements. Without these elements the offer does not legally exist and so cannot be accepted. The requirements of a valid offer are set out below.

1.3   The offer must be a definite and unequivocal statement of willingness to be bound in contract. It cannot be vague or uncertain in its interpretation. So, an offer to sell someone a particular car for £5,000 will be an offer. But a statement that a person will sell '… one of my cars for a reasonable sum' will not be an offer.

1.4   There must be a clear intention to be bound by the offer. The offeror must not merely be negotiating. All the offeree has to do is to accept the terms as laid down by the offeror and the contract will be complete.

1.5   The offer can be made to a particular person, to a class of persons or even to the whole world. Where X is buying an apple from the greengrocer, X is the offeror, making an offer to a single person, the greengrocer. The circumstances in which an offer can be made to the whole world are sometimes a little more complicated. This can be illustrated by the case cited in the previous chapter: **Carlill v Carbolic Smokeball Co** (1893).

The manufacturers of a medicinal 'smokeball' advertised in a newspaper that anyone who bought and used the ball properly and nevertheless contracted influenza would be paid a £100 reward. Mrs Carlill used the ball as directed and did catch 'flu. The manufacturers claimed that they did not have to pay her the £100 as an offer could not be made to the whole world.

Held: An offer could be made to the whole world, the wording of the advert amounted to such an offer, and Mrs Carlill had accepted it by buying and properly using the smokeball.

1.6   Another example of an offer to the world at large is a more typical advert for reward, say when someone has lost their cat and they offer a financial incentive for the finder to return it.

1.7   The offer must actually reach the person to whom it was made. In other words the offeree must know of it. An offer will not be valid unless the offeror has clearly communicated it to the offeree and that person is aware of it. This is illustrated by the case of **R v Clarke** (1927).

The Government of Western Australia offered a free pardon to the accomplices of certain murderers if they gave evidence that would lead to their arrest and conviction. Clarke provided the information but admitted that he was not aware of the reward at the time he gave it to the authorities.

Held: He could not claim the reward because he was not aware of the offer at the time he gave the information. He had not acted 'in exchange for' the offer.

1.8   This rule is also relevant to 'cross-offers'. Suppose that A writes to B offering to sell certain property at a certain price. B writes to A offering to buy the same property at the same price. These were the facts considered in **Tinn v Hoffman** (1873), and it was held that there would be no contract in this situation.

Termination of the offer

1.9 The offer must be 'open' (ie still in force) when the offeree accepts it. Once an offer has been closed it can no longer be accepted. One of the most important ways in which an offer can be closed is by a **revocation**. A revocation is an act of the offeror which effectively cancels or annuls the offer. It can no longer be accepted by the offeree.

1.10 An offer can be revoked at any time before it has been accepted by the offeree. The revocation may be by express words, or it may be implied by the offeror's conduct: **Dickinson v Dodds** (1876).

1.11 The revocation will not take effect until it has been received and clearly understood by the offeree. Until then, it remains open, and can be accepted: **Byrne v Van Tienhoven** (1880).

An offer was posted by the defendant in Cardiff on 1 October. It was received by the claimant in New York on 11 October. He at once cabled an acceptance (effectively accepting on this date). In the meantime the defendant had changed his mind and had sent a letter of revocation from Cardiff on 8 October. This letter of revocation reached New York on 15 October. The question before the court was whether the contract had been accepted or revoked.

Held: The revocation was not complete until it had been properly communicated to the offeree. This was on 15 October. In the meantime, however, the offer had been accepted. As a result, the revocation was ineffective and the contract **did** exist. The defendant was then liable under the contract.

1.12 The revocation can be communicated by the offeror or by a reliable third party: **Dickinson v Dodds** (1876).

The defendant, on 10 June, gave the claimant a written offer to sell a house for £800, 'to be left open until 12 June at 9.00am'. On 11 June the defendant sold the house to a third party for £800, and that evening another person told the claimant of the sale. Before 9.00am the next day the claimant accepted the offer.

Held: As the claimant knew that the defendant was no longer in the position to sell the property to him the defendant had validly withdrawn his offer. If a reasonable person would have been aware of this withdrawal the offer is withdrawn.

1.13 With unilateral contracts (where an offer is to be accepted by conduct) the offer cannot be revoked once the offeree has begun to try and perform whatever act is necessary to constitute acceptance: **Errington v Errington** (1953).

1.14 The rule that an offer can be revoked at any time before acceptance applies even though the offeror has stated that he will keep the offer open for a stated time: **Routledge v Grant** (1828).

Grant offered to buy Routledge's horse and gave him six weeks to decide whether or not to accept. Before the six weeks had elapsed Grant withdrew his offer.

Held: Since Routledge had not yet accepted, Grant was entitled to withdraw his offer.

1.15   An offer can also be terminated by a **rejection**. This is the action of the offeree turning down the offer. This is either outright, by the offeree stating that he will not accept it, or by a **counter-offer**. A counter-offer is where the offeree does not accept the offer unconditionally but imposes his own terms on the acceptance.

1.16   An example of a counter-offer is where the offeree offers a lower price or in any other way barters with the offeror. This is imposing conditions on the acceptance and, as we will see, an acceptance must be unconditional. The rejection closes the offer.

1.17   A counter-offer has two main effects.

•   It closes the original offer, which is no longer capable of being accepted.

•   The offeror in the original negotiations now becomes the offeree once the counter-offer has been made. The original offeree by making the counter-offer now becomes the offeror: **Hyde v Wrench** (1840).

Wrench offered to sell Hyde a farm for £1,000. Hyde made a counter-offer, by offering £950. Wrench rejected this. Later Hyde came back and said that he now accepted the original offer of £1,000. Wrench rejected it.

Held: Hyde could no longer accept the original offer. It had been terminated by the counter-offer and was no longer capable of acceptance. His 'acceptance' was merely a fresh offer which Wrench was free to turn down.

1.18   Note that a mere request for further details does not constitute a counter-offer: **Stevenson v McLean** (1880).

M offered, in writing, to sell a quantity of iron to S at a given price. S replied querying delivery times, but before receiving a reply sent a further letter accepting the offer. This acceptance crossed in the post with a letter of revocation from M to S. M refused to supply the iron to S, arguing that S's query was a counter-offer.

Held: M could not treat the query as a counter-offer. S had not intended to prejudice M's position, just to establish the parameters of the deal. Therefore M's offer was still open when S wrote accepting it.

1.19   Finally, an offer may be terminated by lapse. If the offer is stated only to be open for a specific time period it will end after the expiration of this time. If there is no specific period of time mentioned by the offeror the offer will lapse after a reasonable length of time. This is usually a matter for the parties to decide, looking at all the circumstances and at the type of offer that was made. If there is a dispute about the time period the court will decide what is reasonable. It is a question of fact to be decided in each case.

1.20   If the offer was made subject to a condition it will lapse on failure of that condition. An example of this would be an offer to supply an establishment with alcohol as long as it had a licence to sell alcohol. If the establishment for any reason lost its licence, the offer would lapse and would no longer be capable of acceptance.

1.21   If the offeror dies the offer can no longer be accepted once the offeree knows of the death.

1.22   If the contract is for personal services, such as those of a plumber or a musician, the offer can clearly not be accepted after the offeree has died, as the contract could not be performed.

1.23　In summary, an offer must be:

- clear, definite and unequivocal
- one that the offeror intends to be bound by
- made to a person, a group of persons or to the whole world
- communicated to the offeree
- still in force at the time of acceptance.

1.24　Unless all of these conditions are present the offer will not be valid and so cannot be accepted. If one or more of the above pre-requisites are missing there cannot be a contract and so neither of the parties can be sued for breach of contract if they do not act in accordance with the purported agreement.

2　Situations where there is no offer

An invitation to treat

2.1　When considering an examination question it is vital to decide whether or not the facts amount to an offer. Not all statements amount to an offer and only an offer can be accepted, so leading to a contract. It is vital to distinguish the offer from the other possibilities.

2.2　An invitation to treat is not an offer in itself but is an invitation to others to make an offer. An invitation to treat is part of the negotiations. A good example is the display of goods in a shop: **Pharmaceutical Society of Great Britain v Boots Cash Chemists** (1953).

Statute requires that the purchase of certain pharmaceuticals must be carried out under the supervision of a qualified pharmacist. Boots operated a store where the drugs were sold on a self-service basis and the customers paid at a cash desk for the goods they had selected. A pharmacist was present at the cash desk but not at the shelves where the goods were displayed with a price tag. The Pharmaceutical Society claimed that the statute was being contravened.

Held: The display of goods in a shop was not an offer but an invitation to treat. It was the customer who made the offer at the cash desk and Boots could either accept or reject this offer (in the presence of a qualified pharmacist).

2.3　A similar case is **Fisher v Bell** (1961): a shopkeeper who displayed flick knives in his shop window was not guilty of offering knives for sale.

2.4　An advertisement to sell an item will not be an offer in itself: **Partridge v Crittenden** (1968). At that stage the owner has no intention to be bound to any person who answers the advertisement. It could be, for example, that the person advertising is selling something quite precious and would not agree to sell it to just anyone who answered, especially if they appeared unsuitable. Similarly, a catalogue or prospectus will constitute an invitation to treat, and not an offer.

Statement of intention and statement of price

2.5   A mere statement of intention is not an offer: **Harris v Nickerson** (1873).

An auction sale of furniture was advertised in a newspaper. A London broker saw the advert and travelled up to attend the sale in order to bid for various lots. Unknown to him the items had been withdrawn from the sale before he arrived. He claimed that his action of turning up at the auction sale amounted to an acceptance of the offer contained in the advertisement. As a result he claimed that the auctioneers had breached the contract in not selling the items of furniture to him. He then sued for damages to cover his loss.

Held: The advertisement did not amount to an offer. It was not clear, definite or unequivocal from the advertisement that the auctioneers wanted to sell the items of furniture to the broker. Also, the auctioneers had no intention to be bound to this broker. Accordingly, the critical pre-requisites for an offer were not all present and this advertisement was a mere statement of intention.

2.6   A statement of price in answer to an enquiry is not an offer, but merely the supply of information: **Harvey v Facey** (1893).

Harvey sent a telegram to Facey saying, 'Will you sell us Bumper Hall Pen? Telegram lowest cash price.' Bumper Hall Pen was a piece of land owned by Facey. Facey replied, also by telegram, 'Lowest cash price £900.' Harvey then sent another telegram saying, 'We agree to buy Bumper Hall Pen for £900.' Harvey claimed that there was now an enforceable contract to sell the land for £900. It was claimed that the telegram stating the lowest cash price was an offer and that Harvey had accepted that offer in his final telegram.

Held: There was no contract. The first telegram was a request for information and the second telegram was merely an answer to the question posed in the first. The final telegram embodied an offer to purchase the land for £900, but there was no acceptance from the landowner.

2.7   In response to a request for information it is common for a purchaser to be given a quotation. The request is clearly not an offer but, depending on the facts, the quotation could be construed as being an offer capable of acceptance. To be so, it must be detailed and specific enough to be capable of acceptance simply by saying 'yes'. If there are other matters that would still need clarifying, such as whether the actual items are in stock, then the quotation probably is not an offer. Instead, an offer would be deemed to be made when an order form which refers to the quotation is submitted by the buyer.

2.8   Auctions are a special case. We have already seen that the advertisement of an auction is not an offer, but what happens in the saleroom itself? The rules are as follows based on the case of **British Car Auctions Ltd v Wright** (1972).

- Advertisements and the auctioneer standing up and referring to a lot are invitations to treat.
- A bid from the floor is an offer.
- The fall of the auctioneer's gavel is acceptance of the last offer.

3 Acceptance

The meaning of acceptance

3.1 Acceptance is an unconditional assent to all the terms of an offer. This is because a contract must embody a **consensus ad idem** – agreement on the same thing.

3.2 We have already seen that if an offeree attempts to change the terms of the offer or qualify its effectiveness in any way it will close the offer and be classed as a counter-offer. This is as in the case of **Hyde v Wrench** above. It is only when the offeree has accepted the offer unconditionally that the parties can be said to be in agreement. This complete agreement about the terms and conditions of the contract is fundamental in English contract law.

3.3 Remember that not all enquiries about the form of the contract will amount to a counter-offer by the offeree. The offeree may only be enquiring about delivery times or other less essential terms of the contract. Only that which amounts to a complete rejection of the terms suggested by the offeror will close the offer, rendering it incapable of acceptance. However, an enquiry about the price will almost certainly be a counter-offer. It depends upon the facts of the question and what the parties consider are the conditions (or fundamental terms) of the contract.

3.4 The acceptance must also not be 'subject to contract'. This phrase is frequently used in the buying and selling of land, and denotes that the parties have reached a measure of agreement but there will be no binding commitment until they enter into a formal contract, usually in writing. (In English law this will be at the 'exchange of contracts' stage.)

Form of acceptance

3.5 Any form of acceptance is valid, whether oral, written, or merely inferred from the conduct of the parties (as in the Carlill case already described). Another example is that of **Brogden v Metropolitan Railway** (1877).

The company submitted a draft agreement to Brogden for the supply of coal. Brogden sent back the document to the company having added new terms. The company did not expressly agree these new terms but coal was supplied on the amended terms.

Held: The parties had, by their conduct, agreed to act on the basis of the amended draft contract and so it had become binding.

3.6 An offeror may stipulate a mode or method of acceptance. If he makes his stipulation mandatory (eg by stating that acceptance must be in writing) then no other form of acceptance will be valid. If instead he makes his stipulation as a request, then any other equally advantageous form of acceptance is valid: **Yates Building v R J Pulleyn & Sons** (1975).

The offeror asked for the offer to be accepted by registered or recorded delivery letter. The offeree accepted by an ordinary letter, which arrived promptly.

Held: The offeror had suffered no disadvantage in the way that the offer had been accepted. As the offeror had not specified that the acceptance could only be made in a particular form the acceptance was in a form that was equally quick and reliable, and was therefore valid.

3.7   An offeror may not stipulate that silence shall amount to acceptance: **Felthouse v Bindley** (1863).

F wrote to his nephew, after a series of negotiations, offering to buy his horse for thirty guineas. The letter stated that if he did not hear from the nephew he would consider that the horse was his at that price. The nephew never replied.

Held: The Court said that there was no contract because the offeror cannot impose acceptance merely because the offeree does not specifically reject the offer. Also, silence can never be clear, absolute and unqualified so it complies with none of the rules about acceptance.

Communication of acceptance

3.8   It is the responsibility of the offeree to ensure that the acceptance is properly and clearly communicated to the offeror. This can either be done by the offeree personally or by a reliable third party.

3.9   The general rule for acceptance of an offer is that the acceptance will only be complete when the offeror has received and understood the acceptance. Usually it is a sensible move for the offeree to check that the acceptance has been received.

3.10   The offeror may expressly or by implication dispense with the need for communication. He may dispense altogether with communication or may merely dispense with communication direct to himself.

The postal rule

3.11   The postal rule constitutes an exception to the general rule of acceptance. It states that the acceptance will be complete and effective when the letter is posted or placed into the hands of the relevant postal authorities: **Adams v Lindsell** (1818).

3.12   The postal rule will only apply when acceptance by post is either the chosen, obvious or reasonable method of acceptance.

- It will be the chosen method of acceptance where the offeror has stipulated that posting the acceptance is the only acceptable method.
- It will be the obvious method of acceptance in a standard business situation or where the parties are communicating at a distance and the offeror requires a record of the reply. Also where the offer was by letter.
- It will be the reasonable method of acceptance if an ordinary person, looking at all the circumstances, would assume that to reply by post was the proper way.

3.13   The letter must be properly stamped, addressed and posted. Handing a letter to a postman is not equivalent in law to posting a letter: **Re London and Northern Bank ex parte Jones** (1900).

3.14   The postal rule does not extend to acceptance by telex (though it does apply to telegrams). Being effectively a telegraphic medium telex is treated in the same way as other instantaneous communications. As a result the normal rule of acceptance applies: **Entores v Miles Far East Corporation** (1955).

3.15 In contrast to the rules applying to revocation, acceptance can only be communicated by a person authorised to accept.

3.16 Another circumstance where the strict application of the postal rule has been questioned is where the offeree seeks to revoke his posted acceptance. When the offeree uses a speedier means to communicate the revocation of his postal acceptance, the offeror may receive that revocation before the acceptance. In such circumstances, it can be argued that the offeror would not be in any way prejudiced if, contrary to the strict application of the postal rule, the court were to hold that no contract came into existence. The objection to this is that such a view unduly favours the offeree who is thereby allowed a brief period to gamble on market movements. However, the offeree can always stipulate that acceptance must be communicated within a particular time or by an expeditious means.

4 Tenders

Introduction

4.1 A tender is an offer to supply specified goods or services at a stated cost or rate.

4.2 Tenders are often used in commercial situations. An example would be where a local authority or government body invited various suppliers to bid for a contract, say to supply heating oil for the region's schools. Competing businesses would then, as offerors, send in bids or tenders to do the work and these would be the offers.

4.3 If this tender is an offer to work on a 'one-off' job, such as building a by-pass, it is an offer that can be accepted by the relevant local authority. The contract would then be complete when the local authority accepts the tender in the usual way.

4.4 Alternatively, a tender may be in the form of a standing offer. A standing offer is where there has been a general invitation to supply a series of things, such as school meals or refuse collection services, if and when required. The tender is open to a series of acceptances whenever an order is placed.

4.5 Each acceptance then completes a distinct contract. The standing offer can be revoked at any time unless there is a binding obligation to keep it open for a certain period of time. This obligation to keep the offer open has to be supported by consideration or be embodied in an agreement under seal, where no consideration is needed: **Great Northern Railways v Witham** (1873).

Witham successfully tendered for the contract to supply iron goods to GNR for the period of one year. The wording of the tender was to supply such quantities as GNR 'may order from time to time'. GNR placed several orders but after a time Witham refused to service the orders.

Held: Witham's tender was a standing offer which GNR accepted every time it placed an order. As a result Witham was bound to supply orders that had already been placed, but he was free to revoke the standing offer in the usual way. Witham was not liable to supply any iron after the revocation had been clearly received by the offeree.

The buyer's obligations under a tender

4.6   The simplest case is where the buyer wants a particular quantity of a particular product. A supplier who tenders for the business is making an offer. If the buyer accepts he is obliged to purchase from the supplier the stated quantity of the product at the agreed price.

4.7   A more complicated case is that of standing offers, illustrated above in the case of **GNR v Witham**. When the buyer places an order, a contract comes into being – that is why Witham was bound to supply orders that had already been placed. However, what happens if the buyer does not place any order under the standing offer, or orders less than the full quantity originally contemplated? The answer is that the buyer is not in breach of contract: **Percival v London County Council** (1918).

P tendered to supply goods to LCC to the extent ordered and in any quantity. Estimates of required quantities were set out in a schedule to the tender. P's tender was accepted, but LCC did not order the estimated amounts.

Held: LCC were under no obligation to order any goods, but P was obliged to deliver any goods ordered.

4.8   Another possibility is illustrated by the case of **Kier v Whitehead Iron Co** (1938).

A buyer invited tenders for his usual requirements of certain goods and agreed to take all his requirements from the successful tenderer.

Held: The buyer is not obliged to order anything from the successful tenderer, but he is in breach of contract if he orders goods of the stated kind from anyone else.

4.9   In general, a buyer is not required to accept the lowest tender (or indeed to accept any tender at all). However, if the buyer states in the invitation to tender that he will accept the lowest tender, then he is bound to do so: **Harvela Investments Ltd v Royal Trust Company of Canada** (1986). In this case it was also stated that if referential bids were to be considered, this fact should be made known to all tenderers. A referential bid is one which is related to another – eg '£5,000 less than the other lowest bid'.

4.10   Although the buyer is not obliged to accept any of the tenders received, it has been held that he is obliged to give due consideration to such tenders provided they arrive by the stated deadline and comply with the requirements of the invitation to tender: **Blackpool & Fylde Aero Club Ltd v Blackpool Borough Council** (1990). (This is known as a **collateral obligation**.) In this case a tender was placed in the buyer's letterbox one hour ahead of the deadline. The buyer's staff failed to empty the letterbox, and the tender was therefore deemed to have arrived late. The court held that this was unwarranted: the buyer was obliged to consider the tender.

4.11   We shall see more about tenders in Chapter 18.

5 Reconciliation of buyer's and seller's terms

Contracts on standard terms

5.1 Most commercial concerns do not go to the trouble of drawing up a special contract every time they purchase or sell goods or services. Instead, they rely on standard terms. Each firm will draw up its own standard terms of business and will seek to ensure that these terms are accepted by other firms with whom they deal.

5.2 Clearly this can lead to problems if one firm's terms of purchase differ from another firm's terms of sale. This situation is often referred to as the **battle of the forms**. The buying firm may send a written enquiry to a supplier or potential supplier. The enquiry may be on a preprinted form stating that any purchase made pursuant to the enquiry will be governed by the buyer's standard terms printed on the reverse of the form.

Offer and counter-offer

5.3 Typically, the supplier will reply quoting details of price and availability, and stating that any sale will be governed by the supplier's own standard terms, printed on the reverse of the form. This is an invitation to treat.

5.4 It can go on and on. The buyer may place an order (make an offer) on a standard form repeating his own terms. The supplier may reply with an acknowledgement of order, again on a standard form containing the supplier's terms. These may be repeated on the supplier's delivery note. The question of importance to the buyer is: once the contract is completed, whose terms of business govern it? Both the acknowledgement and the delivery note are actually counter-offers, but if the buyer then signs the delivery note containing the terms, the counter-offer has been accepted and the contract is formed on the seller's terms.

5.5 The courts have usually approached these situations by analysing them in terms of offer and counter-offer. Each new step in the proceedings is regarded as a counter-offer which negates any terms mentioned previously. This approach is illustrated in the case of **Butler Machine Tool Co Ltd v Ex-Cell-O Corporation** (1979).

B offered to sell on their standard terms. E placed an order using their own standard terms which differed from B's. E's order form contained a slip at the bottom which the supplier was required to tear off and return in acknowledgement of E's terms. B did so.

Held: The return of the tear-off slip amounted to acceptance by B of E's terms, and E's terms therefore governed the contract.

5.6 In the Butler case, judgement was given in favour of the buyer. Often it will go the other way. The analysis of offer and counter-offer is sometimes said to favour the person who 'fires the last shot'. Usually it is the seller who is best placed to do this. For example, the supplier may deliver the goods along with a delivery note repeating his standard terms. When the buyer accepts and uses the goods he may well be deemed to have accepted the terms stated on the delivery note.

5.7 This is especially so if the buyer attempts to take advantage of some other term appearing on the seller's standard form. For example, if the seller's terms include a discount for prompt payment and the buyer takes advantage of such discount when paying, this is supporting evidence that the seller's terms have been accepted.

5.8   It is possible for the buyer to make it expressly clear, in writing, that acceptance of the contract by him is done on his terms and not on the seller's. However, it is also possible that, because of very careful counter-offers, both sides could be shown not to have accepted the other's terms. In such a case, where goods may have passed and been used but not paid for, the law uses the idea of **quasi-contract**: under the principles of equity the buyer must pay what the goods are worth under the principle known as ***quantum meruit***.

5.9   In the previous section of this chapter we looked at the use of tenders for the purchase of supplies and services. Many organisations use a formal tender process for high-value and high-risk purchases as it is a method of resolving the issues associated with the battle of the forms. The invitation to tender issued by the buyer will state clearly that any offer made by the seller will be accepted by the buyer only on the buyer's conditions of contract. The seller is asked to sign his agreement to this as part of the tender submission.

5.10   The examiner has made it clear that he expects candidates to analyse each stage of the dealings between buyer and supplier in terms of offer and acceptance. Although it is tempting to proceed straight to the question of 'who fired the last shot?' you may well lose marks by doing so.

Chapter summary

- An offer is a clear and unequivocal statement of willingness to be legally bound on defined terms. It can be made to a particular person, a class of persons, or the whole world.

- An offer is not valid unless it has been communicated.

- An offer may be terminated by revocation at any time before acceptance. It may also be terminated by a rejection, including a counter-offer, or by lapse.

- An offer must be distinguished from an invitation to treat, a statement of intention and a statement of price.

- Acceptance is an unconditional assent to all the terms of an offer. It may be oral, written or inferred from conduct. It must be communicated to the offeror.

- A tender is an offer to supply specified goods or services at a stated cost or rate. A buyer's obligations when accepting a tender depend on the terms of the invitation to tender.

- A buyer who invites tenders is not generally obliged to accept the lowest one received, or to accept any tender at all. However, he is obliged to give due consideration to any tenders received which comply with the stated requirements.

- The use of standard terms by commercial concerns often leads to a 'battle of the forms'. Usually such battles are decided in favour of the party who fires the last shot.

Self-test questions

Numbers in brackets refer to the paragraphs above where your answers can be checked.

1   Can an offer be made by implication? (1.1)

2   Explain why Clarke did not receive the promised reward in the case of **R v Clarke** (1927). (1.7)

3   What is a counter-offer? (1.15)

4   In what circumstances may an offer terminate by lapse? (1.19)

5   What is an invitation to treat? (2.2)

6   What are the consequences if an offeror stipulates a particular mode of acceptance? (3.6)

7   What is the basic postal rule established in **Adams v Lindsell**? (3.11)

8   Explain the obligations of a buyer under a standing offer from a seller. (4.7)

9   Why is the battle of the forms often resolved in favour of the seller? (5.6, 5.7)

CHAPTER 4

Consideration

Learning objectives and indicative content

1.1 Analyse the legal problems that may arise from the process of contract formation and the problems of reconciling the buyer's terms and conditions with those of the seller when faced with the battle of the forms.

- Consideration

Chapter headings

1   The nature of consideration

2   The rules relating to consideration

3   The problem of part-payment

4   The doctrine of promissory estoppel

Introduction

In this chapter we continue our examination of the basic elements required to form a binding contract.

In most cases, a contract is only binding if the promises of the parties are supported by consideration. The simplest case is where a seller agrees to provide goods and the buyer agrees to pay money. Each is handing over something valuable to the other, and in broad terms this is what is meant by consideration.

To begin with we look at the nature of consideration. Then we discuss the somewhat complicated rules that have evolved in relation to consideration. Finally, we look at the particular problem of part-payment: when is payment of only part of the agreed sum sufficient to discharge a contract? This includes the related issue of promissory estoppel.

1   The nature of consideration

Definition of consideration

1.1 Every **simple contract** must be supported by consideration. However, this basic rule does not apply to **specialty contracts** – contracts made by deed.

1.2 The case of **Currie v Misa** (1875) laid down an accepted definition of consideration. It can be defined as: 'some right, interest, profit or benefit accruing to one party, or some forbearance, detriment, loss or responsibility given, suffered or undertaken by the other'.

1.3   This can be difficult to understand and to quote but in an exam question there are some key words that can be used to show the examiner that you do understand the concept. It is essentially where one person (being a party to the contract) does something, omits to do something or promises to do or omit something in exchange for another person (the other party) doing, omitting or promising something.

1.4   It must be an exchange; one person does something, etc **because** the other person does something. A simple everyday example is where a person purchases a drink from a vending machine. One party inserts the money into the machine and in exchange for this receives the canned drink.

1.5   Both parties are receiving a benefit (the person inserting the money takes the canned drink, and the vending machine company takes the money), and simultaneously they are each suffering a detriment. The purchaser is losing the purchase price and the drinks company the can that has been vended.

1.6   A more modern definition, and one which reflects more the importance of respective promises, rather than the concept of benefit/detriment, is given by the case of **Dunlop v Selfridge** (1915): 'consideration is an act or forbearance (or the promise of it) on the part of one party to a contract as the price of the promise made to him by the other party to the contract'.

Executed and executory consideration

1.7   'Executed' consideration is given where a promise is made in return for the performance of an act. For example, where an offer of reward is made, one party promises to pay if and when another performs the specified act. This is illustrated by the now familiar case of **Carlill v Carbolic Smokeball Co Ltd** (1893).

The company promised to pay £100 to any person complying with various conditions. Mrs Carlill made no reciprocal promise, she merely complied with the terms of the offer.

Held: Here the consideration, provided by Mrs Carlill, was the doing of the act, ie executed consideration.

1.8   'Executory' consideration is given where there is an exchange of promises to do something in the future. Executory means 'yet to be done'. There is a contract even though at the time it is concluded or agreed neither of the parties has actually done the thing that they have promised to do.

1.9   An example is where you get into a taxi and ask to be taken to a particular destination. You have given your promise to pay the fare when you arrive at your destination and the taxi driver has promised to take you there.

Quasi contract

1.10   In certain cases where one party has been enriched at the expense of another the law may require him to make restitution, even though there is no contract between the two parties. This situation is referred to as **quasi contract**. For example, when A pays money which B is liable to pay, at the implied request of B, then B may be liable to repay the money to A.

2   The rules relating to consideration

Consideration must be valuable, but need not be adequate

2.1   There are three main rules that you should be familiar with. Each is analysed in detail below.

- Consideration must be valuable, but need not be adequate.
- Consideration must be sufficient.
- Consideration must move from the promisee.

2.2   In law, the parties to a contract are free to conclude their bargain on whatever terms they think are appropriate. The courts will not question the adequacy of the consideration agreed upon by balancing the respective promises or acts of the parties to ascertain whether the agreement is fair in an objective or commercial sense, but they must be satisfied that there is something of real value provided by the parties. As long as the parties are of equal bargaining power and there is no duress they will not investigate the motives behind the transaction or check the consideration given.

2.3   Valuable consideration means money or money's worth, that is to say something upon which a monetary value can be placed such as rendering a service.

2.4   The consideration provided must be valuable in the sense that it must have some value, however slight. In **Thomas v Thomas** (1842) a promise to convey a house to a widow on her promise to pay £1 per year rent and keep the house in repair was binding; the promise to pay £1 per year and keep the house in repair amounted to valuable consideration.

2.5   However, the consideration need not be sufficient in an objective sense to pay for the promise received: **Chappell & Co v Nestlé Co Ltd** (1960).

Nestlé offered records for sale to the public for 1s 6d (7.5p in today's currency) and three chocolate wrappers each.

Held: The chocolate wrappers were part of the consideration even though they were of minimal value and, in fact, thrown away by Nestlé as soon as received.

2.6   However, where the consideration for a transaction is highly inadequate it may raise a suspicion of fraud, duress or undue influence on the part of the person gaining the advantage.

2.7   **Valuable consideration** must be distinguished from consideration in the moral sense. For example, a promise from feelings of natural love and affection for the promisee is not legally enforceable, as where a father promises to buy a house for his daughter who is homeless after her husband's death: **White v Bluett** (1853).

The alleged consideration was a son's promise to his father that he would cease complaining to him.

Held: Such a promise could not be measured in value and was too insubstantial to amount to real consideration.

Consideration must be sufficient

2.8   The consideration provided must be 'sufficient' in the sense that it must be something the law recognises as consideration. Various acts and omissions have been held by the courts not to constitute sufficient consideration. These include the performance of an existing duty already imposed by law, the performance of an existing duty already imposed by contract, and past consideration. These are discussed in turn below.

Performance of an existing duty imposed by law

2.9   Where a person is **obliged to do something by law** the discharge of that duty will not amount to consideration and cannot support a contract: **Collins v Godefroy** (1831).

A witness, subpoenaed (legally required) to attend court, was promised payment if he would attend court and give evidence. He attended court and sued for the payment promised.

Held: He had not provided consideration, as he was legally obliged to attend under the subpoena. He had done no more than he was legally obliged to do already, and so had not provided sufficient consideration for a contract to exist.

2.10   However, if an act is performed over and above that required by law or public duty, that act is sufficient consideration for any promise to confer a benefit in return: **Glasbrook Brothers Ltd v Glamorgan County Council** (1925).

Glasbrook Brothers Ltd promised to pay the police authority if it stationed police officers on company premises to protect that property from apprehended damage during a miners' strike. The company had rejected a recommendation by the superintendent in charge that a mobile force movable to any trouble spot constituted an adequate safeguard.

Held: The police authority was entitled to payment of the promised remuneration. The police have a public duty to provide only that degree of protection that is reasonably necessary in the circumstances of the individual case. A permanent force of policemen on company property was an additional protection which provided the consideration necessary to enforce the promise to pay.

Performance of an existing duty imposed by contract

2.11   If a person is **obliged to perform an act under an existing contract** and the other party then promises to pay him an additional sum of money to ensure that he finishes the work on time there will be no new contract in respect of the extra sum of money.

2.12   This is because the person doing the work has provided no new consideration (no 'sufficiency' of consideration). He has done no more than he is already obliged to do under the pre-existing contract. Without new consideration there can be no new contract and so he cannot make a claim that this new contract has been breached. The classic case is **Stilk v Myrick** (1809).

A ship's captain, unable to replace two deserting seamen from the crew, promised those remaining that if they completed the voyage the wages of the deserters would be divided amongst them, in addition to their contractually agreed wage.

Held: The extra payment need not be paid since the remaining seamen, by completing the voyage, did no more than they were originally contractually obliged to do.

2.13   This case may be compared with **Hartley v Ponsonby** (1857).

A high number of desertions from a merchant ship rendered the vessel unseaworthy since it was now undermanned. Extra pay was offered to the crew if they remained loyal.

Held: The promise of extra money was recoverable by the seamen who remained loyal since they were now working in a dangerous situation not contemplated by their original contractual undertaking (ie they were doing more than required by their original contract).

2.14   Performance of an existing contractual obligation is sufficient consideration to support a promise from a third party: **Shadwell v Shadwell** (1860).

C promised his nephew, A, an allowance if he would marry his fiancée, B (in those days an agreement to marry was legally binding).

Held: The promise was binding, even though A was already obliged to marry B. A had provided consideration for the uncle's promise as he was initially under a duty to the fiancée not to the uncle.

2.15   The more recent case of **Williams v Roffey Brothers** (1990) is rather difficult to reconcile with **Stilk v Myrick**.

Williams agreed to do some carpentry in a block of flats for Roffey at a fixed price of £20,000. There was an agreed date by which the work was to be completed. The work ran late and Roffey agreed to pay an extra £10,000 to ensure that the work was completed on time. If the work was not completed on time Roffey would have suffered a penalty in his own contract with the owner of the flats.

Held: The court decided that even though Williams was in effect doing nothing over and above the original agreement to complete the work by a stated time there was a new contract here for the £10,000. The court decided that both Williams and Roffey benefited from the new contract.

2.16   Two reasons were given for this decision.

•   The new consideration given by Williams was that of enabling Roffey to avoid the penalty sum (and not merely finishing the work on time). As such he had provided 'something new'.

•   Roffey's promise to pay the extra £10,000 had not been extracted by fraud or pressure. It would be inequitable to go back on this promise.

Past consideration

2.17   Finally, **past consideration** is not regarded as sufficient. The act or promise of one party and the act or promise of the other must constitute one single transaction. One party must do something because the other party is doing something. If one party makes a promise in return for an act or promise which has already been performed unilaterally, the two promises are not a response to one another and do not support a contract: **Re McArdle** (1951).

A man and his wife spent £488 on improvements to a bungalow in which they resided with the husband's mother. When the mother died the house would become the joint property of the husband and his brothers and sisters. The man attempted to enforce a promise made by the brothers and sisters to repay the cost of the improvements after completion of the work.

Held: Since all the work had been carried out before the promise was made, this past consideration could not support the later promise to reimburse the cost so as to bring a binding obligation into existence. Past consideration is no consideration.

2.18　Past consideration must be distinguished from the situation where a promise of payment in return for an act carried out some time in the past, at the request of the promisor, is enforceable by the promisee, provided that both parties contemplated throughout that some payment should be made: **Re Casey's Patents** (1892).

Casey spent two years promoting a patent jointly owned by two persons who encouraged him so to act. Later, Casey was given a written assurance that he would receive a one-third share of the patent in payment for his work.

Held: This assurance was legally binding; an implication existed when Casey agreed to work for the owners that he would ultimately be paid for his services.

2.19　However, there are exceptions to the rule that past consideration is insufficient.

- Bills of exchange can be supported by past consideration: s 27 Bills of Exchange Act 1882. A bill of exchange is a written order by one person to another to pay a sum of money to the former or to another person (eg a cheque is a bill of exchange drawn on a banker and payable on demand).

- Past consideration is sufficient to support a written acknowledgement of a debt in order to re-start time running for the purposes of the Limitation Act 1980. This somewhat technical provision is not important for exam purposes.

2.20　One final rule is that the doing of, or promise of doing, an illegal act is insufficient to amount to consideration.

Consideration must move from the promisee

2.21　A person wishing to enforce a contract must show that he personally provided consideration. It is not enough that someone else provided consideration to the party being sued. For example, Alan services Brian's car in return for Brian's promise to pay the agreed charge of £20 to Colin. If Alan completes the service Colin cannot sue for payment of the £20 since, as promisee, he did not personally supply consideration to Brian. Only Alan can sue Brian.

2.22　This principle is often confused with the rule called 'privity of contract' (see Chapter 15), that only a party to a contract can enforce it. Though interconnected, these are in fact two separate rules which operate independently of each other.

2.23　For example, Jim has recently married Margaret and their respective fathers promise to pay Jim £5,000 each. Each father suffers a detriment, and also receives a benefit in the form of an equivalent payment by the other father to make suitable provision for their children, whom they wish to see settled for life.

2.24 If only Jim's father pays, then he may sue Margaret's father for failing to implement his promise. Jim cannot sue however, since he did not provide any consideration in return for his father-in-law's promise. Further, Jim might not be a party to the contract between his father and his father-in-law. Even if Jim had been expressly joined as a party to a written contract he could not have enforced his father-in-law's promise, since he did not provide any consideration in return.

2.25 On the other hand, if the agreement is concluded by deed and if Jim is joined as a party to the deed, then he may personally enforce his father-in-law's promise. Not only is he a party to the contract, but also his failure to supply consideration is immaterial in a specialty contract.

2.26 A leading case in this area is that of **Tweddle v Atkinson** (1861).

The claimant's father and father-in-law agreed with each other to pay the claimant £100 and £200 respectively in consideration of his then intended marriage and after the marriage had taken place they confirmed their agreement in writing. The £200 was not paid and the claimant sued his father-in-law's executor to recover this sum.

Held: His action must fail as no stranger to the consideration can take advantage of a contract, although made for his benefit. A promisee cannot bring a successful action unless the consideration for the promise moved from him.

3 The problem of part-payment

The rule in Pinnel's case

3.1 The rule in **Pinnel's case** (1602) states that payment of a lesser sum in satisfaction of a greater sum cannot be any satisfaction for the whole sum. This rule has been affirmed by the House of Lords in the case of **Foakes v Beer** (1884).

Mrs Beer obtained a judgement against Dr Foakes for a sum of £2,090 with interest. She agreed to payment of the debt in instalments and also promised that further proceedings on the judgement would not be taken. After receiving the £2,090, Mrs Beer sued for £360 interest on the judgement debt which Dr Foakes refused to pay.

Held: The interest was recoverable. Payment of the debt and costs, a smaller sum, was not consideration for the promise to accept this amount in satisfaction of a debt, interest and costs, a greater sum. The debtor had not provided any consideration for the promise not to claim interest.

3.2 A creditor who agrees to accept £50 from a debtor in payment and satisfaction of a debt for £100 does not receive any benefit for his promise not to claim the balance; consequently the creditor's promise is unenforceable at common law. The creditor cannot be restrained from breaking his promise and taking legal action to recover the balance of the debt still unpaid.

3.3   This is really an example of the rule that a promise to do something one is already bound to do by contract is insufficient consideration to enforce a promise. But note the following points.

- **The rule only applies to liquidated claims,** ie claims for fixed amounts (eg the price of goods), and not for unliquidated amounts (eg damages for defective goods).

- **The rule only applies to undisputed claims**; where the claim is disputed in good faith, the value is again uncertain. Unless this were so, all legal actions compromised to avoid litigation could be reopened at a later stage.

3.4   It seems unfair that a party can apparently dupe another party by accepting a smaller sum in full and final settlement of his claim and then go back and sue for the full amount. So the law has found ways around the problem. These are discussed below.

Variation of terms at the creditor's request

3.5   Where the payment of a lesser sum in discharge of a greater debt is accompanied by the introduction of some new element at the creditor's request, the new element is sufficient consideration to support the creditor's promise not to claim the balance of the debt still unpaid. This is often called **accord and satisfaction**. The accord is the agreement to accept less and the satisfaction is the new consideration.

3.6   The new element introduced at the creditor's request, which is the consideration he receives for not claiming the balance, may take a number of forms. Examples include:

- payment of the debt on a date earlier than that originally agreed

- payment at a different place to that stipulated in the agreement

- payment of a smaller sum accompanied by the transfer of another item (eg £10 plus a book in satisfaction of a £15 debt).

3.7   A vitally important case in this area is that of **D&C Builders v Rees** (1966).

The defendant owed £482 to the claimant (a building company) for work carried out. The defendant, knowing that the claimant was in desperate need of money to stave off bankruptcy, offered £300 by cheque in settlement of the debt saying that if the claimant refused he would get nothing. The claimant accepted the £300 reluctantly in settlement.

Held: The claimant could successfully sue for the balance.

3.8   Several reasons contributed to the court's decision.

- In view of the pressure put on the claimant and the claimant's reluctance to accept there was no true accord.

- Payment by cheque and cash are, in these circumstances, no different. Therefore the payment by cheque did not amount to consideration: it conferred no benefit over and above payment in cash.

3.9   If the promise to accept less than is owed, or nothing at all, is made by deed it will be binding. Remember that an agreement made by deed does not require consideration. So if the agreement to accept a lesser sum is made by deed no satisfaction is required to make that accord binding.

Part-payment by a third party

3.10 A creditor who has agreed to accept a smaller sum from a third party, in full satisfaction of a debtor's obligation to pay a larger sum, is prevented from claiming the balance of the debt from the debtor himself, since this would be a fraud on the third party: **Hirachand Punamchand v Temple** *(1911)*.

The defendant had given the claimant a promissory note (this is evidence of a promise to pay the bearer a certain sum of money in the future). The claimant accepted a smaller sum from the defendant's father in full and final settlement of the debt.

Held: The claimant could not sue the defendant for the balance. The position was as if the promissory note had been cancelled as the original debt had been discharged by payment by another person of the smaller sum.

Composition with creditors

3.11 A debtor who is unable to pay his debts in full may make an arrangement with his creditors in consequence of which they all agree to accept part-payment of outstanding debts in full satisfaction of their claims.

3.12 If an individual creditor went back on his promise by attempting to sue for the balance of his debt, this would constitute a fraud on the other creditors who were observing the composition.

3.13 The consideration between the creditors themselves, supporting their individual promises not to sue, is the promise of each creditor not to claim the full debt so that no creditor benefits at the expense of the others.

3.14 The debtor's consideration is the procuring of a promise from each individual creditor to accept less than the full amount so that creditors generally will share whatever property is available.

4 *The doctrine of promissory estoppel*

The nature of the doctrine

4.1 Another way around the part-payment problem is to apply the principle of equity or fairness. As has already been seen, the rule that a gratuitous promise is unenforceable (unless it is given by deed) can produce hardship.

4.2 There is no question that if a certain sum is owed under a contract, the party to whom the money is owed can invoke the common law to sue for the debt. This is the case even if it appears unfair to go back on his word as in **Foakes v Beer**.

4.3 However equity can act to interpret or modify the common law where it appears harsh or inflexible. The equitable concept of **estoppel**, referred to as **promissory estoppel**, may operate to prevent a person going back on his promise to accept a lesser amount. The promise which the claimant is prevented by equity from breaking is a promise relating to his future conduct.

4.4   The leading case is that of **Central London Property Trust Ltd v High Trees House Ltd** (1947).

In 1937, the claimant company ('the lessor') let a block of flats in London to the defendant company ('the lessee') on a ninety-nine year term, at a ground rent of £2,500 per year. During the war, because of the blitz, few flats could be let to tenants by High Trees House Ltd, and the lessor agreed to reduce the rent by one-half. By 1945, all the flats had been let and the lessor claimed full rent for the last two quarters of 1945.

Held: The lessor's claim should be allowed since the wartime conditions giving rise to the promise to reduce the rent had now ended and the agreement was no longer operative.

4.5   Although the claimants were not claiming the full rent during the war the court commented on whether they could have claimed it. (This was *obiter dicta*.) The lessee had not provided any consideration for the lessor's promise to reduce the rent, but if payment of full rent had been demanded for the years during which the flats were unoccupied, then the doctrine of **equitable estoppel** would have barred any such claim.

4.6   The promise not to claim the full rent was 'intended to be acted upon, and in fact acted upon, [and] is binding so far as its terms properly apply. It is binding as covering the period down to 1945, and from that time full rent is payable.' In this way Lord Justice Denning let promissory estoppel in through the back door of *obiter dicta*.

4.7   It must be clear that one party has made an unequivocal representation whether by words or conduct, which he intends the other party to rely upon.

4.8   The exact scope of promissory estoppel is not clear and there are difficulties with it as it does conflict with the rule in **Pinnel's case**. Partially as a result of this confusion, certain limitations have been put on the principle. These are discussed below.

4.9   Firstly, the doctrine is *'a shield not a sword'* (ie it is a defence, but cannot be used as a weapon). The doctrine may be used by a defendant as a defence to an action claiming the debt which the claimant promised to waive, but equitable estoppel cannot be used by a person in the position of a claimant to demand rights not supported by consideration.

4.10   Secondly, **it may have only a suspensory effect**. The obligations imposed by the original contract, later modified by mutual agreement, may be reverted to after the promisor has given sufficient notice to the promisee of his intention to do so, or where the situation giving rise to the modification comes to an end. The future relationship between the parties is then governed by their original contractual undertaking.

4.11   The effect of the principle on periodic payments such as rent or hire-purchase instalments is clear: arrears which have been waived are irrecoverable but future payments may be demanded in full. This was the actual decision in the **High Trees** case.

4.12   A party relying on equitable estoppel must also have acted fairly and in accordance with equitable principles: for example, the doctrine would not have supported the rather unscrupulous action of the defendant in the **D&C Builders** case.

Example

4.13 Bev offers to sell Raman her car for £12,000. Raman accepts and promises to pay in two equal instalments; the first instalment due in three months and the balance after a further three months. Raman pays the first instalment but then loses his job and he realises that he will be unable to pay the balance.

He approaches Bev and asks her if she will accept a further £4,000 in full and final settlement of all of her claims. She agrees and he pays her a cheque.

The next day Bev issues proceedings in the County Court for the outstanding £2,000. Her action is based on the original contract. Raman serves a defence upon her which is based upon the fact that the money is not, in fact, owed at all. He claims that there is a new contract in which she has agreed to accept £10,000 in full and final settlement of all claims. Raman says that this is contractually binding.

Write a brief summary of the competing contractual claims in this situation concentrating upon the matters surrounding the mutual consideration.

Solution to example

4.14 Bev claims that there is no consideration for the new contract.

- Raman did not offer her anything other than that which he was contractually obliged to do (ie pay money under the existing contract; £12,000 was owed).

- As a result there was insufficient consideration to support the new contract and it did not exist.

- The case of **Stilk v Myrick** applies: Raman has not exceeded his existing contractual duty and so is still bound by the original contract.

4.15 Raman is claiming that there is a new contract. He can support this claim as follows.

- By paying the smaller sum early he has provided new consideration (under the rules of 'accord and satisfaction'.) Being paid earlier is valuable and so it will be regarded as sufficient consideration.

- Alternatively, the doctrine of promissory estoppel may apply. The creditor has waived part of the original consideration in exchange for no new consideration. She has promised not to go back on her word and if Raman can fairly show that he has in some way suffered detriment from her action she will be estopped by the court from going back on her promise.

Chapter summary

*   With minor exceptions, a contract is not binding unless supported by consideration.

*   Consideration must be valuable, but need not be adequate.

*   Consideration must be sufficient. Several cases illustrate examples of insufficient consideration, eg performance of a pre-existing duty. Past consideration is generally not sufficient.

*   Consideration must move from the promisee.

*   In general, payment of a lesser sum does not prevent the creditor from pressing for payment of the balance. However, in some circumstances this rule is overturned: for example, accord and satisfaction, or a composition with creditors.

*   A creditor may be estopped from pursuing the unpaid amount if he has promised to waive it and the debtor has acted on this promise. This is the doctrine of promissory estoppel.

Self-test questions

Numbers in brackets refer to the paragraphs above where your answers can be checked.

1   Define what is meant by consideration. (1.2, 1.6)

2   Distinguish between executed and executory consideration. (1.7, 1.8)

3   What is the difference between 'value' and 'adequacy' in relation to consideration? (2.3–2.5)

4   What principles are established by the cases of **Glasbrook v Glamorgan CC** and **Stilk v Myrick**? (2.10, 2.12)

5   Summarise the details of **Williams v Roffey Brothers**. (2.15)

6   What is meant by the rule that consideration must move from the promisee? (2.21)

7   What is the rule in **Pinnel's** case? (3.1)

8   Summarise the details of the **High Trees House** case. (4.4)

CHAPTER 5

Intention, Capacity and Form

Learning objectives and indicative content

1.1   Analyse the legal problems that may arise from the process of contract formation and the problems of reconciling the buyer's terms and conditions with those of the seller when faced with the battle of the forms.

- Letters of intent
- Electronic contracting

Chapter headings

1   Intention to create legal relations

2   Capacity to contract

3   Contract form

4   Electronic contracting

Introduction

In this chapter we complete our discussion of the essential elements of a binding contract. The three final elements are:

- intention to create legal relations
- capacity to contract
- contract form.

In business contexts an intention to create legal relations is usually present, but we look at exceptions to this rule and glance briefly at the situation in non-business contexts.

Most individuals have full contractual capacity. We mention briefly the exceptions to this rule, and then describe how contractual capacity applies to 'artificial' persons such as companies. This is important for your professional work, because of course most contracts you undertake as buyers will be in the name of the organisations you work for.

Although commercial contracts do not normally have to be in any prescribed form, there are certain contracts which must be executed in a particular legal form.

We will also look at the formation of contracts by electronic means. E-commerce in purchasing typically takes two forms: a traditional exchange of correspondence, but by e-mail, or making limited choices from a company's website. The basic principles of contract formation remain as in non-electronic transactions, but the new rules relating to electronic commerce are a small step forward for purchasers in imposing some basic standards for electronic commerce.

1   *Intention to create legal relations*

Domestic and social agreements

1.1   Some agreements are not intended to be legally enforceable, their nature being such that a reasonable man viewing the words and conduct of the parties objectively would not conclude that they intended to create legal relations. For example, a reasonable man would not expect an enforceable legal obligation to spring from a mere social engagement, such as an invitation to lunch, despite the presence of all the other essential elements necessary to create a binding agreement. Even a 'car pool' arrangement in which one party contributes to the running costs of another's vehicle does not rank as a contract: **Coward v MIB** (1963).

1.2   In domestic and social arrangements there is a presumption that there was no intention for the agreement to be legally binding. Arrangements in a domestic or social context include agreements made between members of a family and between friends. A presumption means that the claimant in the action need not prove certain matters on a balance of probabilities; the court presumes that they exist.

1.3   A case to illustrate this is that of **Balfour v Balfour** (1919).

The defendant, who was about to go abroad, promised to pay his wife £30 per month in consideration of her agreeing to support herself without calling on him for any further maintenance. The wife contended that the defendant was bound by his promise.

Held: There was no legally binding contract between the parties. As it was a domestic agreement it was presumed the parties did not intend to be legally bound.

1.4   However this presumption may be rebutted. Thus the court may reach a contrary conclusion after examining words used and surrounding circumstances: **Simpkins v Pays** (1955).

Pays and her granddaughter, together with Simpkins, a paying lodger, submitted an entry each week in a fashion competition appearing in the Sunday Empire News. All three devised a separate solution to the competition, but they were submitted on one coupon only, in Pays' name. The entry fees and postage were shared equally. The granddaughter made a correct forecast and Pays received a prize of £750. Simpkins claimed a one-third share of the prize money.

Held: Although this was an arrangement in a domestic context the normal presumption was rebutted: it was a legally enforceable joint enterprise and the parties clearly intended to share any prize money. 'There was mutuality in the arrangements between the parties and an intention to create legal relations.' It was decided that on the facts this went beyond a mere friendly agreement and became a joint enterprise.

1.5   The normal presumption will also be rebutted where the evidence shows that the parties made formal and/or detailed financial arrangements: **Parker v Clark** (1960).

1.6   The usual presumption that agreements between spouses living happily together are not legally enforceable does not apply when they are about to separate, or have already separated: **Merritt v Merritt** (1970).

Commercial agreements

1.7 In the case of ordinary commercial dealings (for example buying and selling) there is a strong presumption that the parties intended it to be legally binding. This presumption can be rebutted if a contrary intention is clearly expressed in the agreement itself: this was the ruling **in Rose and Frank Co v Crompton** (1925) and also in **Jones v Vernon's Pools Ltd** (1938).

Jones contended that he had forwarded a winning entry to the defendant company of football pools promoters, but they denied having received it. In order to deal with this type of eventuality, a clause was printed on the pools coupon which Jones had signed, stating that 'any agreement... entered into... shall not... give rise to any legal relationship... but... is binding in honour only'.

Held: A contract did not exist between the parties, since the wording of the agreement clearly negated any such intention. Jones could not, therefore, sue the pools company for breach of contract.

1.8 Another illustration is given by the case of **Edwards v Skyways** (1964).

An employer agreed to make an ex gratia payment to a redundant employee. (Ex gratia means non-contractual and at the will of one of the parties.)

Held: The use of the term *ex gratia* was only a denial of a previous liability. It did not rule out an intention by the parties to be legally bound, and in this case the employer's promise was enforceable.

Collective agreements

1.9 A collective agreement is defined as an agreement or arrangement made by, or on behalf of, one or more trade unions and one or more employers' associations, concerning working conditions of the employees.

1.10 Collective agreements are conclusively presumed not to have been intended by the parties to be legally enforceable unless there is a written term stating that the agreement is intended to be wholly or partially enforceable by legal action; then it is conclusively presumed to be so to the extent indicated.

1.11 In practice, trade unions and employers resist agreeing to the legal enforceability of a collective agreement to which they are party, especially if it embodies a clause restricting the right of the workers to strike or take other forms of industrial action. Such agreements are binding in honour only and the terms agreed upon may be violated without giving rise to any right of legal redress for the innocent party.

Letters of intent

1.12 One final point on the subject of intention is highly relevant to buyers. This is the use of a letter of intent.

1.13 Such letters can arise frequently in commercial contexts, where the parties are not yet ready to sign a formal contract, but intend to do so once final terms are agreed. It often happens that one party will commence work on his side of the bargain on the strength of a letter of intent from the other party.

1.14 This is a risky procedure. Until terms have been formally agreed, or can be established with a degree of certainty, no binding contract exists and either party completing work under such circumstances does so at his peril.

1.15 The leading case in this area is that of **British Steel Corporation v Cleveland Bridge & Engineering Co Ltd** (1984).

The defendant, CBE, negotiated with the claimant, BSC, to buy steel nodes for use in a construction project. CBE needed the nodes urgently and, before terms had been agreed, asked BSC to commence manufacture on the strength of a letter in which CBE expressed their intention to complete a formal contract. While negotiations dragged on, BSC began to manufacture and then deliver the nodes, retaining only the last one to strengthen their bargaining position. This last node became trapped as a result of a strike. When it was finally delivered, BSC claimed for the price of the nodes and CBE counterclaimed damages for late delivery.

Held: CBE had no claim for damages as no contract existed. BSC were entitled to claim a reasonable price (*quantum meruit*) for the nodes delivered.

2 Capacity to contract

Persons who lack capacity to contract

2.1 In order for a contract to be valid the parties must have the legal capacity (or ability) to contract. Most individuals have such capacity automatically. However, there are a number of instances where this is not the case.

2.2 Those who are deemed incapable by the law to contract include:

- minors
- the mentally disordered
- drunkards.

2.3 Clearly these cases are not very relevant to the examination syllabus or to your professional work, and they are not examined in detail here.

Corporations

2.4 A more interesting case for purchasing specialists is the contractual capacity of corporations. A corporation is a recognised legal person having a distinct legal personality. As such it has the capacity to make contracts in its own name.

2.5 A corporation is required to have a formal description of its activities (in a document called a Memorandum of Association). If a corporation makes a contract which is unconnected with those stated activities the contract is said to be *ultra vires* the corporation (beyond the corporation's powers).

2.6 At common law an *ultra vires* contract is void. Thus the corporation cannot sue the other party on the contract nor can the other party sue the corporation. Exceptionally, the common law effect of the *ultra vires* rule does not apply to contracts made by corporations created by registration under the Companies Act 1985 (such a corporation is commonly referred to as a company). Thus if a company makes an *ultra vires* contract that contract is **not** void for lack of capacity.

2.7   No corporation has contractual capacity before it is formed. A corporation becomes a legal person on the date it is incorporated. Before that date it does not exist as a legal person so cannot make contracts – **Kelner v Baxter** (1866). Any person who acts on behalf of a company not yet formed will generally be personally liable on the contract under company law.

3   Contract form

3.1   As we saw in Chapter 2, no particular form or writing is usually required for commercial contracts. However, certain contracts – such as for the sale of land, or marine insurance – must be in writing. In the absence of writing, if one of the parties refuses to abide by the terms of the contract, the other party cannot sue under the contract in court. Such contracts will either be void or unenforceable.

4   Electronic contracting

4.1   Many businesses use websites and e-mail for commercial purposes. Many firms are also moving towards electronic contracts and thinking about whether to use electronic signatures on them. Those involved in purchasing and supply need to consider the changes to English law that have resulted from the implementation of two EU directives in 2002 – on electronic signatures and electronic commerce.

4.2   The Electronic Signatures Directive 1999 was implemented into UK law by virtue of the Electronic Communications Act 2000, which recognises digital signatures as legally valid.

4.3   Many of the contracts companies deal with do not need a signature to be valid. As we have seen previously, no particular form or writing is required for commercial contracts. Most companies e-mail draft contracts to each other freely, but for the bigger deals they print off the final version for signature. It is not that these documents must be signed to be legally valid, but if the other party denies agreeing the terms, a signature makes it easier to prove they did so. An e-signature rather than one on paper could be used for these contracts if the parties so wish. It will be entirely voluntary.

4.4   The Electronic Communications Act only implemented part of the EC directive. A minor part remained, which has now been brought into force. The Electronic Signatures Regulations 2002 (SI 2002/318) relate to the supervision of certification service providers, their liability in certain circumstances, and data protection requirements concerning them.

4.5   The Electronic Commerce Directive 2000 was implemented into UK law by virtue of the Electronic Commerce (EC Directive) Regulations 2002 (SI 2002/2013) and sets out to remove many of the existing legal barriers and uncertainty with e-commerce. The Directive sets out basic information that should appear on a company's e-mails and website, whether goods and services are sold from the site or not. Many companies do not give this information and should now do so. The Directive also includes provisions relevant to those who sell online to consumers, and deals with the liability of internet service providers.

4.6   Regulation 6 requires companies to include the following information in any commercial e-mail they send: name; geographic address; details including e-mail address; trade register in which registered and number; supervisory authority, where relevant; for regulated professions, the regulator; VAT number, where relevant. In addition, where goods or services are being provided, companies must include a clear statement of the price and whether it includes tax and delivery costs.

4.7   Regulation 7 sets out further rules on commercial communications – they must be clearly identifiable as such – and about promotions and competitions. Regulation 8 places a duty on sellers to check opt-out e-mail registers.

4.8   Regulation 9 concerns information for web orders. Before the order is concluded, the buyer should be given information on: technical steps to conclude the contract; whether the contract will be filed with the supplier and how it can be accessed; technical means for identifying and correcting input errors before the order is placed; and languages offered for conclusion of the contract. These measures are not required where the order is placed by e-mail rather than via a website. Regulation 11 requires receipts to be issued for orders placed via a website. Regulations 13 to 15 state that in case of failure to provide the means for the buyer to identify and correct input errors in compliance with Regulations 6 to 9 and 11, the buyer shall have the right to rescind the contract.

Chapter summary

- In domestic and social contexts it is presumed that agreements **are not** meant to be legally binding.

- In commercial contexts it is presumed that agreements **are** intended to be legally binding.

- Both of these presumptions may be rebutted if the facts of the case so indicate.

- Collective agreements are presumed **not** to be intended as legally enforceable unless there is a written term to the contrary.

- A firm doing work on the strength of a letter of intent has no contract to rely on, but may have a claim to be paid on a *quantum meruit* basis.

- Most individuals have full contractual capacity, though some exceptions exist. Companies also have contractual capacity.

- Commercial contracts do not generally have to be in a particular form.

- Additional rules apply to the normal rules on contract formation for electronic transactions.

Self-test questions

Numbers in brackets refer to the paragraphs above where your answers can be checked.

1   What was the principle laid down in **Balfour v Balfour**? (1.3)

2   Describe two cases illustrating exceptions to the usual rule that intention to create legal relations is normally assumed in commercial contexts. (1.7, 1.8)

3   Describe the principles arrived at in the case of **British Steel v Cleveland Bridge**. (1.15)

4   In what circumstances may an individual lack contractual capacity? (2.2)

5   What is meant by the term *ultra vires*? (2.5)

6   What is meant by contract form? (3.1)

7   What are the two recent UK Regulations relating to the formation of electronic contracts? (4.4, 4.5)

CHAPTER 6

The Terms of a Contract

Learning objectives and indicative content

1.2 Distinguish between different types of contractual terms and assess the legal validity of specific types of contractual clauses.

- Expressed and implied terms
- Conditions, warranties and innominate terms
- Exclusion and limitation clauses
- Indemnity clauses
- *Force majeure* clauses

Chapter headings

1 Terms and representations

2 Express and implied terms

3 Conditions and warranties

4 Exclusion clauses and unfair contract terms

5 Guarantees and indemnities

6 *Force majeure* clauses

Introduction

Having dealt with the main elements in the formation of a binding contract we look in this chapter at the contents of the contract: the terms and conditions by which the parties are bound. These can include simple matters such as price and date of delivery but they can also contain complicated references to the passage of title in the goods and the exclusion of liability in the event of a breach of contract. They can also include special clauses including *force majeure* and retention of title.

In determining the contract terms there are a number of areas which need to be considered.

- Whether a statement made in negotiations has become a term of the contract or not
- The need for certainty of essential terms of the agreement
- What, if any, terms will be implied into a contract
- The importance of any particular term and what happens if it is broken
- Whether a term in a contract excluding or limiting a party's liability for breach is effective.

1 *Terms and representations*

The distinction between terms and mere representations

1.1 A statement, written or oral, made during negotiations leading to a contract, may be a term of the subsequent contract or merely a representation inducing the contract.

1.2 It is important to ascertain whether a statement becomes a term of the contract or remains a mere representation because the remedies available to a wronged party will differ depending on whether there is a breach of a contractual term or merely a misrepresentation.

1.3 The differences between terms and representations are as follows.

- If the representation is subsequently included in the contract as one of its terms and if it is then later found to be untrue, the party misled has remedies for breach of the term, as well as for misrepresentation.

- If, however, the representation does not become a term of the contract, the party misled will have remedies **only** for misrepresentation. Misrepresentation and the related remedies are discussed in Chapter 7.

Intention of the parties

1.4 Whether a statement becomes a term of the contract or not depends on the intention of the parties. The test of the parties' intentions is objective and will depend on what was said and the circumstances in which the statement was made.

1.5 In deciding whether a statement is a term or a representation the following paragraphs provide relevant guidelines.

1.6 When the statement was made is important. The greater the interval of time between making the statement and making the contract the more likely it is that it will be a mere representation.

1.7 Whether the statement was reduced to writing after it was made is also important. If it was, it is more likely to be a term of the contract.

1.8 The importance of the statement to the recipient is also relevant. For example, where a statement on the quality of the goods being sold is the whole basis upon which the contract is made as far as the buyer is concerned then it will be a term: **Bannerman v White** (1861).

A buyer of hops asked the seller whether sulphur had been used in the treatment and added that if it had he would not buy. The seller assured him that sulphur had not been used. Sulphur had in fact been used.

Held: The court decided that as the use of sulphur was a vital part of the contract, around which the whole deal revolved, it was a term.

1.9 Where a party negotiating the contract suggests that the other party should check the accuracy of his assertions before finally concluding the contract (eg suggesting to a potential house-purchaser that a survey should be made and a report of the probable defects in the structure be given), the statement will probably not be a term.

1.10 However, it has been held to be a term where a forceful or emphatic assertion suggests that a potential buyer need not bother to check its accuracy: **Schawel v Reade** (1913).

Schawel was examining a horse which he was considering buying for stud purposes. The seller stated: 'You need not look for anything, the horse is perfectly sound. If there was anything the matter with the horse I should tell you'. Schawel then ceased his examination. A few days later a price was agreed upon and three weeks later Schawel bought the horse relying on the seller's statement. The horse proved to be unsuitable for stud purposes.

Held: The seller's statement was a contractual term. It was obvious from the words and actions of the parties that the responsibility for the soundness of the horse should rest upon the vendor.

1.11 If the person making the statement has special knowledge or skill his statements are more likely to be regarded as a term of the contract. For example, where goods are sold by an expert who guarantees to the buyer that they have stated qualities which, in fact, they lack the statement has been held to be a term of the contract: **Dick Bentley Productions Ltd v Harold Smith (Motors) Ltd** (1965).

Bentley was interested in purchasing a Bentley car with an ascertainable history. The defendant, a car dealer, persuaded Bentley to purchase a car which was described as having a replacement engine and gearbox with only 20,000 miles on the odometer since replacement. The assertion relating to the mileage was false.

Held: The dealer's statements became a term of the contract of sale, for breach of which damages were recoverable. The special skill and knowledge of the car dealer placed him in a stronger position than the purchaser. Consequently the court could more easily infer that the statements relating to the condition of the car formed the basis of a contractual term rather than a mere representation.

1.12 However, where a layman who does not normally deal in the kind of goods being disposed of makes an assertion to an expert the statement is unlikely to be a term of the contract: **Oscar Chess Ltd v Williams** (1957).

Williams, on selling a car to the claimant company of car dealers, asserted that it was a 1948 model. The registration book appeared to confirm this statement, but it had been altered by some previous owner and the car was in fact a 1939 model.

Held: The statement was an innocent misrepresentation but not a term of the contract. The seller, who was not a car dealer with expert knowledge, did not intend to be bound contractually by his statement concerning the age of the vehicle. The dealers should have checked the engine and chassis numbers to verify the date of manufacture.

1.13 A representation is something that is said by the offeror in order to induce the offeree to enter into the contract. It only becomes a term of that contract if it becomes formalised (eg written down and inserted into an agreement) or if it can be said to be a very important part of the contract (for example, a statement on which the other party relies). This is especially the case if the party is an expert in the relevant matters or has certain information which is critical to the decision making process of the other side.

1.14   If what is said is merely a representation and is untrue the innocent party's action is for misrepresentation; see Chapter 7.

1.15   By contrast, if what is said is not only a representation but also becomes a term of the contract and is untrue the innocent party may sue for misrepresentation and/or breach of contract at his choice.

2   Express and implied terms

Introduction

2.1   Terms can be implied into a contract or they can be expressly inserted by either or both of the parties. A common example of an express term is an exclusion clause (sometimes known as an exemption clause). This is discussed later in this chapter.

2.2   A common example of implied terms is the group of terms inserted into contracts by the Sale of Goods Act 1979. These will be discussed in detail in Chapter 11.

2.3   Express terms may be written or oral or partly written and partly oral. Normally, an oral contract is as enforceable and as valid as a written contract. Express terms are terms specifically inserted into the contract by either or both of the parties.

Certainty of terms

2.4   An agreement can only be enforced as a contract if it contains, implies or provides for the necessary terms on all essential points. Thus the terms of the contract must be complete and certain of meaning: **King's Motors (Oxford) Ltd v Lax** (1969).

The parties agreed to an option to renew a lease 'at such rental as may be agreed upon between the parties'.

Held: The agreement was void for uncertainty since it was incomplete – the vital term as to amount of rent still being subject to negotiation.

2.5   Another example is the case of **Scammell v Ouston** (1941).

An agreement provided for the balance of the price '... on hire purchase terms over a period of two years'.

Held: The words 'hire purchase terms' were considered too imprecise and there was no contract.

2.6   It would however be sufficient if the agreement provided that the price under the contract should be the price ruling in an existing market on the completion date, or that a dispute over price should be decided by an arbitrator or valuer.

2.7 The course of dealing between the parties or the custom of their trade may suffice to indicate the missing term which they intended to adopt but did not express: this was the ruling **in Hillas v Arcos** (1932) and also in **Foley v Classique Coaches** (1934).

In a contract to supply the petrol requirements of a bus company, no price was expressed or provided for but, for some time before the dispute, petrol had been supplied at the supplier's standard price to all his customers.

Held: This practice indicated what was to be implied (there was also arbitration on disputes if necessary).

2.8 In addition, the Sale of Goods Act 1979 and the Supply of Goods and Services Act 1982 provide that in a contract for the sale of goods or supply of services a reasonable price must be paid. Thus, a valid contract will exist even though there is no express term as to price or the method of fixing the price.

2.9 The parties may have included meaningless words in their contract; this is particularly likely to happen when they use standard printed conditions not adapted to their transaction. If the words are unnecessary they may be disregarded. This is illustrated by the case of Nicolene **v Simmonds** (1953), in which the phrase used was 'usual conditions of acceptance apply'. However, there were no usual conditions, and the contract was construed without them.

2.10 If, however, the words used are essential but imprecise then the contract is void.

Implied terms

2.11 Implied terms are terms which are not expressly included by the parties but which nevertheless are still part of the workings of the contract. They can be implied by:

- the nature of the contract
- business efficacy
- Acts of Parliament
- custom.

2.12 As a general rule, implied terms take second place to the express provisions of the contract. However, some of the statutory implied terms cannot be excluded even by express provision or can only be excluded to a limited extent.

Terms implicitly required by the nature of the contract

2.13 In some situations, for example employment contracts, many matters are not expressly agreed. The courts have implied terms which are required by the contractual relationship. These terms are implied into all similar contractual relationships unless excluded or inconsistent with the express terms.

2.14 In employment contracts there are implied terms expressed as duties of the employee, eg to give honest and faithful service to his employer, and duties of the employer, eg to use reasonable care in providing a safe place of work for his employees. These terms are implied as a result of the court deciding the content of these types of contracts generally rather than deciding what the intentions of the parties were in one particular situation.

2.15   This is illustrated by the case of **Liverpool City Council v Irwin** (1977).

The claimants owned a block of flats in which the defendants were tenants. The block was a tower block in which tenants had the right to use the lifts and rubbish chutes, but these frequently did not work. There was no formal agreement and no express undertaking by the claimants.

Held: The nature of the contract implicitly required an obligation on the claimants as landlords to take reasonable care to maintain the common parts (including the lifts and rubbish chutes) in a reasonable state of repair, as, given the provision of the lift, etc, it was necessary to imply some term to cover this. The claimants were in breach of the implied term.

Terms necessary to give business efficacy to the contract

2.16   The courts may imply a term where the parties have failed to cover a particular matter which, unless remedied, makes the agreement unworkable. The courts imply a term to implement the parties' presumed intentions, to make the contract workable, 'to give it business efficacy'.

2.17   The test of what will be implied in this way is whether, if an officious bystander had said to the parties, when they were making the contract, 'You agree on this point?', both would have replied, 'Oh, of course'. An illustration is provided by the case of **The Moorcock** (1889).

There was an agreement by a wharf owner to permit a ship owner to unload his ship at the wharf. The ship was damaged when, at low tide, it was grounded on the bottom of the river on a hard ridge.

Held: The court implied a term into the agreement that the river bottom would be reasonably safe. Such implied terms are based on the presumed but unexpressed intention of the parties.

Terms implied by Acts of Parliament

2.18   Examples are the Sale of Goods Act 1979; the Partnership Act 1890; the Consumer Credit Act 1974; and a number of Employment Acts. Many of these implied terms are only effective in the absence of express terms to the contrary. Others, however, are automatically included in the contract and cannot be excluded.

Terms implied by custom

2.19   Any contract (oral or written) may be deemed to incorporate any relevant custom of the market, trade or locality in which it is made unless the custom is inconsistent with the express terms or the nature of the contract.

Interpretation of contract terms

2.20   In many cases it falls to the court to interpret the terms of a contract. The usual starting point is the assumption that the parties mean what they say and say what they mean. The words of a contract are interpreted by giving them their ordinary and natural meaning.

2.21   If there is ambiguity in a contractual term (ie more than one meaning of the term is possible) the courts employ the following rules of interpretation.

- They favour an interpretation that will give effect to the contract, as opposed to an interpretation that will or may nullify the contract.

- They interpret a term in a way that tells against the person seeking to rely on it. This rule – known as the ***contra proferentem rule*** – is especially relevant in the case of exclusion clauses, discussed later in this chapter.

3   Conditions and warranties

Distinction between conditions and warranties

3.1   It has been common practice to classify each term of a contract as either a condition or a warranty.

3.2   A **condition** is a vital term of the contract, breach of which may be treated by the innocent party as a substantial failure to perform a basic element of the agreement. The innocent party has the choice of either treating the contract as repudiated (or ended) and claiming damages for any loss suffered, or merely claiming damages for the breach.

3.3   The individual circumstances of the case will usually indicate quite clearly which of these two alternatives is more appropriate. For example, James may buy a washing machine from Bernard, with the intention of using it in his launderette. If the washing machine is defective, James may wish to treat the contract as repudiated for breach of condition, by refusing to accept the machine and seeking a refund of the purchase price. James may also claim damages for business lost by being unable to hire out the machine to customers.

3.4   Alternatively, after a complete overhaul by a mechanic, James may decide to affirm the contract, keep the washing machine, but claim damages for the inconvenience, expenses and loss of profits incurred.

3.5   A **warranty** is a less important term which is incidental to the main purpose of the contract. Failure to observe it does not cause the whole agreement to collapse: consequently the innocent party may claim damages for its breach but may not treat the contract as repudiated.

3.6   If the washing machine supplied to James works but looks shoddy owing to damage to the exterior casing caused during delivery by Bernard, a claim for damages may take the form of a reduction in the purchase price, probably by mutual agreement between the two parties.

3.7   Compare the following two cases.

- **Poussard v Spiers** (1876)

    A soprano, Madame Poussard, agreed to sing in a series of operas for Spiers. She failed to appear on the opening night and Spiers refused her services for subsequent nights.

    Held: The obligation to appear on the opening night was a condition and since Madame Poussard was in breach of this condition Spiers was entitled to treat the contract as at an end and was therefore not himself in breach by refusing her services for the remaining nights.

- **Bettini v Gye** (1876)

  A tenor, Bettini, who agreed to sing in a series of concerts and to attend six days of rehearsals beforehand, failed to appear for the first four rehearsal days. Gye in consequence refused Bettini's services for the balance of the rehearsals and performances.

  Held: The obligation to appear for rehearsals was a warranty and therefore Bettini's breach did not entitle Gye to treat the contract as at an end. Gye was accordingly in breach of contract when he refused Bettini's services for the remainder of the contract.

3.8 The parties may expressly declare that some term is to be a condition, as when time of performance is declared to be of the essence of the contract. But the mere use of the word condition or warranty is not of itself conclusive.

Innominate terms

3.9 Recently, the courts have tried to avoid too rigid a classification of terms on these lines and have recognised an intermediate category described as innominate or intermediate terms: **Cehave NV v Bremer (The Hansa Nord)** (1975).

   Citrus pulp pellets were sold for £100,000. One of the conditions of the contract was: 'shipment to be made in good condition'. On arrival, not all the pellets were in good condition, and their market value was reduced by £20,000. However, even if all the goods had been sound the market value, which had fallen between sale and delivery, was only £86,000. The buyers rejected the goods, which were later sold and eventually re-acquired by the original buyers for £34,000.

   Held: On the question of whether the buyers' rejection had been justified, the provision as to shipment in good condition was neither a condition nor a warranty, but an intermediate stipulation. The effect of the breach was not sufficient to justify treating the contract as discharged. The buyers' only remedy was in damages, namely compensation for the difference in value of the sound goods and the defective goods.

3.10 An intermediate stipulation is neither a condition nor a warranty at the time the contract is made; instead, one must consider the effects of a breach of that term. If these are serious, then remedies should be granted as if it were a breach of condition. If less serious, then only remedies for breach of warranty can be obtained. This was the conclusion in **Hong Kong Fir Shipping Co v Kawasaki** (1962).

3.11 It is also possible for the parties to agree, once a clause has been breached, whether it should be treated as a condition or a warranty, ie whether the effects of breach are fundamental or not: **The Mihalis Angelos** (1971). While this may seem a reasonable approach, it means that there is fundamental uncertainty still over innominate clauses.

4 Exclusion clauses and unfair contract terms

Definition and effect

4.1   The term exclusion clause is applied both to clauses which totally exclude one party from the liability which would otherwise arise from some breach of contract (such as the supply of goods of inferior quality), and to clauses which restrict liability in some way or offer some dubious 'guarantee' in place of normal liability for breach of contract. Such clauses used to be very common in printed contracts and conditions of sale put forward by manufacturers, distributors or carriers of goods. In a purchasing environment exclusion clauses are often seen in relation to liability for late delivery, to the use to which goods supplied to specification are later put, and to the timescale in which notification of shortages may be made.

4.2   The tendency of modern statutes is to limit the use of exclusion clauses, especially in dealing with private citizens who frequently do not read or do not understand the effect of the printed document put before them for acceptance.

Applicability and validity of exclusion clauses

4.3   In order to be valid the exclusion clause must pass two separate tests: the common law test and the statutory test.

4.4   The common law test is broken down into two parts.

- The clause must be incorporated into the contract and not added after the contract is complete.
- The clause must be clear and precise; any vagueness will be construed against the party who is attempting to rely on it. (The technical phrase is that exclusion clauses are construed **contra proferentem**.)

4.5   The statutory test is laid down by The Unfair Contract Terms Act 1977 (often known as UCTA 1977). This will be explained later.

4.6   It is important to be aware of these two tests when answering examination questions. It is also important to be aware that if the exclusion clause does not pass the first test there is no need to consider UCTA 1977.

The common law test – incorporation into the contract

4.7   It must be shown that the party who is to be bound by the clause did in fact agree to it. If he signed a contractual document in which the clause is included he will generally be treated as having agreed to it even if he did not read the document: **L'Estrange v Graucob** (1934).

The proprietress of a cafe bought a cigarette vending machine and signed a contract of sale, which she did not read, and which contained the clause 'Any express or implied condition, statement or warranty, statutory or otherwise, not stated herein is hereby excluded'. The machine was defective.

Held: She was unable to recover the price or obtain damages. She was bound by the clause as she had signed the contract.

4.8   However, a signatory is not bound by an exclusion clause where his signature to the document was induced by fraud or misrepresentation by the other party, or his agent: **Curtis v Chemical Cleaning Co** (1951).

The claimant took a white satin wedding dress to the defendants for cleaning. She was asked to sign a document which contained a clause 'that the dress is accepted on condition that the company is not liable for any damage howsoever arising'. Before she signed, she was told that the effect of the document which she was about to sign was to exclude liability for damage to beads or sequins. Without reading all the terms of the document the claimant then signed as she was asked. The dress was stained owing to the negligence of the defendants.

Held: The defendants were liable and could not rely on the exclusion clause because of the misrepresentation as to its extent.

4.9   If the document was not signed then the offeree is not bound if it can be shown that he did not know that the document contained terms of the contract, or that reasonable notice of those terms was not given to him, and that the term was 'onerous': **Interfoto Picture Gallery Ltd v Stiletto Visual Programmes Ltd** (1988) and **Parker v South East Railway** (1877).

4.10 An exclusion clause cannot be introduced into a contract after it has been made unless the other party agrees: **Olley v Marlborough Court** (1949).

A notice in a hotel room excluded liability for loss or damage to guests' property.

Held: This was ineffective because the contract for accommodation had been made at the reception desk. (The same would be true of an exemption clause in a receipt given after conclusion of the contract, as was held in **Chapelton v Barry UDC** (1940).)

4.11 However, an exclusion clause can be incorporated into a contract even if it is not explicitly stated in the contract. This can happen if the parties to the contract have a history of dealing with each other and the term is known to the parties even though not explicitly written down: **Spurling v Bradshaw** (1956).

The common law test – construction of the clause

4.12 The party relying on an exemption clause to relieve him from some or all of the consequences flowing from his breach of contract must prove that it was a term which, when properly construed, covered the loss or damage suffered by the other party: **Andrew Bros (Bournemouth) Ltd v Singer & Co Ltd** (1934).

A contract for sale of 'new' cars contained a clause exempting the seller from liability for breach of all terms implied by common law, statute or otherwise. One of the cars was not new.

Held: The exemption clause did not protect the seller because there had been a breach of an express term, whereas the clause referred only to implied terms.

4.13 If there is any doubt as to the clause's meaning and scope, the ambiguity will be resolved by interpreting the clause in a manner restricting the interests of the party who inserted it into the contract and who is now seeking to rely on it as a protection against his legal liability. This is called the *contra proferentem* rule. An example is the case of **Hollier v Rambler Motors** (1972).

A car was damaged by fire due to the negligence of a garage employee. The contract contained a clause excluding the garage from liability for damage to cars caused by fire. This was ambiguous as it could mean either fire damage caused without negligence or fire damage caused by the garage's negligence.

Held: The court interpreted the clause in the narrower sense, ie as exempting liability only for non-negligent damage. The garage was therefore liable as the liability for broader negligence was not covered.

The Unfair Contract Terms Act 1977

4.14 All of the cases cited in illustration so far arose before the passing of UCTA 1977. This Act provides important limitations on the validity of exemption clauses. If the clause passes the common law test it may still fail this statutory test.

4.15 The Act restricts the extent to which a person can exclude or limit his liability for negligence and for breach of contract. **Negligence** includes any express or implied term of a contract to take reasonable care and the common law duty in the tort of negligence to take reasonable care. The Act provides that:

- a person in business cannot exclude or restrict liability for death or personal injury resulting from negligence, by contract or any notice. In other words, any clause purporting to do this is totally prohibited (s2(1)).

- a person in business cannot exclude or restrict liability for negligence causing loss other than death or personal injury unless the exclusion clause is reasonable. This requirement is discussed further below (s2(2)).

4.16 As regards liability for **breach of contract**, any term in a standard term contract or in any consumer contract purporting to exclude or restrict liability for breach is effective only if it is reasonable.

- Standard term contracts are contracts whereby one party deals on the other party's written standard terms of business (s3).

- Consumer contracts are contracts whereby one party acts in the course of business and the other party does not (nor does he hold himself out as acting in the course of business), **and** where any goods purchased are of a type ordinarily for private use (s3).

The requirement of reasonableness

4.17 The burden of proving reasonableness is on the party wishing to rely on the clause. To be reasonable the term must be a fair and reasonable one to be included having regard to the circumstances which were, or ought reasonably to have been, known to or in the contemplation of the parties when the contract was made. An example is the case of **George Mitchell (Chesterhall) Ltd v Finney Lock Seeds Ltd** (1983).

A farmer purchased seeds for about £200, but they were defective and the farmer lost all the costs involved in their cultivation, a sum of about £50,000.

Held: a clause in the supplier's standard term contract to the effect that only the cost of the seeds would be refunded in the case of defectiveness was held not to be reasonable in the circumstances, which included the fact that the suppliers should have had insurance, and the farmer had no choice but to accept the term as all suppliers of seeds had it.

4.18   Similarly, in **Smith v Eric S Bush** (1989) it was held to be unreasonable for a property valuer to disclaim liability for negligence to the purchaser of the property, even though it was not the purchaser who paid him for his service (it was the lender, a building society). These cases can be contrasted with **Photo Productions Ltd v Securicor Ltd** (1980), where the suppliers of security services were held not to be liable for loss through their employee's negligence, as the buyer had insurance and the service was very cheap. We can conclude from this that the test of reasonableness will be applied to the facts of each case.

4.19   By way of supplement to the statutory test, s11 and Schedule 2 UCTA 1977 lists five guidelines indicating which matters in particular are to be taken into account.

•   The strength of the bargaining positions of the parties relative to each other, taking into account (among other things) alternative means of supplying the buyer's requirements.

•   Whether the buyer received an inducement to agree to the term, or in accepting it had an opportunity of making a similar contract lacking such a term with other persons.

•   Whether the buyer knew or ought to have known of the existence and the extent of the term, having regard to trade custom and any previous course of dealing between the parties.

•   Whether it was reasonable to expect when the contract was made that it would be practical for the buyer to comply with a condition such that liability of the seller would be excluded or restricted if he did not.

•   Whether the goods were manufactured, processed or adapted to the special order of the customer.

4.20   These guidelines are specifically applied by UCTA 1977 to ascertain reasonableness in the context of contracts for the sale of goods and other transfers of goods (hire, hire purchase and contracts of exchange or for work and materials). However, they are also used when ascertaining the reasonableness of exemption or limitation clauses in relation to other breaches of contract.

4.21   Where the clause is attempting to limit (rather than exclude) liability the courts must have regard to the resources which the party could expect to be available to him for the purpose of meeting the liability should it arise and how far it was open to him to cover himself by insurance.

The Unfair Terms in Consumer Contracts Regulations 1999

4.22   A further statutory protection relating to unfair contract terms in consumer contracts only is provided by the Unfair Terms in Consumer Contracts Regulations 1999.

The scope of the regulations

4.23   They apply to the provision of goods and/or services. They apply a 'fairness' test to terms in contracts between 'consumers' and 'sellers and suppliers' which have not been individually negotiated. They include insurance contracts, which are outside UCTA 1977, and can apply to contracts relating to succession and family law, and the incorporation of companies.

The meaning of 'consumer'

4.24 A consumer is defined under Regulation 3 as 'any natural person … acting for purposes outside his trade, business or profession'. A seller or supplier is defined as 'any natural or legal person … acting for purposes relating to his trade, business or profession, whether publicly owned or privately owned'. A company or business is therefore outside the protection offered by these regulations.

Exclusions

4.25 Certain ('core') terms are excluded from the regulations provided that they are in 'plain intelligible language'. These 'core terms' are exempt from the fairness test (see below). To be classified as 'core', a term must:

- define the main subject matter of the contract, or
- concern the adequacy or price of the remuneration.

In practical terms, difficulties are expected to arise in interpreting the first of these conditions. While there is, as yet, little case law, some guidance on the attitude of the Courts is offered by **Director General of Fair Trading v First National Bank** (2000). In the case, a term in the bank's loan agreement allowed the bank to claim interest on judgements. The bank argued that the clause was excluded from the regulations since 'it defined the subject matter of the contract, or concerned the adequacy of the price'. The Court of Appeal disagreed, since the clause only came into operation after a borrower defaulted.

The test of fairness

4.26 The regulations state that an unfair term is one which 'if contrary to the requirements of good faith causes a significant imbalance in the parties' rights and obligations arising under the contract to the detriment of the consumer'.

4.27 The 1999 regulations merely provide that the assessment of unfairness will take into account all the circumstances attending the conclusion of the contract. To render the term unfair, the 'significant imbalance' which it creates must be 'contrary to good faith'. This is likely to oblige the parties to deal with each other openly and honestly, bearing in mind their respective bargaining strengths.

4.28 The regulations offer further assistance by giving a non-exhaustive list of terms which may be regarded as unfair. There are 17 of these. Examples include:

- Terms excluding or limiting the liability of the seller or supplier for death or personal injury to a consumer resulting from act or omission of the seller/supplier.
- Terms requiring any consumer who fails to meet his obligation to pay a disproportionately high sum in compensation.
- Terms excluding or hindering the consumer's right to take legal action, particularly requiring the consumer to take disputes to arbitration.

The effect of an unfair term

4.29   The inclusion of an unfair term does not necessarily destroy the contract, provided that the contract remains workable without the term.

4.30   The regulations oblige the Office of Fair Trading (OFT) to consider any complaint made to it about the fairness of any contract term drawn up for general use. It may seek an injunction preventing the continued use of such a term. They also empower the OFT to require traders to produce copies of their standard contracts.

4.31   In addition, other qualifying bodies are given similar powers. These include statutory regulators, trading standards departments and consumer associations. They are under a duty to inform the OFT of any undertakings given to them about the continued use of an unfair term, and of the outcome of any Court proceedings. The OFT is empowered to arrange for the publication of such information. It will also supply enquirers with details of particular standard terms, along with details of any undertakings and Court orders.

Interaction between the Regulations and UCTA

4.32   There is considerable overlap between the regulations and UCTA, so that a term may infringe both. The following points of difference should be noted.

- The Regulations protect consumers only and do not apply to contracts made between businesses.

- The regulations apply to **all** terms in contracts except 'core clauses' – and even these are caught if they are not in 'clear and intelligible language'. UCTA applies only to exemption clauses.

- The protection afforded by the Regulations may in fact be wider than that under UCTA, although case law on this is still awaited.

- Under the Regulations, the OFT is given power to prevent the continued application of unfair terms in general use.

- The definition of 'consumer' is narrower in the Regulations than in UCTA in that it is limited to 'natural persons'.

5   *Guarantees and indemnities*

Contracts of guarantee

5.1   In a contract of guarantee, one party, the guarantor, promises to be answerable to the other party for the debt, default or miscarriage of another person.

5.2   For example, if Ian wishes to borrow money the bank may be unwilling to lend to him because they doubt his ability to repay, unless he can find a financially sound guarantor, say Carl, whom the bank can trust. In effect Carl, the guarantor, says to the bank, 'let Ian borrow £1,000, then if he fails to settle his indebtedness with you I will settle on his behalf.' In this type of situation three contracts exist.

- As between the principal debtor (Ian) and the principal creditor (the bank) there is a contract giving rise to the debt.

- As between the guarantor (Carl) and the principal creditor (the bank) there is a contract of guarantee under which Carl makes himself secondarily liable to settle the principal debtor's loan if it is not repaid by the principal debtor himself.

- As between the guarantor and the principal debtor there is always an implied contract, and often an express agreement, whereby the principal debtor promises to repay the guarantor any money that he has to hand over to the principal creditor.

5.3 The main effect of a guarantee is that the principal debtor is able to raise a loan that would otherwise be denied him, while the principal creditor transfers any risk of loss onto the shoulders of the guarantor, a person not expected to default if called upon to meet payment of the debt.

5.4 The Statute of Frauds 1677 requires a contract of guarantee to be evidenced in writing. It provides that no action shall be brought unless the agreement or some memorandum or note thereof is in writing and signed by the guarantor or some other person lawfully authorised by him.

5.5 Thus, the contract itself need not be committed to writing at the time when the parties conclude their agreement. However, there must be a note or memorandum in writing, signed by the guarantor or by his duly authorised agent, setting out the main terms of the contract, with the following details.

- The parties to the contract must be named or sufficiently described in order to be identifiable.
- The subject matter of the contract must be described in such a way that it can be identified.
- All material terms of the contract must be set out.

5.6 The memorandum need not be in any special form and may be contained in more than one document. But documents not signed by the defendant may be introduced as evidence only if documents which **are** signed refer to them expressly or by implication.

5.7 Note that a contract of guarantee which is not evidenced in writing is not void, merely unenforceable (ie no court action may be brought). Thus if the guarantor refuses to pay under an oral guarantee which is not evidenced by writing, the creditor cannot sue him to make him do so. The guarantor may, however, choose to pay and cannot then sue to recover the money from the debtor.

Indemnities

5.8 Somewhat similar to a contract of guarantee is an indemnity. However, there is a crucial difference. You need to bear this in mind because in common usage the terms are often used as though they referred to the same thing.

5.9 The key point of distinction is that in a contract of guarantee there is both a primary and a secondary liability. In the example above the primary liability to the bank is that of Ian. Only if Ian defaults does the secondary liability – that of Carl – come into play.

5.10 By contrast, an indemnity is a primary liability, and no secondary liability exists. Contrast these two situations, discussed in the case of **Birkmyr v Darnell** (1704).

- A and B go into a shop. B says to the shopkeeper 'Let him (ie A) have the goods. If he doesn't pay you, then I will'. This is a contract of guarantee: the primary liability is with A, and the secondary liability with B.

- A and B go into a shop. B says to the shopkeeper 'Let him (ie A) have the goods. I will see that you are paid'. This contract is one of indemnity. B has assumed the primary liability and there is no secondary liability.

5.11 The relevance of this in commercial contexts is clearly seen in the common situation where a contractor carries out work for a subsidiary company in a group. Often the contractor seeks an assurance from the group's parent company that payment will be forthcoming. It is important from the contractor's point of view to determine whether the parent company is acting as a guarantor or providing an indemnity.

5.12 A clause covering the issue of indemnities is very often incorporated into a commercial contract between buyer and supplier. It is essentially a clause which states what the legal position is anyway. It makes it plain to the supplier that should the buyer, for example, incur costs through defending an action in relation to the goods (or services), then the supplier shall be liable for such costs as legal fees. This may be the case where goods are found by the buyer to be defective and cause damage to a third party, or infringe a third party's patent or trade mark.

5.13 A typical indemnity clause is given below.

The supplier shall indemnify the buyer against all those claims, costs and expenses which the buyer may incur and which arise, directly or indirectly, from the supplier's breach of any of its obligations under this contract.

Letters of comfort

5.14 The situation is further complicated by the use of so-called 'letters of comfort'. In the case of **Kleinwort Benson Ltd v Malaysia Mining Corporation Berhad** (1989) the defendant company had refused to give a formal guarantee in relation to its subsidiary company's debts, but did state in writing a policy to ensure that the subsidiary was at all times in a position to meet its liabilities. It was held that these words of assurance amounted to a policy statement only, and not a promise by which the defendant was contractually bound.

5.15 Note that, unlike a guarantee, an indemnity does not have to be evidenced in writing.

6 *Force majeure clauses*

6.1 The purpose of *force majeure* clauses is to release the parties from liability in circumstances where their failure to perform a contract results from circumstances which were unforeseeable, for which they are not responsible and which they could not have avoided or overcome. Note that the clause provides for what is to happen when the *force majeure* event is over or it extends for a long time. This is necessary because, unlike frustration, *force majeure* does not automatically end a contract. (See Chapter 8 on the doctrine of frustration.)

6.2 As the term *force majeure* is not a term of art in English law and its precise meaning is unclear, it is better to use an English paraphrase such as 'matters beyond the parties' control'. The specimen clause reproduced below protects both the seller and the buyer. There is no reason why its protection should not be confined to the buyer alone, but many business managers may think it fairer for its range to be extended to both parties, as here. The clause below identifies specific causes which might disrupt production or delivery in particular industries. The list, however, should usually be kept short and there should be no general phrase added at the end as a catch all for other unspecified events.

6.3 The model *force majeure* clause below is the copyright of CIPS, which we acknowledge. Members are licensed to use it in support of their employment.

6.4 *Model clause 1: force majeure*

1 For the purpose of the contract the term *force majeure* shall mean:

(a) war and other hostilities (whether war be declared or not), invasion, act of foreign enemies, mobilisation, requisition or embargo;

(b) rebellion, revolution, insurrection, military or usurped power or civil war;

(c) riot, commotion or disorder except where solely restricted to employees of the supplier or its subcontractors or sub-suppliers;

(d) earthquake, flood, fire or other natural physical disasters except to the extent that any such disaster is caused by, or its effects contributed to by, the party claiming *force majeure*;

(e) a general industrial dispute not limited to the employees of the supplier or the employees of any of its subcontractors or sub-suppliers.

2 If either party considers that any circumstance of *force majeure* has occurred which may affect materially the performance of its obligations then he shall forthwith notify the other in writing to that effect giving full details of the circumstances giving rise to the *force majeure* event.

3 Neither party shall be considered to be in default of its obligations under the contract to the extent that it can establish that the performance of such obligations is prevented by any circumstance of force majeure which arises after the date of the contract and which was not foreseeable at the date of the contract.

4 If the performance of the obligations of either party under the contract is so prevented by circumstances of *force majeure* and shall continue to be so prevented for a period of less than 30 days then during that period the contract shall be considered as suspended. Upon the ending of the *force majeure* event the contractual obligations of the parties shall be reinstated with such reasonable modifications to take account of the consequences of the *force majeure* event as may be agreed between the parties or, in default of such agreement, as may be determined by an expert under sub-clause .... Notwithstanding such suspension, the supplier shall use his best endeavours to assist the purchaser in the performance of the contract.

5 If performance of the obligations of either party under the contract is so prevented by circumstances of *force majeure* and shall continue to be so prevented for a period in excess of 30 days then the contract shall be terminated by mutual consent and, subject to sub-clause 6 below, neither party shall be liable to the other as a result of such termination.

6 If the contract is so terminated then, subject to the transfer to the purchaser of the benefit referred to in sub-clause 7 below, the purchaser shall pay to the supplier such reasonable sum as may be agreed between the parties or in default of agreement as may be determined by expert determination in accordance with sub-clause ... in respect of costs incurred and commitments already entered into by the supplier at the date of the *force majeure* notice, less the amount of any payments already made to the supplier at the date of the *force majeure* notice. If the amount of such advance payments made to the supplier exceeds the sum due to the supplier under this clause then the supplier shall repay the balance to the purchaser.

7   The supplier shall transfer to the purchaser the benefit of all work done by him or his subcontractors and sub-suppliers in the performance of the contract up to the date of the *force majeure* notice, and if applicable it shall include the rights in any licensed and developed software and licensed firmware so far as the rights in the same have accrued to the purchaser prior to the *force majeure* notice or will do so on the payment under sub-clause 6 above.

Chapter summary

- Statements made during negotiations may either become terms of the subsequent contract, or may be regarded as mere representations. The remedies for breach will differ as a result of this distinction.

- Terms may be expressly inserted in a contract by the parties, or they may be implied. An agreement can only be legally enforced if its terms are certain.

- Terms may be implied into a contract by various means: the nature of the contract; business efficacy; Acts of Parliament; and custom.

- Contract terms may be divided into conditions (vitally important) and warranties (less important). A middle class called innominate terms is also recognised.

- Exclusion clauses are only enforceable if they satisfy both a common law test and a statutory test. The common law test is that they must be incorporated into the contract, and they must be clear (any vagueness being construed *contra proferentem*). The statutory test is laid down in UCTA 1977: such clauses are only valid if reasonable, and never valid in respect of death or personal injury.

- In a contract of guarantee a guarantor promises to be answerable for a debt if the person with primary liability defaults. Such contracts must be evidenced in writing.

- In an indemnity, only a primary liability exists.

- A letter of comfort is not legally binding.

Self-test questions

Numbers in brackets refer to the paragraphs above where your answers can be checked.

1   What is the importance of the difference between a representation and a term? (1.2)

2   What were the facts in the case of **Dick Bentley Productions Ltd v Harold Smith Motors Ltd**? (1.11)

3   What are the four situations where the courts will imply terms into a contract? (2.11)

4   What are the differences between conditions and warranties? (3.1–3.5)

5   Explain the distinction between **Bettini v Gye** and **Poussard v Spiers**. (3.7)

6   What is meant by an exclusion clause? (4.1)

7   If a contract is signed when will an exclusion clause contained in that contract not be valid? (4.8)

8   What is the *contra proferentem* rule? (4.13)

CHAPTER 7

Void and Unenforceable Contracts

Learning objectives and indicative content

1.3   Determine the factors that may vitiate consent to a contract.

- Duress
- Misrepresentation
- Mistake
- Undue influence

4.2   Examine the common law rules relating to confidentiality and the protection of trade secrets in English law and analyse their importance in purchasing and supply.

- Solus agreements
- Restraint of trade clauses

Chapter headings

1   Misrepresentation

2   Mistake in contract

3   Duress and undue influence

4   Void, voidable and illegal contracts

Introduction

In this chapter we look at the factors that 'vitiate' or invalidate a contract once it has been formed.

To begin with we look at the rules relating to misrepresentation. This is where a party to a contract relies on a statement made by the other party, and that statement turns out to be false or misleading.

We then deal with the topic of mistake in contract. In general a contract is binding in the terms agreed by the parties. However, there may be cases where a mistake is so fundamental that the true intention of the mistaken party is not reflected in the terms actually agreed.

Thirdly we look at cases where the genuine consent of one party is absent, because his apparent consent has been obtained by duress or undue influence.

Finally, we look at the general issue of when a contract is void, voidable or illegal, and the consequences that ensue. We focus in particular on contracts in restraint of trade.

1 *Misrepresentation*

Definition of misrepresentation

1.1   A misrepresentation may be defined as a false statement of material fact (not law) made by one of the contracting parties before or at the time of entering into the contract which was intended to and did induce the other party to make the contract.

1.2   This definition of misrepresentation can be broken down into five main parts, each of which is examined further below. A misrepresentation is:

- a **statement**
- of **fact**
- which is **false**
- which is made by one **contracting party**
- and which **induced** the contract.

A misrepresentation is a statement

1.3   The statement may be express or implied by conduct. The general rule is that silence does not constitute a misrepresentation. There are exceptions to this general rule.

1.4   One exception relates to contracts 'of utmost good faith' (contracts *uberrimae fidei*, as they are sometimes known by a Latin term). In contracts of utmost good faith, where one party only is in possession of vital information, it must be communicated to the other party so that he can assess the advisability of entering into a contractual relationship.

1.5   A common example is a contract of insurance. Usually the only person aware of key information about the risk taken by the insurance company is the person seeking insurance cover. For example, if you seek a policy of life assurance the insurance company must depend on information from you about your medical history and current medical condition, so that they can assess the level of risk. You are therefore under an obligation to pass on such information, even if the insurance company does not specifically ask.

1.6   Another exception to the general rule is where silence distorts a positive representation: a half truth may be false because of what it leaves unsaid. The case of **Nottingham Patent Brick v Butler** (1886) is relevant.

The potential purchaser of a house asked if there were any restrictive covenants in relation to the property. The solicitor replied that he was 'not aware' of any such covenants. This was a true statement because the solicitor had not actually looked for any covenants. He should have done this type of search; if he had done so he would have discovered certain restrictions.

Held: This statement amounted to a misrepresentation because it was a misleading statement in the context it was given.

1.7 Another exception is where a party makes a representation during the course of negotiations which is true at the time, but which becomes false before the making of the contract is concluded. He is then under a duty to disclose this fact to the other party. If he does not, the original statement has become a misrepresentation: **With v O'Flanagan** (1936).

O'Flanagan correctly told With that his medical practice produced an income of £2,000 a year, but when With bought it some four months later it was practically worthless, owing to neglect while O'Flanagan was ill during that period.

Held: Failure to correct his earlier statement amounted to a misrepresentation by O'Flanagan.

A misrepresentation is a statement of fact

1.8 A statement of law is not a statement of fact and thus a false statement of law will not amount to a misrepresentation.

1.9 Neither will a statement of opinion which turns out to be ill-founded: **Bisset v Wilkinson** (1927). But the opinion must be honestly held: to say that you hold a particular opinion when in fact you do not is a misstatement of fact.

1.10 The same can be said of a statement of intention. In the case of **Edgington v Fitzmaurice** (1885) the directors of a company invited loans from the public stating that the money would be used to improve the company's business. The directors' real intention was to pay off the company's existing debts. This was held to be a misstatement of fact: the directors did not have the intention they claimed to have.

1.11 A tradesman's praise of his wares – 'this product washes clothes whiter than white' – is usually regarded as a 'mere puff' and not a representation.

A misrepresentation is a statement which is false

1.12 A statement is false not only if it is untrue, but also where it is true but misleading in the context. See for example **Nottingham Patent Brick v Butler** (1886).

A misstatement must be made by a contracting party

1.13 The statement must be made by the contracting party or his agent. A statement made by a contracting party which reaches the other party indirectly is actionable provided the misrepresentor intended it to reach the misrepresentee.

A misstatement must induce the contract

1.14 The misrepresentation must have induced the other party to enter the contract. Thus, the innocent party cannot avoid the contract if the false statement was made after the contract had been entered into, or if he did not know of the misrepresentation: **Horsfall v Thomas** (1862).

Horsfall made a gun for Thomas which had a defect that Horsfall concealed. However, Thomas did not examine the gun before paying for it.

Held: As Thomas was unaware of the misrepresentation (the concealment of the defect) it had not induced him to enter into the contract.

1.15 Equally, the innocent party cannot claim a misrepresentation if he knew the statement was false, or if he did not actually rely on the statement (perhaps because he ignored it or made his own independent investigation, as was the case in **Attwood v Small** (1838)).

1.16 The misrepresentation need not be the sole inducement: **Edgington v Fitzmaurice** (1885).

A man was induced to take debentures in a company partly because of a misstatement in the prospectus and partly because of his own mistaken belief that he would have a charge on the company's assets.

Held: The fact that the misrepresentation was not the sole inducement did not disentitle him to rescission for misrepresentation.

Fraudulent misrepresentation

1.17 A misrepresentation is fraudulent if the person making the statement did not honestly believe it to be true, either because he knew it to be false or because he made it recklessly, not caring whether or not it was true. Information which is inaccurate but which the defendant thought was true does not constitute fraudulent misrepresentation: **Derry v Peek** (1889).

1.18 Remedies for fraudulent misrepresentation are rescission or damages.

- Rescission is an equitable remedy. The misrepresentee in effect elects to consider the contract as no contract. (He may instead, if it suits him, elect to affirm the contract despite the misrepresentation.) This remedy puts the parties back into their exact precontractual positions.

- A claim for damages for the tort of deceit depends on clear evidence of fraud.

Negligent misrepresentation

1.19 This is a misrepresentation made when the party making the misrepresentation has a duty to take care when making the statement but breaches this duty by failing to take reasonable care. This might arise if the misrepresentor is in a position of trust (such as a professional person or someone who is regarded as an expert) and makes a statement without properly and fully checking the facts. But the case of **McCullagh v Lane Fox** (1995) shows that an estate agent acting for a seller has no liability to a purchaser for negligent misrepresentation if a disclaimer for such liability is clearly expressed.

1.20 Remedies for negligent misrepresentation are:

- rescission of the contract (though again the misrepresentee may elect not to rescind but rather to affirm the contract). Note that s2(2) Misrepresentation Act 1967 authorises the court to award damages instead of rescission if it would be equitable to do so (ie if it would be too severe a penalty to impose rescission on a person guilty of a relatively minor negligent misrepresentation)

- a claim for damages under s2(1) Misrepresentation Act 1967.

1.21 Under the Misrepresentation Act 1967, where a party has been induced to enter into a contract after a misrepresentation has been made to him, and as a result has suffered loss, then if the person making the statement would be liable for damages had the misrepresentation been made fraudulently, that person should still be liable unless he proves that he had reasonable grounds to believe and did believe up to the time of the contract that the facts represented were true: s2(1) Misrepresentation Act 1967. The misled party is more likely to bring an action for negligent rather than fraudulent misrepresentation as the former is much easier to prove, the onus being on the representor to disprove negligence.

1.22 A claim for damages may also be made at common law in the tort of negligence. The tort of negligence is discussed more fully in Chapter 16. In brief the claimant has the duty of proving three things.

- That the defendant owed him a duty of care
- That the defendant has breached his duty of care by failing to exercise reasonable care. Notice here that the burden of proof is on the claimant: compare this with s2(1) Misrepresentation Act 1967
- That as a result the defendant has suffered loss which is not too remote.

Innocent misrepresentation

1.23 In this case the representor has reasonable grounds for his statement but it was nonetheless untrue.

1.24 The sole remedy for innocent misrepresentation is to rescind the contract (although again the injured party may elect not to rescind but rather to affirm the contract). Note that under s2(2) Misrepresentation Act 1967 the court may award damages in lieu of rescission (as for negligent misrepresentation).

1.25 Affirmation is any act by a party entitled to rescind which has the effect of showing his continuing intention to be bound, eg voting with shares bought under a voidable contract.

1.26 The court has no power under the 1967 Act to award damages in lieu of rescission where the right to rescission has been lost. If there is no longer a right to rescind there can be no award of damages in lieu. Thus if rescission is not available, perhaps because the parties cannot be restored to their original position or because the contract has been affirmed, there is no remedy available for an innocent misrepresentation.

The equitable remedy of rescission

1.27 Rescission is an equitable remedy (and is therefore at the discretion of the court) which restores the parties to their exact pre-contractual position. Rescission can mean a formal order of the court or the act of a party cancelling or 'avoiding' the contract. The contract in such a case is said to be 'voidable'. Rescission takes effect when notified to the other party and releases the aggrieved party from his obligations. It sets aside the contract as thought it had never existed.

1.28   In practice the right to rescind is of less importance than it might appear because it is lost in the following circumstances.

- **Affirmation.** This is where a party, knowing of the misrepresentation, shows an intention nevertheless to continue with the contract.

- **Lapse of time.** All equitable remedies must be sought within a reasonable time – 'delay defeats the equities'.

- **Restitution is impossible.** The parties can no longer be restored to their original position, eg the goods have been consumed or have deteriorated.

- **Intervention of innocent third party rights.** A third party has acquired rights which would be prejudiced by rescission (eg if he has bought the contract goods from the party who made the misrepresentation).

2   *Mistake in contract*

The effect of mistake

2.1   Since a contract is made by acceptance of an offer the parties are, in principle, bound by the terms which have been agreed between them: **Leaf v International Galleries** (1950) – a case where both buyer and seller mistakenly believed a painting to be by Constable. The principle here is *caveat emptor*, or 'let the buyer beware'. As a general rule neither party can escape liability by saying afterwards that what was agreed is not what was intended, ie that he was mistaken: **Tamplin v James** (1880).

The defendant had bid successfully at an auction sale for a public house believing that the property offered for sale included an adjoining field, which had always been used by the publican.

Held: The court decided that the sale particulars clearly excluded the field. The defendant was bound by the contract.

2.2   However, there are some exceptional situations where a mistake operates to vitiate the contract. The significance of mistake in contract is twofold.

2.3   First there is the obvious question of whether a party is bound by a contract to which he did not, when the true position is discovered, intend to commit himself.

2.4   An **operative mistake** is one which the common law recognises as being so fundamental as to destroy any intention on the part of the person mistaken to be bound by the contract. If mistake is an operative mistake at common law then the contract is **void**, the mistake nullifying the consent.

2.5   A void contract is one which has no legal effect. It cannot be enforced. Assets mistakenly transferred can be recovered. However, even if there is a binding contract at common law, equity may sometimes grant relief (eg rescission): **Solle v Butcher** (1950). This relief is always discretionary and may be granted on terms laid down by the court.

2.6   Secondly the other party may, before the true position is discovered, have resold the goods to an innocent third party. What then is the position of the third party?

2.7   If the contract was **void for mistake** the other party had no title to the goods and therefore could give no title on resale. This is the principle known as *nemo dat quod non habet* — one cannot transfer that which one does not have. This means that the third party does not own the goods and would have to return them to the true owner. This rule and its exceptions are discussed more fully in Chapter 12.

2.8   If, on the other hand, the contract was not void for mistake but is merely **voidable** (eg for misrepresentation) then the party misled may be entitled to avoid or rescind the contract. However, until he does so it is a valid contract under which title to goods passes and can be passed on under a resale to an innocent purchaser.

2.9   If the misled party avoids the contract after the resale it is too late — he cannot recover the goods from the third party who purchased them although he may still claim damages from the dishonest party. It is a question of which innocent person is to suffer the loss caused by the dishonesty of the party who made the misrepresentation.

Types of mistake

2.10   There are several different types of mistake.

- Common mistake — where both parties have made the same mistake. Each knows the other's intention but both are mistaken about the same thing. Not all common mistakes are operative.
- Mutual mistake — where the parties believe that they have agreed but in fact there is a misunderstanding. Mutual mistakes are operative.
- Unilateral mistake — where there is again misunderstanding but one party is aware of it and may indeed have dishonestly induced it by misrepresentation. Unilateral mistake is frequently concerned with the identity of the parties. Not all unilateral mistakes are operative.

Common mistake

2.11   An agreement may be reached on the basis of a mistake which is common to both parties, and thus they are both labouring under exactly the same misapprehension. Since the terms of both the offer and the acceptance correspond with one another, an agreement does exist. It must then be determined whether the underlying mistake affects the validity of the contract concluded (ie is it an operative mistake?)

2.12   As an example, both parties may believe that the subject matter of the contract is in existence at the time when the agreement is concluded, whereas in fact the property has been destroyed or does not exist. In this case, there is an operative mistake because the mistake is fundamental and the contract is void. The buyer is not required to pay for the goods, and any payment already made may be recovered: **Couturier v Hastie** (1852).

Some corn on board a ship travelling between two countries was sold while in transit. Unknown to either buyer or seller, the cargo had become overheated, and therefore dangerous, in the course of voyage. Consequently the captain had sold it at a port of call. The buyer repudiated the sale on learning the true facts, but the court had to decide whether an obligation to pay for the goods still existed.

Held: There was a basic assumption by both parties at the time of contracting that the goods being sold were still in existence, whereas in fact this was not true. The parties had made a contract which was void and destitute of effect since they were negotiating about goods which no longer existed.

2.13   A common mistake by the parties concerning the **quality** of the subject matter of the contract does not render the agreement void at common law, since the parties have agreed in the same terms on the same subject matter: **Bell v Lever Bros** (1932).

2.14   Where a common mistake is not operative, relief in equity may be available provided that the party seeking relief is not personally at fault in failing to detect his error. Usually the court imposes terms that are fair to both parties, rather than casting the loss wholly on the shoulders of one party.

Mutual mistake

2.15   This is where the parties are at cross purposes although neither party is aware of this. For example, one party offers a horse for sale and the other believes he is offering a house. In such cases the court resolves the confusion by looking objectively at the parties' conduct to determine whether the actions of the parties support one interpretation rather than the other.

2.16   The court is not concerned with intention but with conduct, so if someone conducts himself so that a reasonable man would infer the existence of a contract in a given sense, the court notwithstanding the mistake will hold the contract binding, and the party who correctly understood the contract is then able to enforce it: see **Tamplin v James** above.

2.17   The attitude of the court is that where there has been no misrepresentation and no ambiguity in the terms of the contract the defendant cannot be allowed to evade the performance of the contract by the simple statement that he has made a mistake. However, if the contract is so ambiguous that it could mean what either party asserts, there is no agreement between them and therefore the contract is void: **Raffles v Wichelhaus** (1864).

The defendants agreed to buy '125 bales of Surat cotton... to arrive ex Peerless from Bombay...'. The ship mentioned in the agreement was intended by the defendants to be the 'Peerless' which sailed from Bombay in October, whereas the claimant offered 125 bales of Surat cotton from another ship called the 'Peerless' which sailed from Bombay in December.

Held: There was no binding contract between the parties, as there was ambiguity on one objective test.

2.18   If the contract is unambiguous but A, who was not mistaken, must have known that B was mistaken as to the terms of the contract, A cannot hold B to an agreement which A knew did not exist. This is a case of unilateral mistake (see below).

2.19   A contract requires consensus (agreement) in order to be binding on the parties. If there is no agreement because the parties are at cross-purposes there can be no contract. Since the parties' mutual mistake is fundamental it is operative.

Unilateral mistake

2.20 A unilateral mistake occurs when one party is mistaken as to the terms of the contract whilst the other knows of his mistake. In such cases the mistake negates the consent and the contract is void. In this context a man is deemed to know what would be obvious to a reasonable man in the circumstances: **Webster v Cecil** (1861).

A vendor of land, who had refused an offer of £2,000, wrote a letter offering to sell at £1,250 which was a mistake for £2,250. The purchaser was quick to accept before the mistake was corrected.

Held: He plainly knew that a mistake had been made and there was no contract.

2.21 Most cases of unilateral mistake have been cases of mistaken identity. In this type of case, Adam, a rogue, persuades Brian, the seller, to sell goods on credit to Adam by falsely pretending to be Colin, a creditworthy person. Adam then resells to David, an innocent third party, and disappears. (These are essentially the facts in the case of **Cundy v Lindsay** (1878), in which it was held that no contract had been created.) Is the contract between Brian and Adam void for mistake or merely voidable for misrepresentation? The difference will determine which of two innocent parties will suffer the loss caused by the rogue Adam. Any mistake is unilateral since Adam himself deliberately induced it.

2.22 If the contract is void for mistake, there would be no contract. Adam would never own the goods and could not pass title to David. David would therefore be obliged to return the goods to Brian. David suffers the loss.

2.23 However, if the contract is not void for mistake but merely voidable for misrepresentation, Adam would obtain a good title to the goods, and if David bought the goods before Brian rescinded the contract, David would have title to the goods and could keep them. Brian suffers the loss.

2.24 To establish that the contract is void for mistake over identity of the other party, the seller must show that:

- he intended to sell to some person other than the actual buyer
- the buyer was aware of the mistake, ie it was unilateral
- the identity of the buyer was a matter fundamental to the contract
- he (the seller) took reasonable steps to check the identity of the person with whom he was dealing.

Mistake as to the nature or effect of a signed document

2.25 As a general rule, a person is bound by his signature to a document whether he reads or understands it or not. Exceptionally his mistake is operative to render the document void if he can plead *non est factum* (it is not my deed). This is a plea available to a person who wishes to avoid a contract on the basis of its being completely different in nature from that which he intended, as seen in the case of **Lewis v Clay** (1897):

Lewis persuaded Clay to sign as witness to a document which he covered over, stating that its content had to remain confidential. In fact the document was a promissory note for about £1,000, which Lewis tried to get Clay to pay.

Held: the signature was *non est factum*, as the document turned out to be something entirely different to what Clay had been led to expect, and Clay had not been negligent as he had made enquiries and had accepted Lewis's explanation reasonably.

2.26   Another example is the case of **Saunders v Anglia Building Society** (1970), also often referred to by its Court of Appeal title of **Gallie v Lee**. It is a decision of the House of Lords which established clear principles from the confused case law.

Mrs Gallie, a widow, had agreed to transfer her house as a gift to her nephew on condition that she was to remain in occupation for the rest of her life. The nephew asked Lee, a solicitor's clerk, to prepare the transfer. However, he prepared a transfer of sale to himself and persuaded Mrs Gallie, at a time when her spectacles were broken, to sign the document which she had not read. He then mortgaged the house to a building society. It was argued, on the basis of earlier decisions, that Mrs Gallie (and after her death Saunders, her executor) could treat the transfer as void.

Held: A successful plea of *non est factum* requires three conditions.

*   The person signing is mistaken as to 'the object of the exercise' for which the document is required, ie what he signed was a fundamentally different document from that which he thought he signed.
*   His signature was obtained by a trick.
*   The mistake was not caused by carelessness.

2.27   Mrs Gallie's claim failed under the first condition. Mrs Gallie knew that she was transferring the ownership of her house and that the nephew might, subject to her rights of occupation, use it as security to raise money. The House was divided on the question of whether or not Mrs Gallie had been careless. The assignment was however voidable because of the fraud inducing Mrs Gallie's signature, but it was too late to set aside the contract when the third party rights in the property were acquired by the building society for value without notice of Mrs Gallie's claim.

Rectification of a written agreement

2.28   Where parties have reached an oral agreement and have subsequently embodied it in a written document but the document contains a mistake in recording the terms, the court may grant an order of rectification to cause the document to reflect accurately the agreement reached. This is a form of equitable relief for mistake.

2.29   Strong evidence is required to show that the document does not accurately reflect the intentions of the parties: **Joscelyne v Nissen** (1970).

Joscelyne, who shared a house with Nissen, his daughter, proposed to her that she should take over his car hire business. In the ensuing conversations, it was made clear that, if the proposal were accepted, she should pay all the household expenses in respect of the part of the house occupied by her father. The terms were included in a written contract which placed no liability on the daughter to pay the household expenses. The daughter refused to pay the expenses.

Held: Rectification of the document was ordered by the court on the grounds that there was an original oral bargain which set out the common intention of the parties.

3 *Duress and undue influence*

3.1   A contract may have been concluded to all outward appearances. However, there may be a vitiating element which prevents the agreement from correctly reflecting the intentions of the parties. To vitiate a contract is to destroy its validity.

3.2   A contract concluded under duress or undue influence is **voidable** at the option of the coerced or influenced party, since that person does not freely consent to the agreement made.

3.3   The old common law doctrine of duress was narrow in scope, being limited to contracts entered into as a result of the use of violence (**Barton v Armstrong** (1976)), fear of unlawful imprisonment (**Kaufman v Gerson** (1904)), or threatened violence to the contracting party or his immediate family: **Williams v Bayley** (1866). A threat against a person's goods (as opposed to his body) was not considered sufficient duress to enable a contract to be avoided: **Skeate v Beale** (1840). This clearly has little application to the work of purchasing professionals. However, modern cases extend the concept to include **economic duress**: **Pau On v Lau Yiu Long** (1979).

3.4   While the courts now clearly recognise the concept of economic duress, it remains to be seen what action will amount to illegitimate pressure or commercial pressure that vitiates free will. Although it will certainly include some threats to break a contract, it will not include all. There is a very thin line between economic duress and legitimate commercial pressure.

3.5   The leading case which often comes up in exams is that of **Atlas Express v Kafco** (1989).

The claimants were carriers who contracted with the defendants to deliver baskets to one of the defendant's important customers, Woolworths, for an agreed price. In due course the claimant's depot manager refused to collect the goods unless the defendants signed an agreement to pay more for the carriage. The defendants signed under protest, but subsequently refused to pay the increased rates.

Held: The claimants could not enforce the higher rate since the defendant's consent had been obtained by economic duress. A similar ruling was made in the case of **Universe Tankships v ITWF** (1983).

3.6   Factors which, taken together, led the court to decide that there had been illegitimate pressure amounting to duress rather than 'hard bargaining' (which is legitimate) were as follows.

- The claimant knew that fulfilment of the basket contract with Woolworths was vital to the survival of the defendant's business.
- On the day the claimant's lorry driver arrived with the new contract he had been instructed not to take the baskets unless the new contract was signed.
- Also on that day the claimant's depot manager deliberately made himself unavailable for contact by the defendant.
- The claimant knew that the defendant would be unable to find an alternative carrier at such short notice at such a busy time of the year.

3.7   The court also gave another reason for its decision: the claimants had not given consideration for the new agreement as they were already obliged to deliver the goods under the original contract. This case could therefore be cited in a question on 'sufficiency of consideration'.

3.8   Case law seems to have established that a claim for economic duress will be weakened if the injured party did not protest at the time the pressure was applied, or if his decision to repudiate the contract only arose after the event. In other words, the injured party will have a stronger case if he immediately protests and makes clear his intention of later repudiating the contract. A delay may be interpreted as the innocent party affirming the contract: **North Ocean Shipping v Hyundai Construction** (1978).

Undue influence

3.9   A person who has been induced to enter into a transaction by the undue influence of another (the wrongdoer) is entitled in equity to set that transaction aside as against the wrongdoer: the transaction is voidable.

3.10   Equity regarded the common law doctrine of duress as very narrow and therefore developed the wide concept of undue influence to cover cases where one party enters into a transaction under influence which prevents him from freely deciding for himself upon the advisability of the transaction.

3.11   The courts have avoided defining undue influence since the existence of a rigid definition might limit the scope of the doctrine. Undue influence is based on the concept that one party has a stronger mind (or will) than the other such that that other is unable to exercise free and independent judgement: the essence, then, is mental coercion. For example, in **Re Craig** (1971) an elderly widower employed a young woman as his secretary and companion, and over a number of years gave her gifts valued at £28,000. The courts held that the close relationship gave rise to a presumption of undue influence, which the secretary had failed to rebut.

3.12   Contracts which may be rescinded for undue influence fall into two categories: first, those where no fiduciary relationship exists between the parties; second, those where a fiduciary relationship exists. In the first case, undue influence must be **proved** as a fact, while in the second it is **presumed** to exist. Such fiduciary relationships include those between parent and child, solicitor and client, trustee and beneficiary and doctor and patient (but not husband and wife).

3.13   The remedy for undue influence is the equitable one of rescission, ie the complainant may have the transaction set aside. Where undue influence is presumed the complainant cannot set aside the transaction unless it is manifestly disadvantageous to him: whether or not the transaction is manifestly disadvantageous is not material to the setting aside of a transaction induced by actual undue influence.

4   *Void, voidable and illegal contracts*

Void contracts

4.1   Some contracts are declared void or illegal because they are contrary to public policy. There is no easy classification of contracts into these two types owing to the fact that there are few consistent principles.

4.2   Void contracts include contracts in restraint of trade, either at common law or by statute, gaming or wagering contracts, agreements to commit a crime, and agreements to pervert the course of justice. You should concentrate on the rules relating to restraint of trade at common law.

Contracts in restraint of trade

4.3   Common law rules render void a wide range of contracts restricting a person's right to practise his trade. The common law rules are covered in some detail first. There is then a brief explanation of the statutory provisions.

4.4   Restraint of trade exists where a contract restricts a person wholly or in part from carrying on his trade, business, profession or occupation as he wishes. There are, however, certain types of commercial contract such as sole agency agreements or restrictions on the use of business premises imposed on a tenant under a lease, which the law treats as inherently reasonable and so outside the scope of the rules.

4.5   Three types of contract in restraint of trade are as follows.

*   Where an employer requires his employee to agree not to solicit his customers or use his trade secrets after leaving his employment, or to enter the employment of a competitor.

*   Where the vendor of a business, including goodwill, covenants with the purchaser that he will not carry on a competing business; the same principle applies to a partner retiring from a partnership.

*   Where a person enters into a long-term agreement with another to purchase all his supplies from that person (a **solus agreement**). This is often found between petrol companies and petrol station proprietors.

4.6   In all these cases, the restraint of trade clause is part of a larger contract. These clauses are sometimes known as 'restrictive covenants'.

*   In an employer/employee agreement there is an employment contract whereby the employer agrees to pay the employee who agrees to work. One clause in the contract is a promise by the employee not to enter employment of a competitor after he leaves his current employment

*   In a vendor/purchaser agreement there is a contract for the sale of a business (ie the seller will transfer the business plus goodwill to the buyer who will pay for it). One of the terms of the contract is that the seller promises not to continue carrying on the business he is selling as this would mean that the goodwill for which the buyer is paying is of no value.

*   In a solus agreement the petrol company usually leases a garage to the proprietor, who pays rent and promises to buy all his supplies from the petrol company.

4.7   In all these cases it is only the validity of the restraint of trade clause which is generally in question (not the rest of the contract). The general rule is that these clauses are contrary to public policy and therefore void at common law. However the clause may be enforceable if the person attempting to rely on it can prove that it is reasonable. The restraint is reasonable if all of the following circumstances apply.

*   It is imposed to **protect a legitimate interest** of a party to the contract.

- As between the parties it is a reasonable safeguard of that interest (ie it is **no wider than necessary**, geographically or in terms of time or skills, to protect that interest).

- It **is reasonable in the interest of the public** (ie it is not prejudicial to the public interest).

Even then, the employer cannot enforce the clause if he has wrongfully dismissed the employee, because in this case the whole of the contract has been repudiated by the employer: **Briggs v Oates** (1990).

4.8   These rules have a long history and the law as developed by precedent in decided cases has somewhat changed with business practice. On the whole the scope of the rules against restraint of trade has tended to widen, and the trend continues.

Legitimate interest to protect

4.9   In each case of this kind the first step is to identify and define the interest which is to be protected. The tests are applied particularly strictly to restrictions imposed by employers on their employees since the bargaining strength of the parties may be unequal. The employer is not allowed to use a restraint of trade clause merely to prevent a former employee from competing with him, from obtaining other employment or from using personal skills or generally available knowledge acquired during the course of employment: **Faccenda Chicken Ltd v Fowler** (1986), **Attwood v Lamont** (1920) and **Morris v Saxelby** (1916). The two interests which are legitimate interests to protect are trade secrets and client connections. One case where a restraint clause was upheld is **Harris v Littlewoods Organisation** (1978).

A former director tried to join a rival company within the 12-month restraint period stated in his contract.

Held: As the nature of the business was particularly competitive and the employee was senior enough to know many of the employer's trade secrets, the restriction was valid. A similar conclusion was reached in **Fitch v Dewes** (1921). Employments which put the employee in contact with customers raise a *prima facie* legitimate interest for the employer to protect: **Home Counties Dairies v Skilton** (1970) and **Dairy Crest Ltd v Wise** (1989), both relating to milkmen.

No wider than necessary

4.10   The next question is whether the restraint imposed is reasonable in scope, geographical extent and duration. If it is excessive it will not be upheld: **Mason v Provident Clothing** (1913), where a restriction covered an area with a 25 mile radius around London.

4.11   The wider the area stipulated, or the longer the period during which it will continue, the greater the burden on the employer to justify its reasonableness.

4.12   The court must balance the restrictions relating to area and time against each other when ascertaining the acceptability of any covenant in restraint of trade. The greater the area covered, the shorter the time limit must be, and vice versa.

4.13   An employer may impose a worldwide restraint over the employee's competitive activities if the business is conducted over such a wide area, provided the employee's influence over clients is also worldwide. By way of contrast, a restraint in the contract of employment of the manager of a butcher's shop covering an area of only five miles may be too wide where customers are drawn from a two mile radius.

4.14   The complete absence of any time limit will not necessarily invalidate a restraint if the area covered is reasonable, but it increases the difficulty of convincing the court that it should be upheld. The tendency of the courts in modern cases is to allow only a short time limit since the present view with the majority of employees (particularly with regard to client connections) is that the employee's influence is largely ephemeral.

4.15   Restraint clauses agreed upon by the vendor and purchaser of a business are more readily upheld by the court as being reasonable than covenants embodied in contracts of employment. The parties are of equal bargaining strength and the risk of one party insisting on terms that protect his interests unfairly at the expense of the other party is a much less likely occurrence than in contracts of employment.

Reasonable in the interest of the public

4.16   What is judged reasonable between the parties will usually pass the test of not being prejudicial to the public interest. In petrol solus cases the petrol company usually provides substantial consideration in the form of a money payment to purchase exclusivity, which is a legitimate interest, and seeks to impose the restriction to protect that interest. The cases on petrol solus agreements decided in the last fifteen years, however, have been concerned more especially with protecting the public interest in free competition.

'Garden leave' clauses

4.17   'Garden leave' is where an employer gives proper notice of termination to an employee, and continues to pay him or her during this period, but requires him or her not to attend work during the notice period.

4.18   This is often used as a tool to reinforce post-termination restrictive covenants, in order to protect the employer's trade secrets and business connections: the employee is thereby denied access to internal information – and is not able to enter the job market (or to join a new employer), because all existing obligations to the employer (such as obligations of good faith) remain in place until termination.

4.19   In order to uphold a garden leave clause against a challenge on the basis of restraint of trade, the employer must show that:

(a)   The right to put the employee on garden leave (and the obligation on the employee not to work for anyone else during this period) is stated as an express term of the contract of employment. Otherwise, the courts will consider whether there is any implied obligation by the employer to provide work: for example, a statement in employee handbooks or training manuals that the employer will 'ensure that staff have every opportunity to develop their skills'. (**William Hill Organisation v Tucker**, 1998)

(b)   The length of the garden leave is no longer than is necessary to protect the legitimate business interests of the employer

(c)   Full salary and benefits are paid throughout the period of garden leave. (Failure will amount to breach of contract by the employer – so both the garden leave obligation and any restrictive covenants will be unenforceable.)

The blue pencil test

4.20 If a court regards a clause as being too wide, it can delete (with a 'blue pencil') the unenforceable phrase: if the clause still makes sense after these deletions, the remainder will be valid and enforceable. (This may partly help to explain why so many contract clauses are so long-windedly written – so that words and phrases can be removed without invalidating the rest!)

4.21 The blue pencil test can only be applied if the unenforceable part of the clause can be removed without needing any additions or changes to make sense of the remaining part. The remaining terms and conditions must continue to make sense, and the removal of the words must not change what the clause set out to do.

Statutory rules

4.22 The statute which renders void contracts to restrict prices or other conditions imposed on sale of goods is the Competition Act 1998. This is discussed in Chapter 19.

Other void contracts

4.23 There are other contracts which are void. One example relevant to buyers is a contract that attempts to oust the jurisdiction of the courts. It is not unusual for a contract to stipulate that disputes between parties shall be submitted to arbitration (see Chapter 10); such a stipulation is perfectly valid if it provides simply that the parties should refer any dispute before going to court. If the contract seeks to prevent disputes going to court at all, it is void.

Illegal contracts

4.24 Some contracts are illegal by statute or at common law. They are void and no action can be based on them; hence, they are quite distinct from a contract void for, say, mistake.

4.25 A contract is illegal at common law, as being harmful to the interests of society, if it offends against the concepts of public policy. This category includes contracts to further a sexually immoral purpose, to commit a crime or tort (eg to defraud the tax authorities) or to promote corruption in public affairs.

4.26 The effect of illegality depends on whether the contract is inherently illegal, or whether it has become illegal by the manner of its performance. If inherently illegal, the contract is illegal as formed and so void. If it is illegal performance of a lawful contract, the party who is responsible for the illegality cannot enforce the obligations owed to him (it is 'unenforceable') but the 'innocent' party may be able to enforce his rights.

Contracts illegal under statute

4.27 A statute or a statutory instrument may expressly or impliedly declare a certain type of contract to be illegal, with the result that they are void.

4.28 Some statutes only intend to penalise a party failing to follow a prescribed statutory procedure, not to invalidate any contract made without observance of that statutory procedure. For example, a tobacconist who has failed to secure the requisite licence to trade is nonetheless entitled to sue for the price of tobacco sold and delivered to a purchaser refusing to pay. Deciding which of the above two principles to apply to a particular case is a question of construction of the particular statute in issue.

Chapter summary

- Misrepresentation is a false statement of material fact made by one of the contracting parties which is intended to and does induce the other party to make the contract. A contract induced by misrepresentation is voidable by the party misled.

- Silence does not usually constitute a misrepresentation, but there are exceptions to this rule: for example, contracts of utmost good faith.

- Misrepresentation may be fraudulent, negligent or innocent. The remedies available depend on which type of misrepresentation is in question.

- In general, a contract is not vitiated by mistake. However, there are some cases where a mistake is operative (ie vitiates the contract). In such cases the contract is void.

- The distinction between void and voidable contracts is important if the goods bought and sold are then re-sold to an innocent third party. Such a third party cannot obtain legal title if the original contract was void, but may do so if it was merely voidable.

- A contract concluded under duress or undue influence is voidable by the injured party. Duress includes economic duress.

- Illegal contracts include restraint of trade contracts. In general such contracts are void, but the party relying on the clause may be able to demonstrate that it is acceptable.

Self-test questions

Numbers in brackets refer to the paragraphs above where your answers can be checked.

1   Define misrepresentation. (1.1)

2   Can silence ever constitute a misrepresentation? (1.4)

3   How does a statement of fact differ from a statement of intention or opinion? (1.8–1.10)

4   Define fraudulent misrepresentation. (1.17)

5   If a person is found liable for a negligent misrepresentation under what section of the Misrepresentation Act 1967 can the misrepresentee claim for damages? (1.20)

6   In what four circumstances may the right to rescind a contract be lost? (1.28)

7   What is the meaning of 'operative mistake'? What are its consequences? (2.4)

8   Why was the ruling in **Bell v Lever Bros** not regarded as being an example of operative mistake? (2.13)

9   What does *non est factum* mean? What are the consequences of such a claim? (2.25)

10   What is the status of a contract that has been entered into as a result of economic duress? (3.2).

11   Describe the facts and the decision in **Atlas Express v Kafco**. (3.5).

12   List three types of contract in restraint of trade (4.5).

13   Give an example of contracts (other than covenants in restraint of trade) which are void at common law (4.23).

14   Give two examples of contracts which are illegal at common law (4.25).

CHAPTER 8

Discharge of Contract

Learning objectives and indicative content

1.4   Evaluate the different common law methods by which a contract is terminated and the remedies available should a contract be breached.

- • Performance
- • Frustration
- • Agreement including variation of a contract
- • Breach

Chapter headings

1   Performance

2   Agreement

3   Breach

4   Frustration

Introduction

This chapter examines the discharge (or termination) of a contract. One party may claim that a contract has not been fully discharged by the other party (part performance) because he does not want to pay out the sum due under the contract.

Another party may claim, for example, that the contract has been discharged by frustration because he does not want to be sued for breach of the contract. If the contract has been discharged it no longer exists as a vehicle to take a court action.

There are various ways in which a contract may come to an end and we look at the main possibilities.

1   Performance

Methods of discharging a contract

1.1   A contract imposes obligations on the parties from which they may be discharged in various ways. The main ways in which a contract may be discharged are described briefly in the paragraphs following.

1.2   **Performance.** When a party has done what is required of him under the contract he no longer has any obligations under it.

1.3   **Agreement.** The parties may agree to terminate unfulfilled obligations. That agreement must itself be a contract subject to the usual rules, especially consideration.

1.4   **Breach**. If one party commits a breach of contract the other may in some cases, at his option, elect to treat the contract as being at an end with the result that his own obligations are discharged. He is accepting that the other's repudiatory breach terminates the contract. Breach of contract is the inexcusable failure by a party to a contract to fulfil some or all of his obligations under it.

1.5   **Frustration**. In certain cases a contract which becomes impossible to perform is thereby discharged.

1.6   We look at all of these possibilities in turn, beginning with performance.

The general rule on performance

1.7   The general rule is that a contract is discharged by performance only when both parties have complied fully and exactly with the terms of the contract: **Re Moore & Landauer** (1927).

Contract for tinned fruit to be delivered packed in cases of 30 tins each. The correct number of tins was delivered but in cases varying between 24 and 30 tins each.

Held: The contract was not performed even though the market value was the same. The buyer could reject all goods and not pay.

1.8   From this general rule it has sometimes been held that if a single price has been agreed for performance of the contract no part of the price is payable unless and until the entire contract has been exactly performed: **Cutter v Powell** (1795).

The defendants agreed to pay Cutter thirty guineas 'provided he proceeds, continues and does his duty as second mate' on a voyage from Kingston, Jamaica, to Liverpool. Cutter began the journey but died when the ship was about three week's sail from Liverpool. His administrator sought to recover a proportion of the agreed wage in respect of that part of the journey for which Cutter had acted as second mate.

Held: She was unable to succeed as Cutter had not performed his part of the contract. (But note that nowadays the doctrine of frustration would apply to the contract.)

Exceptions to the general rule

1.9   The general rule that performance must be complete, accurate and exact in order to be effective could lead to injustice (as in **Cutter v Powell** above). However, in the case of **Reardon Smith Line v Yngvar Hanson-Tangen** (1976) Lord Wilberforce cast doubt on the correctness of the decision in **Moore & Landauer**, on the ground that the law does not normally concern itself with such trifles. The general rule is subject to exceptions, some of which have been imposed by the common law and some by equity to make the rule fairer. One such exception relates to severable or divisible contracts.

1.10   **Cutter v Powell** is an example of an 'entire' contract. However, some contracts may be treated as divisible into distinct and separate obligations, eg a contract for a number of separate consignments of goods. Whether a contract is 'entire' or severable will depend on construction of the contract and the intention of the parties.

1.11 The parties may be deemed to have intended to divide their contract into two or more separate contracts, in which case each individual contract may be discharged separately. For example, in a contract to deliver a consignment of goods by instalments, the buyer may agree to pay for each instalment when delivered.

1.12 If the first instalment delivered conforms with the terms of the contract, the buyer cannot refuse to pay for it on the grounds that the second delivery is defective in some respect, although payment for the second instalment may be validly refused. Such contracts are called **severable** or **divisible** contracts. We look at these in more detail in Chapter 12.

1.13 Another exception to the general rule is the situation where one party is prevented from fully carrying out his contractual duties because of some act or omission by the other party which effectively prevents the contract being duly performed as anticipated. In such cases the party partially implementing the agreed terms may sue on a quan*tum meruit*, or for damages for breach of contract, in order to recover compensation for the amount of work actually completed.

1.14 *Quantum meruit* is a claim for the value of work done or services rendered, rather than for the full contract price. The words literally mean 'as much as is merited'. An example is the case of **Planché v Colburn** (1831).

Planché agreed to write a book for a series of books to be published by Colburn, but the series was discontinued before completion of the work by the author.

Held: The original contract had been discharged by the defendant's breach, but reasonable remuneration was recoverable on a *quantum meruit* basis, independently of the original contract.

Acceptance of partial performance

1.15 Where a party accepts the benefit conferred on him by the other party's partial performance, the court may infer a promise to pay for the benefit received and grant the other party a right to recover a reasonable price on a *quantum meruit* claim.

1.16 For example, a seller may agree to deliver forty bottles of a specified wine to a buyer. If only twenty bottles are tendered, the buyer may refuse to accept delivery; but if he accepts the twenty bottles he must pay a reasonable price for them. However, if he had no choice but to accept partial performance, then no payment can be claimed: **Sumpter v Hedges** (1898.)

Sumpter contracted to erect buildings on Hedges' land, but abandoned the work when it was only partially completed. Hedges took possession of the land and buildings and completed the work himself, using materials which Sumpter had left behind. Sumpter sued on a quantum meruit to recover compensation for the value of the work done prior to his abandonment of the job.

Held: Sumpter could not recover a reasonable price for his work. It could not be presumed from his conduct that Hedges voluntarily accepted partial performance. He had no other option open to him than to accept the half-completed buildings and finish the work himself, or employ another builder to do so. (However, Sumpter was allowed to recover the value of the materials used, because it was open to Hedges to choose whether or not to use those particular materials in completing the building.)

Substantial performance

1.17 A party who has substantially performed his contractual duties in the manner stipulated may recover the agreed price, less a deduction by way of a claim for damages in respect of duties not properly executed. This is an equitable exception to the rule of full performance: **Hoenig v Isaacs** (1952).

The claimant, an interior decorator, agreed to decorate and furnish the defendant's flat for a sum of £750 payable 'as the work proceeds and balance on completion'. When the job was done the defendant moved in but complained of faulty design and bad workmanship and would not pay the £350 balance.

Held: In a contract for work and labour for a lump sum the employer cannot repudiate liability on the ground that the work, when substantially performed and when he has taken the enjoyment of it, is in some respects not in accordance with the contract. The term that required completion was not a contract condition; hence, the defendant should pay for the work less a sum in damages for breach of warranty.

1.18 If the defects are so extensive that it cannot be said that the contract has been substantially performed, then no part of the contract price can be recovered: **Bolton v Mahadeva** (1972).

1.19 The doctrine of substantial performance raises the question of the distinction between conditions and warranties. All terms which are conditions must be strictly performed. By contrast, no breach of warranty justifies non-performance by the other party. In respect of 'intermediate' terms, the test of substantial performance is whether the party has received substantially the whole benefit as intended under the contract.

1.20 If the party abandons the contract the doctrine cannot be relied upon. It is an equitable doctrine and to abandon work in this way would be inequitable.

Time for performance

1.21 When a contract does not specify the time of performance of the obligations, they must be performed within a reasonable time.

1.22 When a contract does specify the time of performance of the obligations, the question arises as to whether 'time is of the essence', ie a **condition** of the contract. In such cases, if there is a delay in performance the injured party may treat this delay as breach of condition and pay nothing (and also refuse to accept late performance if offered).

1.23 The parties may expressly agree in their contract that time shall be of the essence. Even if they do not so provide and there is delay, the injured party may then make time of the essence of the contract by serving a notice requiring performance within a specified but reasonable additional period: **Charles Rickards Ltd v Oppenheim** (1950).

The contract was for delivery of a custom-built Rolls Royce car within seven months; the buyer agreed to wait three months more and then gave four weeks' notice to complete.

Held: At the expiry of his notice he could cancel the order as by serving notice he had made time of the essence, although he could not have done so immediately the original delivery period expired (as he had waived his right).

1.24   In absence of any such explicit provision the question of whether time is to be treated as of the essence depends on the nature of the contract.

- In commercial contracts and any others where lapse in time could materially affect the value of the subject matter, time of performance is of the essence unless there is evidence to the contrary. This was the conclusion in **Bunge Corporation v Tradax** (1981), and also in **Hartley v Hymans** (1920).

- In contracts where specific performance might be ordered, the court (applying equitable principles) will be inclined to treat the time of performance as not of the essence.

1.25   Specific performance is an equitable remedy whereby the court orders a person to complete his obligations under a contract. It is usually only available in contracts for the transfer of land or goods (not work or services).

1.26   Time for payment of the contract price is not of the essence unless so agreed.

2   Agreement

Conditions precedent and subsequent

2.1   A **condition precedent** is a term of a contract preventing its taking effect unless a specified event occurs or a specified act is performed.

2.2   The original contract may itself contain some terms ('conditions') providing for discharge. As this procedure is part of the original contract, no new consideration is required for its application. For example, a contract for the sale of land may contain a condition precedent by which the contract does not become effective unless and until specified planning permission is obtained. If planning permission is refused the contract is discharged.

2.3   A **condition subsequent** is a term of a contract permitting its discharge on the happening of a specified event or performance of a specified act (eg giving notice of termination of employment).

2.4   A contract may provide that it shall be terminated on the happening of some event. For example, a contract of employment is usually terminable by notice given by one party to another; a contract made by a company promoter may be expressed to terminate automatically if the company is not formed or fails to adopt the contract by a certain date. In such cases the contract is in force until terminated by the condition subsequent.

Termination by a new agreement

2.5   The parties may agree to discharge (ie end) the contract. This agreement will be binding only if it is under seal or supported by consideration. The discharge may be **bilateral** or **unilateral**.

2.6   Discharge will be **bilateral** where both parties still have contractual obligations to perform. Any agreement to discharge the contract relieves both parties from further performance. Each party's promise to release the other party from further performance is his consideration for the release from his own obligations.

2.7   Discharge will be **unilateral** where one party has performed all his obligations but the other has not. Any promise by the party who has performed his obligation to release the other ('accord') will not be binding on him unless the other party has given consideration ('satisfaction') or the agreement to discharge is made by deed.

2.8   Where fresh consideration is given (eg a cancellation fee) there is 'accord', ie agreement by which the obligation is discharged, and 'satisfaction', ie the consideration which makes the agreement effective.

2.9   The parties may agree to discharge the original contract and substitute a new one in its place (a process called **novation**). For example, a contract to supply a colour television may be replaced by a contract to supply a radio. They may agree to vary the original contract; for example, a contract to deliver a carpet in January is varied by extending the delivery date to March.

3   Breach

Discharge by acceptance of breach

3.1   A breach of contract occurs:

- when a party fails to perform an obligation under the contract (actual breach); or
- when, before the time fixed to perform an obligation, a party shows an intention not to perform (anticipatory breach).

3.2   If one party commits a breach of condition, ie of an essential term of a contract, or a substantial breach of an intermediate term, or totally renounces the contract, the breach does not automatically terminate the contract. However, the other party may then at his option:

- treat the contract as terminated (discharged) and claim damages for any loss suffered; or
- treat the contract as operative and claim damages for any loss suffered.

3.3   In the first case their outstanding obligations are discharged by the breach followed by the election to terminate, but in the second case the parties continue to be bound by the contract since the contract remains in existence.

3.4   A breach of warranty will not entitle the innocent party to treat the contract as discharged, ie treat his outstanding obligations as discharged by the breach. He may claim damages only: contrast **Poussard v Spiers** (1876) with **Bettini v Gye** (1876). In either case, the injured party must bring his action within six years after the cause of action arose; otherwise, the party in breach will claim **limitation of action**.

Actual breach

3.5   This occurs where one party is in breach of a condition or improperly repudiates (ends) the contract, or if he makes it impossible to perform during his own performance of it or where he prevents completion of the contract by the other party during performance.

3.6 If the contract is an entire one in which the obligations are interdependent or concurrent, then the contract is discharged by such a breach, eg purchase of an item which does not work. Breach of condition by seller discharges the buyer from his duty to pay.

3.7 If the contract is a divisible one, or if the obligations are independent of each other, then the innocent party's only remedy is to sue for damages for the breach; he cannot treat himself as discharged from his own contractual obligations by the other party's breach of performance.

3.8 If the innocent party does have the right to treat himself as discharged from his contractual obligations and wishes to exercise that right, he must, as a general rule, communicate that decision to the party in breach for otherwise silence may be construed as evidence that he waives his right to treat himself as discharged.

Anticipatory breach

3.9 A contract is discharged by anticipatory breach when one party expressly or impliedly repudiates the obligations imposed on him by the contract before the arrival of the time fixed for performance. In any such case the injured party has a choice of action.

3.10 He can, by notifying the other party of his decision, accept the repudiation and treat the contract as immediately discharged and even commence proceedings for breach before the time has arrived. This is known as 'accepting' the breach.

3.11 Thus the party repudiating the contract may be sued immediately for breach of contract even though the date has not yet arrived for the repudiating party to perform his obligations under the contract: **Hochster v De La Tour** (1853).

The defendant, who had agreed to engage the claimant as a courier as from 1 June 1852, wrote a letter on 11 May repudiating the contract of employment. On 22 May the claimant brought an action claiming damages for breach of contract.

Held: Damages were recoverable. It was not necessary to wait until 1 June 1852, the date when his duties as courier were to begin, before suing for breach of contract.

3.12 Alternatively, he can affirm the contract in the hope that performance will be rendered. In this case he must wait until the time for performance arrives before he can sue. In this case the party in default can escape liability if he in fact performs the contract at the due date or if his obligation to do so is meanwhile discharged, eg by frustration. (Frustration is the discharge of a contract by unforeseen events rendering it impossible or pointless to perform.)

3.13 Generally the innocent party is under a duty to mitigate the loss from a breach of contract (ie to take such steps as are reasonable to reduce or contain the loss suffered). However, it would appear that where there is an anticipatory breach and the innocent party elects to affirm the contract and perform his obligations there is no duty to mitigate the resultant loss: **White & Carter v MacGregor** (1961).

3.14 In summary, where one party commits a repudiatory breach of contract the other party has a choice.

   • He may accept that the breach discharges the contract. He is then released from his obligations and can sue the other party for damages.

   • Or he may affirm the contract and treat it as continuing.

3.15 Where the repudiatory breach is anticipatory he may exercise his choice immediately: he is not required to wait for the date of performance to arrive.

4 Frustration

Introduction

4.1 The general rule is that, unless otherwise agreed, a party who fails to perform his contractual obligations is in breach of contract and liable for damages. This is the position whatever the reason given in excuse: **Paradine v Jane** (1647).

   A tenant was sued for rent of premises of which he had been dispossessed for three years by the King's enemies.

   Held: He was nevertheless liable for the rent.

4.2 The doctrine of frustration was developed to mitigate the severity of this rule where performance of a contract subsequently becomes impossible through the happening of a supervening event which occurred through the fault of neither party. Later cases have extended the doctrine beyond strict 'impossibility' to situations where circumstances have so changed that performance would now be so radically different as to destroy the commercial purpose of the contract.

4.3 If a contract is frustrated it is automatically discharged with the result that both parties are lawfully excused from further performance. The doctrine is narrowly applied and the following cases show the limits of the doctrine.

Application of the doctrine

4.4 Frustration has been held to apply in the following circumstances.

   • Destruction of the subject matter: **Taylor v Caldwell** (1863), in which a music hall was hired but was burnt down before the date of the intended concerts.

   • Non-occurrence of the event on which the contract was based: **Krell v Henry** (1903), in which a room was hired for the express purpose of observing the coronation procession of Edward VII; however, the procession was cancelled because of the King's illness.

   • Incapacity in cases where the contract requires personal performance; a prime example of a contract of personal service is the contract of employment and such a contract is always frustrated by the death of the employee.

   • Impossibility caused by some change in the law or by action taken under statutory authority: **Re Shipton, Anderson & Co** (1915), in which a contract for the sale of wheat stored in a warehouse was frustrated when the government requisitioned it under its emergency wartime powers.

- An extensive interruption which alters performance. An extensive interruption to performance may make any further execution of the contract fundamentally impracticable or essentially different to performance as originally contemplated by the contracting parties: **Metropolitan Water Board v Dick Kerr & Co Ltd** (1918).

When frustration will not apply

4.5   A contract is not frustrated if it merely becomes more difficult or expensive to perform in a different way: **Tsakiroglou v Noblee Thorl** (1960).

A contract was entered into for the sale of groundnuts. The contract price included shipment from the Sudan to Hamburg in Germany. The seller costed the contract on the basis of the shortest shipping route (via the Suez Canal) although this was not an express term of the contract nor would the court allow it to be an implied term. After the making of the contract the Suez Canal was unexpectedly closed. As this would have meant a much longer journey around the Cape of Good Hope the seller alleged that the contract was discharged by frustration.

Held: The contract was not impossible to perform – it was merely more expensive for the seller – and therefore not frustrated.

4.6   Another relevant case is that of **Davis Contractors v Fareham UDC** (1956).

The claimant contracted to build a number of houses for the defendant for £94,000 over a specified period. Owing to labour shortages it took much longer and cost the claimant £110,000. They pleaded that the contract had been frustrated and were therefore entitled to claim on a quantum meruit basis for the benefit conferred.

Held: Undue delay which caused extra expense did not amount to frustration.

4.7   A contract is not frustrated merely because one party has expressly undertaken that he will do something which he later finds he cannot achieve – **Cassidy v Osuustukkukauppa** (1957). Nor is it frustrated if one party by his own choice induces impossibility which could have been avoided; 'self-induced' frustration is not frustration: **Maritime National Fish v Ocean Trawlers** (1935).

A contract for hire of a trawler which required a trawler licence was claimed to be frustrated when the owner obtained insufficient trawler licences for all its boats and failed to allocate one to the trawler which had been hired.

Held: The contract was not frustrated. The person claiming the frustration had caused the event himself and so could not rely upon the doctrine. The owner remained liable to the hirer.

4.8   A court will pay very close attention to the wording of the contract, as can be seen in **Hutton v Herne Bay Steamboat Company Ltd** (1903):

As in Krell v Henry, the King's illness, which led to the postponement of his coronation – and the review of the fleet at Portsmouth – spoiled the plans of Hutton, who had hired a steamboat for the day.

Held: The contract was not frustrated as it did not explicitly state that the hire was for the purpose of the coronation.

The effects of frustration

4.9   The position of the parties is governed by the Law Reform (Frustrated Contracts) Act 1943.

- •   All sums paid under the contract must be repaid. Any sums payable (whether overdue or due in the future) cease to be payable.

- •   If one party has incurred expenses under the contract he can deduct them from any sums which have to be repaid, or claim them from any overdue sums, but if there are no such sums, he cannot recover such expenses from the other party.

- •   Where one party has received some benefit under the contract, he must pay for that benefit.

4.10   The Act does not cover:

- •   contracts which themselves contain a provision (a *force majeure* clause) to meet the possibility of frustration (see Chapter 6 under *force majeure* clauses)

- •   shipping contracts

- •   contracts for insurance

- •   contracts for the sale of specific goods which have perished before the property in the goods has passed to the buyer (discussed later in Chapter 12).

Sale of goods

4.11   Special rules exist in relation to the sale of goods, which are dealt with in Chapter 12.

4.12   If the Act does not apply, the common law position is the same in that the contract is void and money is recoverable. However, it does not make any provision for the recovery of expenses or for payment in respect of any benefit received. The operation of the common law principles is seen in the **Fibrosa** case (1939), which pre-dated the 1943 Act.

An English company agreed in 1939 to manufacture machinery for a Polish company at a price of £4,800. The buyer paid a deposit of £1,000 after which the war broke out. Poland was occupied by the German army and the contract became illegal.

Held: It was held that the Polish buyer could recover the £1,000.

Chapter summary

- The usual methods by which a contract is discharged are performance, agreement, breach and frustration.

- 'Performance' in general means full and exact performance. Limited exceptions exist to this general rule: separable (or divisible) contracts, acceptance of partial performance, and substantial performance.

- In commercial contexts, the time of performance is usually regarded as a contract condition, and may be explicitly described in this way by the phrase 'time is of the essence'.

- Agreement to terminate a contract may be expressed by means of a condition precedent or a condition subsequent. Alternatively, the parties may agree to 'novation': replacing the old contract with a revised one.

- Breach of contract may be actual or anticipatory. Breach of a condition entitles the injured party to repudiate the contract. Breach of a warranty leads only to a claim for damages.

- In the case of anticipatory breach, the injured party may accept the breach immediately and treat the contract as discharged. Alternatively, he can affirm the contract.

- If a contract is frustrated, both parties are excused further performance. However, only exceptional circumstances will justify a claim of frustration.

- If a contract is frustrated, the position of the parties is in general governed by the Law Reform (Frustrated Contracts) Act 1943. However, this does not apply in all cases, and in particular does not apply if the parties have included a *force majeure* clause in their contract.

Self-test questions

Numbers in brackets refer to the paragraphs above where your answers can be checked.

1   What are the four ways in which a contract can be discharged? (1.1–1.5)

2   What is the general rule on performance of a contract? (1.7)

3   When can a party to a severable contract who has not completed the whole contract claim payment? (1.11, 1.12)

4   What is meant by *quantum meruit*? (1.14)

5   Is the doctrine of substantial performance a common law or an equitable doctrine? (1.17)

6   Describe the facts and the decision in the case of **Charles Rickards Ltd v Oppenheim**. (1.23)

7   Distinguish between a condition precedent and a condition subsequent. (2.1–2.4)

8   Will a breach of warranty ever entitle the innocent party to 'accept' the breach and end the contract? (3.4)

9   Define frustration of contract. (4.2)

10 What was decided in the case of **Krell v Henry**? (4.8)

11 What is the position of a party who has incurred expenses under a frustrated contract? (4.9)

CHAPTER 9

Remedies for Breach of Contract

Learning objectives and indicative content

1.2 Distinguish between different types of contractual terms and assess the legal validity of specific types of contractual clauses.

- Penalty and liquidated damages clauses

1.4 Evaluate the different common law methods by which a contract is terminated and the remedies available should a contract be breached.

- Assessment of unliquidated damages
- Equitable remedies

Chapter headings

1 Damages

2 Specific performance

3 Injunction

4 *Quantum meruit*

Introduction

In the previous chapter we considered whether or not a contract has been breached. This chapter considers the remedies available for breach of contract, comprising both monetary remedies (eg damages and an action for the price) and also, where a monetary remedy would be inadequate, the court orders of specific performance and injunction (equitable remedies).

1 Damages

Types of remedy arising on breach of contract

1.1 In appropriate cases the party who has suffered a breach of contract may have any of the following remedies.

- Damages
- Specific performance
- Injunction
- *Quantum meruit*
- Action for the price.

1.2   The remedy of 'action for the price' will be discussed in the context of contracts for the sale of goods in Chapter 13. In this chapter we look at the remedies of damages, specific performance, injunction and *quantum meruit*.

The purpose of damages

1.3   The purpose of damages in contract is to put the injured party into the position he would have been in if the contract had been properly performed. Thus in a contract for the sale of goods where the seller has failed to deliver goods, the buyer's measure of damages will be the difference between the agreed contract price and the price the buyer needed to pay in order to get the goods elsewhere, ie the prevailing market price.

1.4   Damages are compensatory; they are not usually intended to be punitive. Thus damages are not usually affected by the motive or intention behind the breach of contract – whether good or bad.

Liquidated damages and penalty clauses

1.5   The parties may agree a sum to be paid in the event of breach, or they may not discuss this point at all.

- Where the contract does not make any provision for damages the court will determine the damages payable. Such damages are referred to as **unliquidated damages**.

- Where a contract provides for the payment of a fixed sum on breach, it may rank as either a **liquidated damages clause** or a **penalty clause**. It is crucial to differentiate these as the results are different.

1.6   If the clause is a genuine attempt at estimating the loss in advance of the breach it is a liquidated damages clause and will be valid and enforceable by either party to the contract. If the actual damages suffered by the innocent party are greater than the damages provided for, he can only claim the liquidated amount: **Cellulose Acetate Silk Co v Widnes Foundry** (1933).

A contract for the building of a factory contained a clause providing for payment of a fixed sum in compensation for each day's delay in completion of the work. The work was finished late and the claimants suffered losses considerably greater than those envisaged when the contract was made.

Held: The claimants were entitled only to the contract rate of damages: that figure had represented a genuine estimate of loss when it was inserted in the contract.

1.7   By contrast, where the clause is framed so as to compel a party to perform his obligations under the contract, it will rank as a penalty clause and will be void as a penalty. The injured party will have to prove the loss suffered and the damages will be unliquidated damages assessed by the court.

1.8   Whether a clause is a penalty or for liquidated damages is a question of construction of the contract; certainly the name that the contract gives to the clause is not conclusive.

Guidelines for construing the clauses

1.9   A leading case in this area is that of **Dunlop Pneumatic Tyre Co v New Garage** (1915).

The claimant supplied tyres to the defendants. The defendants agreed that for any of a number of breaches they would pay Dunlop £5 per tyre sold in breach. The defendants sold tyres at below the listed price, which was one of the breaches mentioned in the contract.

Held: The stipulated sum was for liquidated damages. The figure of £5 was a rough and ready estimate of the possible loss which the claimants might suffer. Moreover, although the sum was payable on the happening of a number of different types of breach, the range of breaches was very limited. They were all fairly trivial.

1.10   Certain guidelines were laid down in the case to help the court construe penalty clauses. The guidelines suggest that there is a presumption that a clause is a penalty clause in any of the following circumstances.

•   The sum stipulated is extravagant and unconscionable.

•   A single sum is payable on the occurrence of one or more breaches, some trifling, others serious. (In the case of **Kemble v Farren** (1829) a clause was held to be a penalty clause for precisely this reason.)

•   If it is a sum payable for a breach, where the breach is non-payment of money, and the sum stipulated is larger than the non-payment.

1.11   However, a clause is not necessarily for penalty merely because the stipulated sum is more than the loss actually suffered. As long as the stipulated figure is a genuine attempt to pre-estimate the loss it will be permissible. These are only presumptions and can be rebutted by evidence to the contrary.

1.12   The burden of proof is on the party alleging that the clause is a penalty.

Calculation of unliquidated damages

1.13   Damages is the common law remedy and is available as of right for every breach of contract. Two questions arise when the court is assessing a claim for unliquidated damages.

•   What losses should be included in the claim? This is the question of **remoteness of damage**.

•   What level of damages will compensate the party claiming? This question concerns the **measure of damages**.

Remoteness of damage

1.14   The basic rule is that damages are awarded to put the innocent party in the same position that he would have been in had the contract been properly performed. However, some losses, albeit flowing from the breach, are nevertheless too remote and not recoverable.

1.15   Consider, for example, the following situation. A builder agrees to build a factory by a certain date. If erection of a new factory is delayed, the manufacturer may lose profits on his trade for the period of delay; he may have to buy products (which he could have made) in order to fulfil contracts to supply customers; he may have to pay interest charges on capital invested in raw materials which he cannot use, or pay wages to employees for whom he has no work. Which of these indirect losses and expenses (loosely called **consequential loss**) can he recover from the builder as damages for breach of contract in failing to complete the factory on time?

1.16   Some important principles relating to this question were laid down in the leading case of **Hadley v Baxendale** (1854).

A carrier was given a mill-shaft to deliver to a plant manufacturer as a model for making a new shaft. The carrier delayed in delivery and, unknown to him, the mill stood idle during the period of delay.

Held: He was not liable for the loss of profit, and a rule was formulated as follows: the loss to be compensated should be such as may fairly and reasonably be considered either arising naturally, ie according to the usual course of things, from the breach of contract, or such as may reasonably be supposed to have been in the contemplation of both parties at the time they made the contract as the probable result of the breach of it.

1.17   So there are two types of loss for which damages may be recovered.

- That which arises naturally in the usual course of things – **general damages**; sometimes known as 'normal loss'

- And also, that which does not occur naturally in the usual course of things but both parties could foresee, when the contract was made, as the likely result of breach – **special damages**; sometimes known as 'abnormal loss'.

1.18   Both branches of the rule arising from the case of **Hadley v Baxendale** are based on a test of foresight and probability. In the first branch the test is what would an outsider with no special knowledge of the circumstances regard as the likely consequence of a breach.

1.19   In **Hadley v Baxendale** it was held that without inside knowledge the carrier could not be expected to realise that delay on his part would keep the mill idle (in many cases mill owners were likely to have a spare shaft to use in an emergency). A similar case is **Pilkington v Wood** (1953): a solicitor was liable to a house buyer for negligently failing to notice that the house had a defective title, but could not be held liable for an additional loss that arose when the buyer sold the house to move to a different part of the country.

1.20   The second branch of the rule starts from the special knowledge (if any) which the parties possessed when they made their contract and asks what, with that knowledge, should reasonably have been foreseen as the likely loss resulting from breach.

1.21   The rule in **Hadley v Baxendale** has been considered and approved in many cases, for example that of **Victoria Laundry v Newman Industries** (1949).

A laundry required a new boiler to enlarge its plant. There was delay in delivery of the boiler and as a result the laundry lost both a normal trading profit from delay in bringing the new plant into use, and also an extra large profit on certain government contracts.

Held: The boiler manufacturer was held liable for the loss of normal profits; under the first branch of the rule, he or anyone else would know that an industrial boiler was essential to the operation of the plant, and, therefore, to earning normal profits from it. He was not liable for the loss of profit on the government contracts, of which he had no information. (If, of course, he had known of them he would have been liable under the second branch of the rule.)

1.22   Where parties contemplate the type of damage which may follow a breach of contract they will be liable for damage of that type even where its extent was not foreseen: **H Parsons Livestock v Uttley Ingham & Co** (1978).

D had supplied a 'feed storage hopper' to P, who was a pig breeder and who needed the hopper to store nuts for his pigs. The hopper proved defective, the nuts went mouldy and a number of pigs died from a rare stomach disease as a result of eating those nuts. P claimed:

(a)   damages for the death of the pigs, and also for

(b)   consequent financial loss from lost sales, etc.

Held: Damages under (a) were recoverable, because the parties would have contemplated at least a 'serious possibility' of some harm coming to the pigs if the hopper failed to keep the pigs' food in a satisfactory condition; it was not relevant that the parties would not have foreseen the extent of the harm (ie a fatal stomach disease). Damages under (b) were not recoverable, being too remote under the guidelines of **Hadley v Baxendale**.

1.23   Recovery of damages in contract is usually for financial loss (eg loss of profits) but other types of loss are also recoverable (eg personal injury and property damage). In an appropriate case damages can be recovered for mental distress and loss of enjoyment, but this takes us into an area where purchasing professionals need not tread.

The measure of damages

1.24   The measure of damages is the amount which will, so far as money can, put the claimant in the position in which he would have been had the contract been performed.

1.25   For example, if a buyer bought goods for £50 which the seller refused to deliver, the buyer's damages would be the cost to him of acquiring the same goods from someone else. So if he had to pay £60 his damages would be £10 (plus the £50 if he had already paid that to the seller). If a buyer refused to accept goods the seller's loss would be the difference between the contract price and the price he can actually sell for.

1.26 If the claimant has suffered no actual loss he will be awarded only nominal damages: **Surrey County Council v Bredero Homes Ltd** (1993).

SCC sold some land to BH and in the contract of sale BH covenanted to build no more than 72 houses on the plot. In deliberate breach of contract BH built 77 houses. SCC claimed damages equal to the profit BH had made on the extra houses.

Held: The remedy at common law for breach of contract was the award of damages to compensate the innocent party for his loss; it was not to transfer to him any benefit which the wrongdoer had gained by his breach of contract. Since SCC had not suffered any loss, it followed that the damages recoverable had to be nominal.

1.27 However, a ruling by the House of Lords, in **Attorney General v Blake** (2000), raises the possibility that judicial attitudes with regard to benefits obtained by defendants who have breached their contracts may be about to change. In the case, Blake, in breach of his employment contract with the Crown, made profits from the sale of his autobiography. The Crown claimed that Blake should be made to account for the profits. The House of Lords upheld the Crown's contention on the ground that it was 'just and equitable that the defendant should retain no benefit from his breach of contract'. However, it remains uncertain how far this principle will be upheld in commercial contracts.

1.28 The court's inability to evaluate the claimant's losses with mathematical accuracy is not sufficient reason for refusing to grant any compensation at all, even though the assessment of damages is almost a matter of guesswork: **Chaplin v Hicks** (1911).

Chaplin agreed with Hicks, a theatrical manager, to attend an interview at which twelve girls would be chosen from fifty contestants to work in the theatre. Hicks's failure to give Chaplin sufficient notice of the interview prevented her attendance. She claimed damages for loss of her chance of being selected. The defendant contended that Miss Chaplin was entitled to nominal damages only since it was impossible to determine objectively whether she would have been chosen.

Held: Although assessment of her loss was problematic, since it could not be determined whether Chaplin would have been chosen, the claimant should nonetheless receive some compensation. Damages of £100 were awarded.

Mitigation of loss

1.29 A duty is imposed upon a claimant to take all reasonable steps to mitigate (ie lessen) any loss caused to him by the defendant's breach of contract. Compensation will not be awarded for any damage incurred which the claimant had a reasonable opportunity to avoid: **Brace v Calder** (1895).

Brace was employed by a partnership for a fixed period of two years, but after only five months the partnership was dissolved, thereby prematurely terminating his contract of employment. He was offered identical employment with a reconstituted partnership which was immediately formed to replace the previous one. He refused the offer and sued for wages he would have earned had his job continued for the agreed two year period.

Held: Brace had not mitigated the loss he suffered by his employer's breach of contract, thus he could only recover nominal damages.

The available market rule

1.30   This special rule applies to contracts for the sale of goods where the breach is either the buyer wrongfully refusing to accept the goods or the seller wrongfully refusing to deliver the goods. By s 51 Sale of Goods Act 1979, if an available market exists, the damages are deemed to be the difference between the contract price and the available market price as at the date of breach. An available market exists where goods of that type can be freely bought or sold at prices fixed by supply and demand.

2   Specific performance

2.1   This is an equitable remedy whereby the court orders the defendant to carry out his obligations under the contract. Like other equitable remedies it is at the discretion of the court to grant it and cannot be obtained as of right (contrast damages which is a common law remedy and is awarded as of right). It therefore follows that it is only given where it is just and equitable to do so. The main principles which determine when specific performance is ordered or refused are discussed in the following paragraphs.

2.2   Where damages are an adequate remedy, specific performance will not be ordered. On a sale of goods (unless they are unique) or an agreement to lend money, damages is an adequate remedy for the extra cost if the claimant can obtain similar goods or money elsewhere. By contrast, specific performance will often be ordered on a contract for sale of land: each piece of the earth's surface is unique.

2.3   Where the court could not adequately supervise the performance of the contract and decide if it was being properly done (in detail) it refuses to order specific performance. Contracts for construction of buildings fall under this head.

2.4   Specific performance will not be ordered in a contract of personal services, such as an employment contract, on the basis that it is contrary to public policy to compel an unwilling party to maintain continuous personal relations with another and that it would require constant supervision.

2.5   The remedy will only be given on the basis of mutuality, ie the remedy will only be granted if both parties could, if necessary, seek the protection of the court. For this reason an infant cannot obtain an order for specific performance since the court would not be able to enforce such an order against him.

3   Injunction

3.1   An injunction is an order of the court which either requires a person to do something (mandatory injunction) or prohibits a person from doing something (prohibitory injunction). This is an equitable remedy and is granted on the same principles as specific performance.

3.2   The court will grant an injunction to restrain a party from committing a breach of contract. Although it is said that an injunction will only be granted to enforce a negative stipulation in a contract it may be extended to cases where a negative term may be inferred: **Metropolitan Electric Supply v Ginder** (1901).

The contract obliged the defendant to take all his electricity from the claimant; the obligation was in substance not to take electricity from another supplier.

Held: An injunction to that effect was issued.

3.3   An injunction will not be granted if it would have the effect of requiring specific performance in circumstances where the latter would be refused: **Page One Records Ltd v Britton** (1967).

The Troggs (a pop group) agreed to employ P as their manager for five years and not to employ any other manager. The Troggs dismissed P, who consequently sought an injunction to restrain them from employing any other manager.

Held: The injunction was refused because, if denied the services of another manager, the Troggs would in effect have had to employ P, since they could not do without a manager.

3.4   However, an injunction may be granted in cases such as that of **Warner Brothers Pictures Inc v Nelson** (1936).

The film star Bette Davis (really Miss Nelson) entered into a contract with the claimants, initially for a term of one year, but giving the claimants the option of extending it, whereby she agreed that she would not undertake other film work without obtaining their written consent. The claimant sought an injunction to restrain her from doing film work for another company in breach of this agreement.

Held: The injunction would be granted since she could still earn her living as an actress, in other ways. A similar conclusion was upheld in the case of **Warren v Hendy** (1989): these cases show that a court will uphold a covenant not to perform services elsewhere, at least as long as the defendant can still earn a livelihood.

3.5   An injunction will be granted only where it is 'just and convenient to do so', and, if it is inappropriate, the court can award damages in lieu of the injunction.

4   Quantum meruit

4.1   *Quantum meruit* is an equitable remedy available when a contract has been part-performed, but where the innocent party is prevented from completing the contract by the conduct of the defaulting party. Although equitable, it is similar to damages in that it involves payment of compensation. In these circumstances, the claimant may be awarded payment for the work done on a provisional basis. Where there is a precise provision for remuneration, a *quantum meruit* cannot usually be used to alter the price, even if extra work is done.

4.2   In **Gilbert & Partners v Knight** (1968), Knight employed a firm of surveyors to supervise building work for a fee of £30. The surveyors did more supervision than Knight had asked for and submitted an account for £30 plus an account for £105 for the additional work. Knight refused to pay the extra £105 and the court upheld his case. The original contract had fixed the payment and it was still in existence.

Chapter summary

- Remedies for breach of contract include damages, specific performance, injunction, *quantum meruit* and action for the price.

- A contract may include a liquidated damages clause, in which the parties attempt a genuine pre-estimate of the damages arising from specified breaches. This is enforceable and determines the measure of damages.

- This must be distinguished from a penalty clause, which is an attempt to coerce performance and is not enforceable.

- Damages are only awarded in respect of losses reasonably foreseeable. If the actual damages arising are too remote to have been foreseen they will not be compensated.

- An injured party is under an obligation to mitigate his loss.

- Specific performance is an equitable remedy under which the court orders the defendant to carry out his contractual obligations. The remedy is not available as of right, and in many circumstances the courts will decline to award it.

- An injunction is an order of the court either requiring a person to do something, or forbidding him from doing something. It is an equitable remedy and not available as of right.

- *Quantum meruit* is an equitable remedy in respect of payment for part-performance.

Self-test questions

Numbers in brackets refer to the paragraphs above where your answers can be checked.

1   What is the purpose of damages? (1.3)

2   Where a contract provides a clause which is a genuine attempt at estimating the loss what is this clause known as? (1.6)

3   What is the name of the case which set out the guidelines for making the distinction between a liquidated damages clause and a penalty clause? (1.9)

4   Is damages a common law or an equitable remedy? (1.13)

5   State the rule in **Hadley v Baxendale**. (1.16)

6   Identify the two branches of the rule in **Hadley v Baxendale**. (1.17)

7   If a person cannot show actual loss as a result of a breach of contract what sort of damages will the court award? (1.26)

8   What equitable remedy will order the defendant to carry out the terms of the contract? (2.1)

9   Why will specific performance not be given in the case of a contract of employment? (2.4)

CHAPTER 10

The Settlement of Commercial Disputes

Learning objectives and indicative content

1.5   Evaluate the alternative methods of resolving commercial disputes.

- Litigation
- Arbitration
- Mediation
- Conciliation
- Adjudication
- Expert determination
- International arbitration

Chapter headings

1   Litigation

2   The nature of arbitration

3   The Arbitration Act 1996

4   Alternative dispute resolution

5   International arbitration

Introduction

Buyers and sellers arrange their dealings with each other in the form of contracts, almost invariably written contracts. They aim to foresee the various eventualities that may arise in the course of their dealings, but inevitably this is not always possible. When things go wrong, they must come to some agreement as to the course of action to be taken. In the vast majority of cases this is done by negotiation – the parties reach an agreement without intervention.

To some extent this process is regulated by the terms of their contract (for example, there may be a liquidated damages, *force majeure*, retention of title or penalty clause) or by judicial precedent or statute. But to take advantage of these rules it may be necessary to go to court in litigation. This can be a time-consuming and costly procedure. Often, businesses seek to avoid this by means of an alternative procedure: arbitration. However, alternative dispute resolution (ADR) – mediation – is gradually winning favour in the UK, following notable successes in the US. We also look at adjudication, a statutory dispute resolution process, which is becoming increasingly popular in the UK construction industry. Finally, we look at some aspects of international arbitration.

1 Litigation

1.1   The English system of civil dispute resolution via litigation (the courts) is adversarial in nature. This means that there are two sides – the claimant and the defendant – who present cases, and who, by and large, control the course of the proceedings. The role of the judge and court is passive compared to the European inquisitorial system, where it is the judge who controls proceedings and the parties who present information.

1.2   Some of these perceived weaknesses have been addressed by Lord Woolf's Civil Procedure Rules. The 'overriding objective' of these is to 'enable the court to deal with cases justly'. This involves:

- Ensuring that the parties are on an equal footing.
- Saving expense.
- Enabling the case to be dealt with in a way that is in proportion to the amount of money involved, the case's importance, the complexity of the issues raised and the financial position of each party.
- Dealing with the case expeditiously and fairly.
- Giving it the appropriate share of the court's time.

1.3   Judges can take much more active control and can limit the amount of time-wasting that the parties engage in as part of their tactics.

1.4   So when a business faces a dispute over a contractual matter it has the option to pursue through the courts in litigation. This option suffers from a number of disadvantages, even with the new Civil Procedure Rules.

- Legal fees are costly.
- The time before the matter comes to court may be lengthy and even then it may not be resolved quickly.
- It is a public method of proceeding, whereas the matters at issue may be confidential.

1.5   If the litigation route is chosen the action may be heard in a County Court (if the dispute is valued below £30,000) or in the High Court (which is a lengthier and more formal procedure).

2 The nature of arbitration

2.1   To avoid all this, it is increasingly common for buyers and sellers to try other options first and to treat court proceedings as a last resort. Often they do so by including a provision in their contract to the effect that any dispute must be referred to arbitration. This allows the parties to choose an arbitrator in whom they both have confidence, and to explain their differences privately.

2.2   An important part of such an arrangement is that the parties agree to be bound by the decision of the arbitrator, which can be enforced as if it were the decision of a court. This of course makes it important to choose someone suitable. In some cases this means a person with legal experience, but often a specialised knowledge of the subject matter of the contract is more crucial.

Arbitration versus litigation

2.3 General advantages of arbitration over litigation include the following.

- The proceedings are held in private, avoiding publicity of issues which parties may not wish to be broadcast.

- The parties can choose the individual or organisation to resolve any dispute.

- Arbitration is less confrontational than litigation. This is especially important if the parties wish to maintain good trading relations after the dispute is resolved.

- Arbitration is intended as a single 'one-stop' process, avoiding the endless appeals that may protract litigation.

- Arbitration should be speedier and less expensive than litigation.

2.4 However, the preference for arbitration is not entirely clear-cut in all circumstances.

- If the parties choose litigation, at least once the procedure is complete the outcome is final. Arbitration may be subject to intervention by the courts, although this should happen only exceptionally.

- The powers of arbitrators are less extensive than those of judges, which can mean a greater possibility of delay in arbitral proceedings.

The legal framework surrounding arbitration

2.5 A statutory framework has grown up around arbitration agreements. Until recently, the relevant statutes were the Arbitration Acts of 1950 (the principal Act), 1975 and 1979. The 1975 Act introduced new provisions to extend the scope of the 1950 Act so as to cover international arbitration agreements. The 1979 Act gave effect to new thinking on the finality of arbitration agreements: judicial intervention in such agreements was to be kept to a minimum.

2.6 The Acts applied only to arbitration agreements evidenced in writing (which they invariably are in dealings between a commercial buyer and seller). In such a case the court would distance itself from the proceedings to enable the parties to reach a conclusion along with the arbitrator. The arbitrator's decision would then be enforced by the court if necessary.

2.7 In addition to the statutes mentioned above, there is an extensive case law relating to arbitration. However, both the statutory rules and the case law are now to large extent embodied in the Arbitration Act 1996 which is discussed below.

2.8 Alongside this treatment of arbitration agreements between commercial enterprises there is also an arbitration service within the County Court structure, sometimes referred to as the 'small claims procedure', for use by consumers. The impact of this is that where the sum in dispute is small – currently £5,000 or less – the district judge can refer the matter to arbitration whether or not the parties have agreed to that effect. The judge usually hears the claim himself, and legal representation is discouraged.

3   *The Arbitration Act 1996*

The principle of party autonomy

3.1   The law relating to arbitration is now contained in the Arbitration Act 1996. The 1975 and 1979 Acts, as well as the 1950 Act with only minor exceptions, are repealed.

3.2   As well as consolidating existing law, the 1996 Act introduces important new provisions. It is based firmly on the principle of party autonomy: the parties in dispute are given maximum autonomy to decide how the arbitration should be conducted. They can tailor the arbitration to suit their own needs, determining for example how many arbitrators should hear their case, what procedures should be adopted, what powers the arbitrators should have and whether appeals can be made to the courts on points of law.

3.3   Under the 1996 Act the courts are not allowed to intervene in the arbitral process unless it is clearly necessary to seek the court's assistance to move the arbitration forward, or where there has been a manifest injustice. As under the previous legislation, the provisions of the Act apply only to arbitration agreements that are in writing.

3.4   The freedom of the parties to the contract is not absolute. There are a few provisions that for reasons of public policy cannot be overridden. These are set out in Schedule 1 to the Act.

3.5   Often an arbitration agreement will include a clause preventing any right to begin court proceedings until arbitration has taken place. This is called a **Scott v Avery** clause after a 19th century case in which such a clause was upheld. The courts have power to 'stay' legal proceedings – ie to restrain the parties from resorting to legal proceedings – but if they refuse to exercise this power (because legal proceedings are held to be necessary) then the **Scott v Avery** clause will cease to have effect.

3.6   The attitude of the courts in these circumstances is illustrated in **Balfour Beatty v Channel Tunnel Group** (1993). This concerned an agreement between the contractors and the concessionaires relating to the construction of the channel tunnel. The agreement provided that, should extra work be required, the parties were to agree a reasonable sum for the extra work. In the absence of agreement, the dispute was to be referred to a panel of experts chosen by the parties to conduct arbitration in accordance with international construction rules. The contractors were dissatisfied with the suggested price and threatened to cease work. The concessionaires applied to the English courts for an injunction preventing them from doing so. The contractors successfully applied for a stay of proceedings. The rules governing the conduct of the dispute empowered the panel to grant an injunction. The court decided that it would not be proper for it to pre-empt the decision of the panel.

3.7   It is usual for the arbitration agreement to contain time limits during which the arbitration must begin. The courts have powers to extend such limits, but these powers are further restricted by the 1996 Act, again following the principle that in general courts should not meddle in the agreements reached by the parties.

Other provisions of the 1996 Act

3.8   The 1996 Act makes it clear that in general an arbitrator enjoys immunity from legal action taken against him in connection with his arbitration. This is necessary to enable him to exercise his duties with impartiality. The immunity is lost if it appears that the arbitrator has acted in bad faith.

3.9   An arbitration is not required to proceed on lines laid down for court proceedings. Indeed, one of the objectives of the new legislation is to encourage flexibility. This is one of the great advantages of arbitration over court action.

Court support for the arbitral process

3.10   Although the principle of party autonomy is upheld, the courts have powers to support arbitral proceedings, for example by compelling the appearance of witnesses and the giving of evidence. Similarly, the courts may be invited to give a ruling on a preliminary point of law, though only if it concerns a matter that substantially affects the rights of one or more of the parties. This is a useful provision in cases where some major event occurs (such as the closure of the Suez canal) which could potentially affect numerous arbitrations; a single preliminary ruling by the court avoids repeated consideration of the same issue.

3.11   Unless the parties agree to the contrary, the arbitrator is obliged to give reasons for the award he eventually declares. It is regarded as a basic rule of justice that someone charged with making a binding decision affecting the rights of others should normally be required to explain his reasons for the decision.

3.12   The courts are empowered to enforce the award made by the arbitrator, though this may be subject to challenge by one or other of the parties. If the court holds that serious irregularity arose in the proceedings or the award, it may remit the award (ie refer it back to the arbitrator for reconsideration) or in exceptional cases set the award aside.

3.13   A party may appeal to the court on a point of law arising out of the award: s69(1). However, the court may only admit such an appeal if it is satisfied either that the decision of the arbitrator is obviously wrong, or that the question is one of general public importance and the decision of the arbitrator is at least open to serious doubt. Additionally, the court must be satisfied that it is just and proper in all the circumstances for it to determine the matter. These limitations on the courts' intervention arise from cases such as **Antaios Compania v Salen Rederierna** (1985).

3.14   A party to the arbitration may also appeal to the court system to determine a preliminary point of law, or to require the arbitrator to give reasons for his decision in more detail.

4 Alternative dispute resolution

The increasing use of ADR

4.1 Alternative Dispute Resolution (ADR) provides a voluntary alternative to the accepted practice of using the courts or arbitration to settle civil disputes. The most common forms of ADR we will look at as part of the syllabus are conciliation, mediation, adjudication and expert determination. There are other forms of ADR but these are the most frequently used at present in the UK.

4.2 In the UK, the Government's main concerns have been to minimise the role played by the courts in dispute settlement in order to save money, to reduce the burden of work on the judicial system and to prevent disputes disrupting commercial relations and economic development.

4.3 The UK Government has introduced a compulsory adjudication process for preliminary dispute settlement in the construction industry. The amended UK Civil Procedure Rules 1998 introduced by Lord Woolf demonstrate that ADR is to play a central role in dispute resolution. Although the Woolf reforms fell short of introducing USA style Court Ordered Mediation, the case management powers of the court allow judges to delay a case to enable parties to go to mediation. Failure to mediate will lead to financial penalties. Lord Woolf also made it compulsory for lawyers to advise clients of the benefits of ADR.

4.4 It is likely that any industry or profession that does not address the problems of speedy, cost-effective dispute resolution could find the Government imposing a compulsory system on them. If the new UK system results in significant savings and commercial advantages it is very likely that other EU member states will emulate it. Indeed, in the spirit of harmonisation and customer satisfaction, the European Union might well choose to impose the UK model on the whole of the community.

4.5 An ADR clause may be expressly written into a contractual agreement. It is even better if the clause specifies the ADR service provider and the rules governing the ADR process. For example, it might specify the dispute resolution services provided by the Centre for Effective Dispute Resolution (CEDR) and their model agreements for the conduct of ADR. This ensures that there is no need to agree these details later. Frequently the parties to an open agreement fail to agree on the details after a dispute arises and are forced to go to court to ask a judge to decide for them.

4.6 If an ADR clause is written into a contract the parties are obliged to exhaust that process before attempting to go to law. It is too late, once a dispute arises, to change one's mind and decide to go to court instead. The voluntary aspect of ADR lies in that the parties choose to adopt the ADR clause in the first place. However, even after a dispute has arisen, the parties can reach a mutual agreement to dispense with ADR and go to court instead.

4.7 Many contracts do not make any provision for dispute settlement mechanisms because it is not something that the parties think about at the time. No one stops to consider what will happen if something goes wrong, how the dispute might be settled, how much time and money it might take to settle the dispute or what adverse effects a protracted dispute might have on their businesses and their relationship.

4.8 Even if there is no ADR clause in the contract, once a dispute arises, the parties are free to agree to refer the dispute to an ADR process rather than go to law.

Conciliation

4.9 Conciliation is an ADR process whereby the parties to a dispute (including future interest disputes) agree to utilise the services of a conciliator, who then meets with the parties separately in an attempt to resolve their differences. The conciliator does this by lowering tensions, improving communications, interpreting issues, providing technical assistance, exploring potential solutions and bringing about a negotiated settlement.

4.10 Conciliation differs from arbitration in that the conciliation process, in and of itself, has no legal standing, and the conciliator usually has no authority to seek evidence or call witnesses, usually writes no decision, and makes no award.

4.11 Conciliation differs from mediation (see below) in that the main goal is to conciliate, most of the time by seeking concessions. In mediation, the mediator tries to guide the discussion in a way that optimises parties' needs, takes feelings into account and reframes representations.

4.12 In conciliation the parties seldom, if ever, actually face each other across the table in the presence of the conciliator.

4.13 A good example of conciliation is the service that the Advisory Conciliation and Arbitration Service (ACAS) provides for employment disputes. Under the ACAS procedures the parties do not meet, but the conciliator speaks to the employer and the employee separately, usually over the telephone.

Mediation

4.14 Mediation is regarded as being the most flexible and the speediest of the ADR techniques, as well as being the most cost-effective. It is a proven means of dispute resolution which can generate a settlement fair to both parties at a reasonable cost.

4.15 Mediation is a voluntary, non-binding, without prejudice process. Trained third party mediators attempt through negotiation techniques to bring the parties together in a binding or non-binding settlement agreement. Where the mediation process ends with a binding agreement between the parties, that agreement can be enforced, simply and quickly, by the courts should the need arise.

4.16 If any of the parties to the mediation process, including the mediator, are dissatisfied with the process at any time, that party can terminate the process. The claimant may then proceed to assert his legal rights through the court system or through arbitration.

4.17 The problem with the court system is that it is adversarial and leads to a 'winner takes all' outcome. Often the court's decision is the result of a very fine distinction drawn on the basis of a mere balance of probabilities. There is little room for compromise and the parties may be left with a feeling that justice has not been done. The system guarantees that at least one of the parties will be dissatisfied with the judicial decision. Mediation avoids these problems. In mediation the parties are in charge of the dispute resolution process.

4.18 There are many different ways of conducting a mediation. However, the model to be adopted should reflect the needs of the industry and the parties it is serving.

4.19   The process begins with a request for mediation, to a mediator or an ADR service provider, by one of the parties. Once the other party consents to the mediation the parties may exchange relevant information and provide the mediator with information. Arrangements for the mediation may be made by the parties, the mediator or the ADR service provider. The mediation may be held at the premises of one of the parties, or their legal representatives, or at an independent venue such as a hotel or at the ADR service provider's mediation suite.

4.20   Most mediations will commence with a joint session with all the parties and the mediator present where the mediation process is explained to the parties. The parties are given an opportunity in the joint session to outline their position, explaining how they feel, what they need and what they hope to achieve out of the process. This sets the parameters for subsequent negotiations. In exceptional circumstances joint session may not be adopted if there is so much animosity present that it might result in an irreconcilable confrontation between the parties. To avoid confrontation, it is possible to brief the parties separately or to show them pre-recorded media (eg on DVD) explaining the process.

4.21   After the opening joint session the mediator will often conduct a series of sequential private meetings (sometimes known as caucuses) with each of the parties and their respective representatives. Private sessions are used to explore each party's situation and possible solutions to the problem as the mediator attempts to help the parties reach an agreement, playing 'devil's advocate' and asking searching questions about the strengths and weaknesses of the case. The mediator will use as many private sessions as circumstances require to broker a settlement. Meetings are entirely confidential. No information will be given to the other party unless expressly agreed.

4.22   The mediation will end with a joint session where the agreement is finalised, committed to paper and signed by the parties.

4.23   Mediation allows the parties to air their views in an informal setting. The mediator explores potential ways of settling the dispute with each party, guiding the parties to a more realistic view of their situation by highlighting the strengths and weaknesses of their case and the risks inherent in failing to reach a settlement. The parties are in control of the process and the outcome.

4.24   Even where a mediation fails the parties often narrow down the scope of the dispute to a single issue which can then be dealt with quickly by the court.

4.25   The advantages of mediation are as follows.

   •   The speed of dispute resolution (usually 3–4 weeks with a 1–2 days mediation)

   •   Cost savings – both in terms of the shortened process involved and also legal fees

   •   An improvement in communication between the parties

   •   A flexible informal procedure

   •   The process addresses unreasonable claims and expectations. It should produce a fair outcome.

Adjudication

4.26 Adjudication is a form of dispute resolution whereby an independent third party considers the claims of both sides and makes a decision. Invariably the adjudicator is an expert in the area related to the dispute. An adjudicator is not bound by the rules of litigation or arbitration. When this form of resolution is adopted, the parties in dispute usually agree in advance to accept the adjudicator's decisions as final. However, in some cases the adjudicator's decision is an interim one, which can be finalised using arbitration or some other process.

4.27 In the context of construction contracts, the term 'adjudication' is used almost exclusively for dispute resolution under Part II of the Housing Grants, Construction and Regeneration Act 1996 (HGCR). Before the passing of the Act adjudication was not a recognised form of ADR. Under the HGCR Act construction contracts must include a provision for adjudication, with the adjudicator giving a decision within 28 days of referral. The adjudicator's decision is binding until a final determination is reached by agreement, arbitration or litigation, or the parties may take the adjudicator's decision as final. For these reasons adjudication is different in kind from other forms of ADR, which are optional and less tied to a single subject area.

Expert determination

4.28 Expert determination is closely related to adjudication. It is a confidential and binding process that can offer a rapid method of settling a technical issue or dispute. This technique offers the following advantages when compared to arbitration or litigation.

- The expert appointed will be a person thoroughly familiar with the technical issues.
- It is usually cheaper, quicker and less formal than arbitration and litigation.
- Being confidential, and less adversarial than other methods, it helps to preserve commercial relations between the parties in dispute.
- Usually, the expert's decision is binding. Unless the parties specifically provide otherwise, it can be challenged only on limited grounds (eg fraud or partiality).

4.29 The parties will pay the expert for his work and there is usually no power for the expert to award costs in favour of either party. Thus each party will have to bear its own costs, even the party who is successful in the dispute.

ADR versus litigation and arbitration

4.30 As already explained, litigation is costly and risky for all parties. It can also be lengthy, inefficient and frustrating. By its adversarial approach it leads to hostility between the parties, which means that future business relations are endangered.

4.31 ADR attempts to overcome these drawbacks. It is based on an idea that there should be no winners and losers in a commercial dispute. It is non-adversarial, speedy, confidential, and inexpensive. It usually avoids the bad feeling that may ruin future business relations.

4.32 These points explain the attraction of ADR compared with litigation. However, they are mostly valid also in a comparison with arbitration. Arbitration is also an adversarial procedure, though admittedly it does not usually involve hostile cross-examination. And despite having greater flexibility than litigation, arbitration is also subject to the possibility of delays, judicial appeals and so on.

4.33 ADR produces a settlement designed by the parties, rather than imposed by a court or an arbitrator. Imagine a case where a buyer claims that certain products were defective and the seller disputes the point. A court or an arbitrator might find in favour of the seller leaving the buyer no alternative but to pay up without compensation. A mediator, or the parties themselves with a conciliator, is more likely to suggest that the buyer is allowed a better price on future supplies, safeguarding the future business relations between the parties and giving some compensation to both.

4.34 Another distinction between litigation and ADR is that whilst many legal practitioners engage in ADR processes, there is no legal or professional requirement for either the ADR practitioner or for party representatives at ADR processes to be legally qualified or to be members of legal professions.

4.35 Many of those who engage in ADR practice are first and foremost experts in particular fields, such as architects, builders, civil engineers, mariners, scientists and social workers, albeit with a thorough understanding of ADR processes and some knowledge and understanding of law. In-house legal experts in large corporate organisations can take part in the entire ADR process without engaging professional lawyers, thus cutting costs further, both in terms of time lost through communicating with the professionals and in respect of legal fees and costs.

4.36 It is also the practical knowledge and understanding of industry and commerce which assures the parties to ADR processes that the people responsible for settling their dispute or assisting them to reach a settlement understand their business and their concerns. It further assures them that the outcome will not be based purely on legal technicalities but will take into account commercial practicalities and technical details which lawyers may not give full weight to.

5   *International arbitration*

5.1 The International Chamber of Commerce (ICC) is committed to best practice in international trade so is well placed to offer advice when it comes to settling contractual disputes with an international dimension.

5.2 Arbitration remains the most commonly used form of dispute resolution particularly for international disputes. The ICC cite three main reasons for this.

- The final and binding character of arbitral awards. The ICC emphasise that arbitration, not being subject to appeal, is much more likely to be final than the judgments of the law courts.

- Wide international acceptance. More than 100 countries have now acceded to the 1958 United Nations Convention on the Recognition and Enforcement of Foreign Arbitral Awards, known as the New York Convention. This is still the most important multilateral convention on international arbitration.

- The neutrality of the forum. Arbitration brings a measure of neutrality. Neither of the disputing parties need be disadvantaged in any of the following regards: place of proceedings; language used; procedures or law applied; nationality of arbitrators; legal representation.

5.3 Therefore arbitration can be conducted in any country, in any language, with arbitrators of any nationality. With this degree of flexibility it is more often possible to structure a neutral procedure offering no undue advantage to either contracting party.

5.4   The buyer must fully understand that arbitration might not be truly international, even when using the services of the ICC court of arbitration or UNCITRAL's rules for arbitration. UNCITRAL is the United Nations Commission on International Trade Law which organised the Vienna Convention to draft a commercial code for use in all international trade transactions. Recourse will still be needed to plug gaps in both the ICC's and UNCITRAL's rules on arbitration. Additionally municipal courts must be used to enforce the award and they may in turn not agree with it.

5.5   However, custom and practice have shown that parties who are conducting international trade and do have disputes prefer to go to institutions such as the ICC or the London Court of International Arbitration and the American Arbitration Association (AAA).

5.6   For any arbitration proceedings the enforcement of any award is of critical importance. Clearly if you cannot enforce an arbitration award its value is meaningless. In international trade a frequent question arises in this regard: is an award made overseas enforceable in the UK, and similarly is an award made in the UK enforceable overseas?

5.7   There are a number of international conventions that have made the enforcement of arbitration less of a problem.

- The Geneva Protocol on Arbitration Clauses 1923
- The Geneva Convention on the Execution of Foreign Arbitral Awards 1927
- The New York Convention on Recognition and Enforcement of Foreign Arbitral Awards 1958

5.8   All three of these have been given legal effect in the UK.

Chapter summary

• Litigation suffers from several disadvantages as a means of settling commercial disputes: it is costly, it is subject to delays, and it is public.

• Arbitration is a binding procedure regulated by statute which attempts to overcome these disadvantages.

• The main statutory regulation concerning arbitration is contained in the Arbitration Act 1996. This Act is based on the principle of minimising court interference in the arbitration process.

• Mediation is an alternative to both arbitration and litigation. It is quicker and less costly than arbitration, but is not usually binding on the parties.

• Adjudication is an adversarial form of ADR used mainly in construction contracts where its use is mandated by the Housing, Grants, Construction and Regeneration Act 1996.

• The International Chamber of Commerce plays a pivotal role in the resolution of international trade disputes.

Self-test questions

Numbers in brackets refer to the paragraphs above where your answers can be checked.

1   What is the overriding objective of the Civil Procedure Rules? (1.2)

2   Describe the general disadvantages of litigation. (1.4)

3   State the advantages of arbitration over litigation. (2.3)

4   What is the small claims procedure? (2.8)

5   What is the principle of party autonomy? (3.2)

6   The parties to a contract have a completely free hand in deciding the terms of any arbitration. True or false? (3.4)

7   In what circumstances may an arbitrator lose his immunity from being sued? (3.8)

8   In what circumstances may a court admit an appeal on a point of law arising out of an arbitrator's award? (3.13)

9   What are the main advantages in the use of mediation? (4.25)

10   Which dispute resolution process is regulated by the Housing, Grants, Construction and Regeneration Act 1996? (4.27)

11   What are the advantages of arbitration cited by the ICC? (5.2)

CHAPTER 11

The Law Relating to Sale of Goods

Learning objectives and indicative content

2.1   Define different types of contract and analyse the statutes applicable to each type.

- Contracts for goods and services
- Contracts for the sale of goods
- Contracts for work and materials
- Contracts for services
- Contracts of hire
- Sale of Goods Act 1979 (as amended)

Chapter headings

1   Contracts for the sale of goods

2   Implied terms in the Sale of Goods Act 1979

3   Exemption clauses

Introduction

Earlier chapters in this text have provided detailed coverage of general principles and rules relating to contract law. For the most part these have been developed by means of case law.

In this chapter we begin our consideration of a particular type of contract: those which relate to the sale (and purchase) of goods. Clearly this is an area of especial relevance to purchasing professionals, and this has been reflected in past examinations.

The rules relating to contracts in general are equally applicable to this particular type of contract, but in addition there is a detailed statutory framework contained mainly in the Sale of Goods Act 1979 (as amended). This Act is the main subject of this chapter and the two that follow.

1   *Contracts for the sale of goods*

The statutory framework

1.1   A contract for the sale of goods, being a contract, is subject to the general principles of the law of contract. However, in the eighteenth and nineteenth centuries there developed out of mercantile custom a number of legal rules relating specifically to the sale of goods, and eventually these were codified in the Sale of Goods Act 1893 ('the 1893 Act').

1.2   Important changes to that Act were made by the Supply of Goods (Implied Terms) Act 1973 ('the 1973 Act'), and these two Acts were consolidated in the Sale of Goods Act 1979 (SGA 1979). The code relating to the sale of goods is therefore now found in the 1979 Act, which must be read together with the Unfair Contract Terms Act 1977 ('the 1977 Act').

1.3   Although certain changes to the 1979 Act were introduced by the Sale and Supply of Goods Act 1994 and the Sale of Goods (Amendment) Act 1995, it is the 1979 Act which remains the leading statute. References to section numbers in this chapter are always to sections of the 1979 Act unless the contrary is stated. Strictly speaking, we should in certain cases refer to 'the 1979 Act (as amended)' but we shall usually omit this.

1.4   Many of the cases decided on the 1893 Act remain relevant to the 1979 Act, which came into force on 1 January 1980. That is why you will see throughout this chapter cases illustrating provisions of the 1979 Act which were decided before that Act came into force.

Definitions

1.5   The provisions of SGA 1979 apply only to a contract for the sale of goods. This is defined in SGA 1979 as a contract whereby the seller transfers or agrees to transfer the property in goods to the buyer for a money consideration called the price. The various elements of this definition are important, because to invoke the provisions of the Act a person must show that the contract in question comes within the definition. Each of these elements will be discussed in turn.

1.6   **Seller** means a person who sells or agrees to sell goods under a contract for the sale of goods.

1.7   **Buyer** means a person who buys or agrees to buy goods under a contract for the sale of goods.

1.8   The word property in this context means ownership (or title). Thus the aim of a contract for the sale of goods is that the buyer becomes owner of the goods.

1.9   The Act provides that a contract of sale is either a sale or an agreement to sell.

1.10   A sale is a contract of sale whereby the property in the goods is transferred from the seller to the buyer at the time the contract is made. Thus as soon as the contract is made the buyer becomes the owner of the goods.

1.11   A sale can be:

- a bargain and sale – where delivery of the goods coincides with the sale – ie the buyer takes possession of the goods there and then; or
- a sale and delivery – where delivery is made subsequent to the sale – ie the buyer takes possession of the goods later.

1.12   In both of these cases the buyer becomes the owner at the time the contract is made.

1.13   An **agreement to sell** is a contract of sale where the transfer of property in the goods is to take place at some time in the future. This could be:

- at a **future time** (an absolute contract of sale, as property will be definitely transferred at an agreed future date); or
- subject to some condition later to be fulfilled (a **conditional** agreement to sell, as property will only be transferred to the buyer on the fulfilment of the condition. Thus an agreement to pay the price by instalments with an agreement that property will be transferred after a specified number of payments is a conditional sale).

1.14   In an agreement to sell the buyer does not become the owner of the goods when the contract is made, but at a later date or when the condition is fulfilled. However, the contract is still a sale of goods because it is agreed that the property or title will be transferred.

1.15   In a sale the buyer becomes the owner of the goods at the time when the contract is made. In an agreement to sell the buyer becomes the owner only at some future date.

Hire and hire purchase

1.16   You must be able to distinguish a contract of sale of goods, where there is a commitment to sell (ie transfer ownership) from a contract of hire and a contract of hire purchase.

1.17   A **contract of hire** of goods arises where the owner merely allows the hirer to have possession of the goods for a specified period. A contract for the hire of goods is also called a contract of bailment. The owner is called the bailor and the hirer is called the bailee.

1.18   A contract of hire is not a contract of sale of goods (neither a sale nor an agreement to sell) because there is never any intention to transfer ownership. SGA 1979 does not therefore apply to contracts of hire.

1.19   A contract of **hire purchase** is where the owner of goods hires them to another, who then has the option to purchase once all the agreed instalments have been paid. A contract of hire purchase is sometimes also called a contract of bailment. The owner (ie the bailor) is the creditor and the hirer (ie the bailee) is the debtor. We shall return to bailment in Chapter 12.

1.20   A contract of hire purchase is not a contract for the sale of goods. It is not a sale because the debtor does not obtain immediate **ownership**: during the currency of the agreement he merely has **possession**. It is not an agreement to sell because the hire purchase contract does not give him a right to ownership once the instalments have been paid: it merely gives him an option to purchase. SGA 1979 does not therefore apply to hire purchase contracts: **Helby v Matthews** (1895).

Credit sales and conditional sales

1.21   A contract where there is a commitment to sell and credit is given will be a contract of sale of goods even if the agreement is that transfer of property (ownership) is conditional on payment of all the instalments. There are two types of contract of sale of goods whereby credit is given: a credit sale and a conditional sale.

1.22   A **credit sale agreement** is where ownership passes to the purchaser at the outset although the purchaser is given credit in that he pays for the goods by instalments over a specified period. This is an absolute contract of sale.

1.23   A **conditional sale agreement** is where ownership of the goods will only pass to the purchaser once he has paid all the instalments. This is a conditional agreement to sell.

1.24   Both are contracts for the sale of goods and therefore SGA 1979 is applicable.

Goods

1.25   Goods are defined by SGA 1979 to include all chattels personal, other than things in action and money and, in particular, to include all emblements, industrial growing crops and things attached to or forming part of the land which are agreed to be severed before sale or under the contract of sale.

1.26   **Chattels personal** means movable property, eg a book or a car, and includes all tangible goods, but does not include land (freehold or leasehold).

1.27   **Things in action** are those intangible forms of property such as debts, shares, copyrights and mortgages (but not leases) which can only be protected by action at law.

1.28   **Emblements and industrial growing crops** are cultivated growing crops (eg potatoes, corn). Other things attached to and forming part of land (eg trees) are not goods unless it is agreed that they are severed before the sale or under the contract of sale.

Work and materials

1.29   Where the substance of the contract is the buying of a skill rather than the buying of a product there is not a sale of goods. The cases abound with fine distinctions. An example is the case of **Stewart v Reavell's** (1952).

A contract for the repair of a car included an agreement to supply the necessary spare parts.

Held: This was a contract for work and materials and was therefore not covered by the SGA.

1.30   The real test is the intention of the parties as to the essential character of the agreement, and the most helpful question is: **was the purchaser or transferee paying substantially for goods or for skills?** If for skills, then the fact that the contract results in the sale of a thing to the transferee who did not have previous property in it does not prevent the contract being one for work and materials and therefore its being outside SGA 1979.

'Money consideration called the price'

1.31 A sale of goods presupposes a price which is money consideration, not goods: **Esso Petroleum v Customs and Excise** (1976). Thus, contracts where the whole of the consideration for the goods is other goods will not come within the definition: such contracts are called **contracts of exchange** or **contracts of barter**.

1.32 The price may be fixed:

- by the contract; or
- in a manner agreed in the contract; or
- by the course of dealing between the parties.

1.33 If none of these methods apply to determine the amount, the buyer must pay a reasonable price: s8 SGA 1979. Where no price has been determined, it may well be difficult to show that there has been a contract at all, since the price is usually an important term.

1.34 But when goods have actually been delivered, accepted and used, or perhaps merely delivered and accepted, the courts will hold that a reasonable price is payable rather than declare that the contract is void.

Types of goods

1.35 A contract of sale of goods includes a range of transactions, from a contract for the sale of a specific item which the buyer selects at the time of the contract, to a contract for the sale of an item which the seller must make or buy himself and then transfer to the buyer. The Act uses two sets of terms to differentiate between the types of goods.

1.36 **Specific goods** are defined in SGA 1979 as goods identified and agreed on at the time the contract of sale is made; for example, X selects a coat in a shop and contracts to buy that particular one.

1.37 **Unascertained goods** are goods not so identified and agreed upon at the time the contract is made. Unascertained goods include:

- goods which have been defined by description applicable to all goods of the same class; for example, a contract to buy a Range Rover of a specific description although you have not identified the actual Range Rover which is the subject of the contract
- goods forming an unidentified part of a specific whole, eg 100 gallons of oil from a particular quantity of oil.

1.38 Notice that unascertained goods will become ascertained because at some stage the parties will know exactly which item is the subject of the contract. Nevertheless it is still a contract for the sale of unascertained goods because SGA 1979 requires the classification between specific and unascertained goods to be done when the contract is made.

1.39 **Future goods** means goods to be manufactured or acquired by the seller after the making of the contract.

1.40 **Existing goods** are those which are in existence and in the ownership of the seller at the time the contract is made.

Conditions and warranties

1.41   It is important to remember the basic contract rules about the difference between a contractual term and a mere representation and the classification of terms into conditions and warranties. Section 11(3) SGA 1979 provides that whether a stipulation in a contract of sale is a condition or a warranty depends in each case on the construction of the contract, and a stipulation may be a condition, even though called a warranty in the contract.

1.42   The Act sets out in ss10, 12, 13, 14 and 15 terms which are implied into all contracts of sale of goods, principally to protect the buyer, for example, by implying that goods will be of a certain quality. Each section also labels the implied term as a condition or a warranty.

1.43   Section 11(3) does not apply to these terms implied by statute as the court will not decide itself whether the implied terms are conditions or warranties but will treat the terms as labelled by the Act.

- • A breach of any of the implied conditions will entitle the innocent party to reject the goods, treat the contract as repudiated and claim any damages he has suffered.

- • A breach of an implied warranty, on the other hand, will only entitle the innocent party to claim damages.

1.44   It is therefore important to note both the terms which are implied and the label given to each term, ie a condition or a warranty.

Breach of condition treated as breach of warranty

1.45   SGA 1979 provides that where a contract of sale of goods is subject to a condition to be fulfilled by the seller, the buyer may waive the condition, or may elect to treat the breach of the condition as a breach of warranty and not as a ground for treating the contract as repudiated.

1.46   SGA 1979 provides that where a contract of sale of goods is not severable and the buyer has accepted the goods or part of them, the breach of condition can **only** be treated as a breach of warranty and not as a ground for rejecting the goods and treating the contract as repudiated, unless there is an express or implied term of the contract to that effect.

1.47   We shall see that this is important when considering the buyer's duty to accept goods and the rules on ascertaining when he has accepted them. The provision about severable contracts will be dealt with in the section on acceptance by the buyer.

Exclusion of implied terms

1.48   Sometimes the contract may specifically state that the terms implied by statute are not to be included, ie the parties themselves agree to contract on their own terms and not those provided by SGA 1979. It is generally in the interests of the seller, as opposed to the buyer, to oust the implied terms as the terms are generally ones which protect the buyer.

1.49   The ability of the seller to exclude the terms has been restricted and is now treated in much the same way as the ability to exempt or limit liability generally. The Unfair Contract Terms Act 1977 specifically deals with the implied terms of SGA 1979. The way in which the 1977 Act applies to each of the terms will be stated as they are covered.

Terms as to time

1.50   Stipulations as to **time of payment** are **not** deemed to be of the essence of a contract of sale (ie are not treated as conditions) unless a different intention appears from its terms: s10. Thus a seller cannot generally repudiate a sale or even an agreement to sell merely because the buyer has not paid for the goods by a stipulated date.

1.51   Other stipulations as to time, such as dates of shipment, transfer or delivery, are normally treated as **conditions**, at any rate in commercial contracts, where time is likely to be an important factor. The approach is fundamentally one of treating a time stipulation as part of the essential description of the goods, so that it is governed by the rule as to implied conditions in relation to description as found in s13 SGA 1979.

1.52   A stipulation as to time may be waived, so that thereafter a buyer cannot insist upon a delivery date specified in the contract. However, on giving reasonable notice, the buyer can once again make time of the essence in the contract. We will see this later in the case of **Charles Rickards v Oppenheim** (1950).

2   Implied terms in the Sale of Goods Act 1979

The implied term as to title: s12

2.1   At present, whatever a contract may say, the seller is deemed to undertake:

- as a **condition**, that he has a right to sell the goods; or in the case of an agreement to sell, that, when the property is to pass, he will have a right to sell then: s12(1) SGA 1979; and

- as a **warranty**, that the goods are and will remain free from any charge or encumbrance not disclosed to the buyer before the contract is made, and that the buyer will enjoy quiet possession of them: s12(2) SGA 1979.

2.2   The condition that the seller has a right to sell is most useful to a buyer when a seller turns out not to have been the true owner of the goods: **Rowland v Divall** (1923).

A claimant who had bought a car and used it for some months then discovered that it had been stolen and returned it to the actual owner.

Held: In an action against the seller, the claimant recovered the full purchase price as being money paid on a consideration which had wholly failed. The defendant's argument that the claimant had accepted the goods and so could only sue for damages as if it were a breach of warranty was rejected. The defendant's argument that the claimant had received a benefit (the use of the car for several months) also failed.

2.3   The s12(1) condition may also be used where a trader buys goods which cannot be marketed in their existing form because they would infringe a patent. The trader can rely on the seller's inadequate title and either reject the goods or claim damages for their reduced value: **Niblett v Confectioners' Materials Co** (1921).

Tins of condensed milk bearing labels which contravened Nestlé's trade mark were sold to a trader. They had to be relabelled before resale by him.

Held: Breach of s12(1).

2.4   If at the time of the contract the seller lacked the right to sell but later acquired it, so that the buyer eventually acquires good title, the buyer loses the right to repudiate the contract for breach of condition as there is no longer a total failure of consideration. He can, however, still claim damages, not least for any expenses which he may reasonably have undertaken to establish the seller's title upon which he relies. He is not, of course, obliged to assist the seller in this way.

2.5   The warranty of quiet possession is rarely invoked in the courts: **Microbeads AG v Vinhurst Road Markings Ltd** (1975).

A seller sold an apparatus for marking roads to a buyer against whom a third party took steps to prevent him using it, on the ground that it infringed a patent granted to the third party.

Held: The seller was in breach of the warranty of quiet possession even though the third party's specification for the patent was not published until after the sale.

2.6   By s6(1) Unfair Contract Terms Act 1977 liability under s12 cannot be excluded, even by an express term of the contract.

The implied term as to description: s13

2.7   In a sale by description the contract includes some description of the goods and the buyer contracts in reliance on that description. If it is a sale by description there is an implied condition that the goods correspond with the description: s13(1) SGA 1979. We saw this illustrated in the case **Re Moore & Landauer** (1921). A similar case is **Arcos v Ronaasen** (1933): the buyer was entitled to reject a consignment of staves which should have been ½ inch thick because some of them were $\frac{9}{16}$ inch thick.

2.8   Most sales involve some description, if only to identify the goods, whether they are specific or unascertained. Where the buyer has not seen the goods, the contract is necessarily a sale by description. But a sale is not prevented from being a sale by description only because, being exposed for sale or hire, the goods are selected by the buyer: s13(3) SGA 1979: **Beale v Taylor** (1967).

A car was described as 'a Herald 1200' in an advertisement and had a plate 'Herald 1200' on it. The buyer saw the car and agreed to buy it. It transpired that the car was only partly a 'Herald 1200': part of another, older, model had been welded on to it.

Held: This was a sale by description notwithstanding the buyer had seen the car. Since the car was not a 'Herald 1200' the condition of compliance with description had been breached.

2.9   Where there is uncertainty about the status of a description the test is: did the buyer rely on it? Was it used to identify the thing sold or was it merely collateral? The case of **Varley v Whipp** (1900) is relevant.

The seller described a secondhand reaping machine which the buyer had not seen as 'new the previous year'.

Held: The phrase formed part of the description.

2.10 A statement which is part of a written advertisement is more likely to be treated as part of the description than one which is made orally in the presence of the buyer.

2.11 The buyer cannot usually rely on s13(3), if he sees the goods before making the contract **and** it is obvious to him that the description is inaccurate, for he could not then claim he had relied on the description.

2.12 Section 6(2) Unfair Contract Terms Act 1977 provides that this term cannot be excluded in a consumer contract and s6(3) provides that the term can only be excluded in any other contract if the term satisfies the requirement of reasonableness. This will be explained later.

The implied terms as to satisfactory quality and fitness for purpose: s14

2.13 The most important of the conditions implied by SGA 1979, though applying only where the seller supplies goods in the course of a business, are in s14. The two conditions are:

- that the goods supplied are of satisfactory quality except in respect of defects specifically drawn to the buyer's attention before the contract is made, and defects which any examination actually carried out by the buyer before the contract ought to reveal: s14(2)

- in a case where the buyer, expressly or by implication, makes known to the seller any particular purpose for which the goods are being bought, that the goods supplied are reasonably fit for the purpose, whether or not it is a purpose for which such goods are commonly supplied, except where either the buyer does not rely, or it is unreasonable for him to rely, on the skill or judgement of the seller: s14(3).

2.14 The term 'satisfactory quality' was introduced by the Sale and Supply of Goods Act 1994 as an amendment to the term 'merchantable quality' originally used in the 1979 Act. The amendment was apparently to benefit the buyer: satisfactory quality is a higher standard than merchantable quality. However, there is little case law yet to illustrate what constitutes satisfactory quality, and earlier cases were all decided in relation to the requirement of merchantable quality. A clear improvement from the buyer's perspective is stated in s14(2B): one aspect of satisfactory quality is 'freedom from minor defects'. In the case of **Rogers v Parish** (1987) the buyer was entitled to reject a motor car, even though it was perfectly functional, on account of a variety of minor faults.

2.15 It is not enough if the goods contracted for are in themselves sound but are so mixed with other contaminating matter as to prevent them being used: **Wilson v Rickett Cockerell and Co Ltd** (1954).

There was a detonator in a sack of coalite.

Held: Goods supplied were not of satisfactory quality.

2.16   The s14 terms are only implied into contracts made in the course of a business. Most if not all transactions that you encounter in your professional work will fall within this description.

2.17   'Quality', in relation to goods, includes their state or condition: s14(2B). Goods should be fit for the purpose or purposes for which goods of that kind are commonly bought. Particular note should be made of:

   •   any description applied to them

   •   the price, if relevant

   •   all other relevant circumstances: s14(2A).

2.18   Thus, a buyer must not expect very cheap goods to be of the same quality as more expensive ones. Other relevant considerations might be that the goods are secondhand, or were made or acquired at great speed to comply with the buyer's special request. Goods used in the way or ways in which goods of that class are normally used and which do not work properly or fail after an unreasonably short time or which are unsafe or injurious are clearly not of satisfactory quality. And even with secondhand goods the buyer is entitled to reasonable expectations of quality: **Shine v General Guarantee** (1988).

2.19   Nor are goods which though originally sound are damaged through having been badly packed by the seller with the knowledge of the kind of journey they would have to make. They are defective in quality notwithstanding that the damage occurs after the buyer has taken them away.

2.20   The degree of fitness required is, of course, a question of fact. But the goods must be fit at the time of sale, and not merely capable of being made so, for instance, by washing: **Grant v Australian Knitting Mills** (1936).

   Underpants contained a chemical which could be removed by washing.

   Held: These goods were not of satisfactory quality.

2.21   Moreover the goods must remain fit for a reasonable time after sale, although in the case of food this may not be very long. If the seller knows the goods have to make a journey before they will be consumed, they must remain fit for the normal period of the journey.

2.22   The seller is protected, however, if:

   •   a defect complained of was drawn to the attention of the buyer or was discovered on examination by him, in either case before the contract was made; or

   •   if the defect was not discovered by the buyer at that stage but ought to have been in the kind of examination actually carried out by the buyer.

2.23   In the great majority of cases, the buyer does make some kind of examination of the goods before making the contract, and the question will depend on what ought to have been discovered in that kind of examination. The buyer is not obliged to make any examination at all. Indeed, the more detailed the examination is intended to be, the more the buyer restricts his rights: a man who knows nothing about car engines may do well not to open the bonnet.

2.24 There is some overlap between satisfactory quality and fitness for purpose. Satisfactory quality is defined in terms of fitness for purposes for which goods of the appropriate class are commonly bought. But the buyer may explain to the seller a **particular** purpose for which he requires the goods. Then if the seller contracts with him, he is in general liable under s14(3) if the goods are not fit for that purpose.

2.25 If the buyer is going to use the goods for a purpose for which they are commonly used (eg a hot water bottle to be used to keep a person warm) then he need not specifically state to the seller the purpose to which he intends to put the goods: **Priest v Last** (1903).

The buyer did not state the use of a hot water bottle for normal purposes. The hot water bottle leaked.

Held: This did not prevent the buyer from successfully suing for breach of the condition that the goods were fit for their purpose: the seller was presumed to have sold the bottle for normal use.

2.26 If the buyer is going to use the goods for a particular (unusual) purpose or there are unusual circumstances then he must notify the seller of this in order to obtain protection under s14(3): **Griffiths v Peter Conway Ltd** (1939).

The buyer was allergic to a Harris tweed coat which was perfectly fit for a normal person.

Held: There was held to be no breach of condition of fitness for purpose as the buyer had not told the seller of the special circumstances (ie her sensitivity to such fabric).

2.27 If the buyer does rely on the seller's judgement, it is unlikely that a court will find it was unreasonable for him to do so, even if both parties trade in the same business. Even a retail shopkeeper can be relied on in this way since he is expected to select his stock with skill and judgement. It is not necessary that the buyer rely **exclusively** on the seller's skill and judgement, provided that the matter complained of arises from that aspect of the goods for which the buyer did rely on the seller.

2.28 Section 6(2) Unfair Contract Terms Act 1977 provides that the s14(2) and s14(3) terms cannot be excluded in a consumer contract and s6(3) provides that the term can only be excluded in any other contract if the term satisfies the requirement of reasonableness. This will be explained later in the chapter.

The implied term as to sale by sample: s15

2.29 A **sale by sample** occurs when the buyer is given the opportunity of examining a small part only of the goods to be bought, but such as to be typical of the whole, in this context usually called the bulk of the goods.

2.30 Thus, corn, toys, pianos or parrots might all be sold by sample if the bulk of the goods was large enough to justify the method. A contract of sale is by sample if, and only if, there is a term in the contract, express or implied, to that effect: s15 (1).

2.31 A contract of sale is not by sample merely because part of the goods was shown to the buyer during the negotiations preceding the contract: both parties must accept as a contract term that the sale is by sample. Trade usage may, of course, raise the necessary presumption without any express agreement to that effect but if the contract is written it will normally be treated as a sale by sample only if stated to be so.

2.32   In a contract for sale by sample there are implied conditions:

- that the bulk shall correspond with the sample in quality;
- that the buyer shall have a reasonable opportunity of comparing the bulk with the sample; and
- that the goods shall be free from any defect rendering them unsatisfactory, which would not be apparent on reasonable examination of the sample: s15(2).

2.33   The test under s15(2) is one of 'reasonable examination' of the sample and not one of thorough examination: **Godley v Perry** (1960).

A boy of six bought a catapult from the defendant's newsagency shop and damaged his eye when it broke in his hands as a result of having been indifferently manufactured. The catapult was part of a quantity bought by sample from a wholesaler and the defendant's wife had tested the sample beforehand by pulling back its elastic.

Held: While the defendant was liable to the boy in damages for the catapult being neither fit for its purpose nor of satisfactory quality, the defendant could also himself claim against the wholesaler because the defect of the goods could not be discovered by reasonable examination of the sample (s15).

2.34   'Reasonableness' is the statutory yardstick. The Act does not even speak of carrying out 'practicable' tests on the goods concerned, but of 'reasonable examination'.

2.35   If the bulk does not correspond with the sample, the buyer is not prevented from rejecting the bulk merely because he has made payment in full. Whenever the bulk does not correspond with the sample, the buyer can either reject the whole or retain the whole, but he cannot accept the part corresponding to the sample and reject the rest, unless the seller agrees.

2.36   If a sale is both by description and by sample it must satisfy the requirements appropriate for each: s13(2). Thus, a contract to sell 'foreign refined rape oil, warranted only equal to sample', was broken when the seller delivered oil corresponding to the sample, but not answering to the description 'foreign refined rape oil': **Nichol v Godts** (1854).

2.37   Section 6(2) Unfair Contract Terms Act 1977 provides that this term cannot be excluded in a consumer contract and s6(3) provides that the term can only be excluded in any other contract if the term satisfies the requirement of reasonableness. This will be explained later in the chapter.

Distance selling

2.38   The Consumer Protection (Distance Selling) Regulations 2000 deal with 'distance selling' (which occurs where the seller does not meet the buyer face to face). They implement the EU Distance Selling Directive. The regulations apply to consumer sales and include contracts made by e-mail, mail order, telephone and fax.

2.39 Under the regulations, the consumer is entitled to receive certain information in writing or by some other 'durable medium'. They give the consumer the right to withdraw from the contract, and to a refund of monies paid. Changes to the rules on cancellation were introduced by the Consumer Protection (Distance Selling) (Amendments) Regulations 2005. This area has now become somewhat technical, but in your professional work you will rarely or never be dealing as a consumer and we therefore spare you the detail!

2.40 Some types of contract are excluded. These include land and auction sales, and financial services. Withdrawal rights do not apply to goods which deteriorate rapidly, such as audio goods, video goods or software packages that have been opened.

2.41 The E-commerce Directive requires that any commercial e-mail sent must include certain information: name, geographic address, details including e-mail address, trade register number if applicable, supervisory authority, regulator if applicable, VAT number if applicable. Where goods or services are being provided, there must be a clear statement of the price and whether this includes tax and delivery costs.

2.42 The directive also requires that websites taking orders should, among other things, give the buyer information on technical steps to conclude the contract, and give the buyer a receipt for orders placed via the website.

3 Exemption clauses

Introduction

3.1 SGA 1979 provides that:

- where a right, duty or liability would arise under a contract for sale of goods by implication of law, it may (subject to the Unfair Contract Terms Act 1977) be negative or varied by express agreement, or by course of dealing between the parties, or by such usage as binds both parties to the contract

- an express condition or warranty does not negative a condition or warranty implied by this Act unless inconsistent with it.

3.2 Thus the basic 'freedom of contract' under which the parties can agree to contract on whatever terms they choose is preserved, subject to the Unfair Contract Terms Act 1977. Thus, subject to the 1977 Act the parties can agree to oust the implied terms. As stated at the beginning of this chapter the courts have treated attempts to exclude the implied terms in much the same way as any exemption or limitation clause.

The requirement of reasonableness

3.3 The requirement of reasonableness (in non-consumer cases) means that the term must have been a fair and reasonable one to be included having regard to the circumstances which were, or ought reasonably to have been, known to, or in the contemplation of the parties when the contract was made: s11(1) UCTA 1977.

3.4   By way of supplement to the test, Sch 2 UCTA 1977 lists five guidelines indicating which matters in particular are to be taken into account. For convenience, these are repeated here from Chapter 6.

• The strength of the bargaining positions of the parties relative to each other, taking into account (among other things) alternative means of supplying the buyer's requirements

• Whether the buyer received an inducement to agree to the term, or in accepting it had an opportunity of making a similar contract lacking such a term with other persons

• Whether the buyer knew or ought to have known of the existence and the extent of the term, having regard to trade custom and any previous course of dealing between the parties

• Whether it was reasonable to expect when the contract was made that it would be practical for the buyer to comply with a condition such that liability of the seller would be excluded or restricted if he did not

• Whether the goods were manufactured, processed or adapted to the special order of the customer

3.5   These guidelines are specifically applied by UCTA 1977 to ascertain reasonableness in the context of contracts for the sale of goods and other transfers of goods (hire, hire purchase and contracts of exchange or for work and materials). However, they are also used when ascertaining the reasonableness of exemption or limitation clauses in other situations as well.

3.6   The provisions of UCTA 1977 are reinforced by the Transactions (Restriction on Statements) Order 1976 (as amended), which makes it a criminal offence to attempt to introduce into a consumer transaction a term which is void by virtue of s6 of UCTA 1977. An example would be a statement that 'no refunds shall be given'.

3.7   Further protection is afforded by the Unfair Terms in Consumer Contracts Regulations 1999, which are discussed in Chapter 6.

Chapter summary

- Sale of goods contracts are subject to the normal rules relating to contracts in general, but are also regulated by statute, principally the Sale of Goods Act 1979.

- The 1979 Act governs contracts of sale and agreements to sell, but not contracts of hire or of hire purchase, nor contracts for work and materials.

- The Act provides that in the absence of contrary agreement, certain terms are implied into all contracts for the sale of goods. In most cases, the implied terms rank as conditions: breach entitles the injured party not merely to claim damages, but to repudiate the contract.

- Section 12 contains an implied term as to title: the seller must have the right to sell and the buyer must be able to enjoy quiet possession.

- Section 13 contains an implied term as to description: in a sale by description the goods must correspond with the description.

- Section 14(2) contains an implied term as to satisfactory quality.

- Section 14(3) contains an implied term as to fitness for purpose.

- Section 15 contains an implied term as to sale by sample: the bulk must match the sample.

- The Unfair Contract Terms Act 1977 refers specifically to the implied terms in the 1979 Act. In non-consumer contracts it is generally open to the parties to vary or exclude the implied terms, subject to the requirement of reasonableness.

Self-test questions

Numbers in brackets refer to the paragraphs above where your answers can be checked.

1   Define a buyer and a seller. (1.6, 1.7)

2   Define an agreement to sell. (1.13)

3   A conditional sale is not a contract falling under the provisions of the 1979 Act. True or false? (1.24)

4   What is a contract for work and materials? Does it rank as a contract for the sale of goods? (1.29)

5   Distinguish between specific and unascertained goods. (1.36, 1.37)

6   Describe the facts and the *ratio* of **Rowland v Divall**. (2.2)

7   Describe the difference between satisfactory quality and merchantable quality. (2.14)

8   What are the implied conditions in a contract for sale by sample? (2.32)

9   What are the five guidelines laid down by UCTA 1977 in relation to the reasonableness test? (3.4)

CHAPTER 12

Transfer of Property, Risk and Title

Learning objectives and indicative content

2.2 Differentiate between ownership, risk, delivery and acceptance of goods and analyse when each passes from the seller to the buyer.

- S16–S20 – Sale of Goods Act 1979 (ownership and risk)
- S30 – Sale of Goods Act 1979 (delivery)
- S31 – Sale of Goods Act 1979 (instalment deliveries)
- Common law rules relating to instalment deliveries
- S34–S35 – Sale of Goods Act 1979 (acceptance)

2.3 Analyse the rules relating to the passing of title by a non-owner under legislation and the exceptions to these rules.

- The *nemo dat* rule
- Romalpa clauses
- Estoppel
- Sale by a mercantile agent
- Sale under a voidable title
- Sale by a seller in possession
- Sale by a buyer in possession
- Sale of a motor vehicle on hire purchase
- Sale under a court order

2.5 Identify and analyse the legal principles that apply to agency and bailment.

- Responsibilities that arise from a bailment relationship

Chapter headings

1 Transfer of property

2 The passing of risk

3 Transfer of title

4 Delivery and acceptance

Introduction

As we saw in the previous chapter, a contract for the sale of goods involves a transfer of property from one party (the seller) to another (the buyer). In many situations it is important to determine exactly when this transfer is legally complete. This can affect the rights of the parties in cases where, for example, damage occurs to the goods, or the buyer sells the goods onwards to a third party.

In this chapter we look at the common law and statutory rules that are relevant in this area.

1   Transfer of property

Why is the time of transfer important?

1.1   The transfer of property means the transfer of ownership. This must be carefully distinguished from the transfer of possession, which means simply physical control of the goods.

1.2   Transfer of property and of possession may operate quite independently. For example, in the case of a cash sale, possession may not be obtainable until the price has been paid; whereas in the case of goods delivered on sale or return, the potential buyer is given possession, but the ownership does not pass until some further action has been performed in relation to the goods.

1.3   The moment when the property in the goods passes from seller to buyer under a contract of sale may be important in many circumstances.

- If the goods are accidentally damaged or destroyed, as the risk may depend on who has the property (ownership)

- If either the seller or the buyer becomes bankrupt, as a bankrupt's property vests in his trustee in bankruptcy

- If the goods are damaged or destroyed through the negligence or other fault of a third party, as the rights of an **owner** to claim for loss are different from those of a person who merely has **possession**

- For the purposes of the *nemo dat* rule and s12 SGA 1979, as it is only a person who owns goods who can sell them. The *nemo dat* rule is dealt with later

- For the purposes of deciding whether an unpaid seller can maintain an action for the price and other remedies. This too is dealt with later.

General principles

1.4   There are two general principles governing the transfer of property in goods.

- Property in unascertained goods cannot pass before they have been ascertained: s16. In **Kursell v Timber Operators** (1927) the contract concerned trees that would be felled over the next 15 years. These were held to be unascertained goods. (However, this decision appears to contrast with that in **Joseph Reid Property v Schultz** (1949).)

- Subordinate to the first rule, property in goods passes from seller to buyer at such time as the parties intend it to pass: s17(1). In the case of **Ward v Bignall** (1967) this was held to be the 'governing rule' in the passing of property.

1.5   The first rule is illustrated by the case of **Hayman v McLintock** (1907).

A seller, having 420 sacks of flour in a warehouse, contracted to sell 100 of them to a buyer. The price was paid and the buyer given a delivery order to present to the warehouseman. But nothing was done to appropriate any particular sacks and before the buyer claimed his 100 sacks the seller became bankrupt.

Held: The goods had not been ascertained and therefore property had not passed. The seller's trustee in bankruptcy was able to claim all the sacks remaining in the warehouse.

1.6   The act of ascertaining may be done by the seller appropriating some of his stock to the buyer, perhaps merely by setting them on one side or placing a mark on them. In addition, it is worth noting that the effect of s16 has to some extent been mitigated by new rules in the Sale of Goods (Amendment) Act 1995, but the new provisions have hardly yet been tested in the courts and their exact effect is hard to estimate.

1.7   A particular problem arose in respect of unascertained goods for buyers who had paid for such goods and who had received documents of title, only for the seller to go into liquidation before the goods became ascertained. In these circumstances, the buyer was merely an unsecured creditor who lost his right to the goods to the liquidator. The Sale of Goods (Amendment) Act 1995 protects a buyer in this situation by providing that if the unascertained goods form part of an identifiable bulk, and the buyer pays for the goods, then the property in these goods passes **at the time of payment** and not when the goods become ascertained.

1.8   With regard to the second rule, the intention of the parties may be evidenced by:

•   the terms of the contract;

•   the conduct of the parties; and

•   the circumstances of the case: s17(2).

1.9   The circumstances of the case include any trade custom as to when property is to pass or, what may amount to the same thing, who is to bear the risk.

The Rules of s18

1.10   If the parties do not indicate their intention as to the time of transfer s18 lays down five rules for determining when property passes. Note that these rules only apply in the absence of a clear indication from the parties or from the circumstances.

Rule 1   In an **unconditional** contract for the sale of specific goods in a deliverable state the property passes at the time of the contract. Goods are in a deliverable state when the buyer would, under the contract, be bound to take delivery of them: s61(5). **Tarling v Baxter** (1827):

A farmer sold a haystack which remained on his farm, to be collected in the spring. Before collection, the stack was destroyed through no fault of the farmer.

Held: Ownership had passed to the buyer, who had to bear the loss.

Rule 2 In a contract for the sale of **specific** goods where the seller has to do something to put the goods into a deliverable state, the property does not pass until this has been done and the buyer has notice of it. **Underwood v Burgh Castle Brick and Cement Syndicate** (1922):

Contract for the sale of a 30-ton engine embedded in a concrete floor, to be dug up by the seller. The seller, in removing the engine from the concrete base, damaged it.

Held: At the time the damage occurred, the goods were not in a deliverable state, so that property in the goods had not passed to the buyer. The seller, therefore, had to bear the loss.

Rule 3 In a contract for the sale of **specific** goods in a deliverable state where the **seller** has to weigh, test or measure the goods in order to ascertain the price, the property does not pass until this has been done and the buyer has notice of it: **Turley v Bates** (1863).

Contract for sale of a heap of clay, buyer to weigh as he loaded.

Held: Since the obligation was on the buyer to weigh, Rule 1, not Rule 3, applied and goods were therefore at his risk. The same conclusion applied in the case of **Nanka-Bruce v Commonwealth Trust** (1926).

Rule 4 Where goods are delivered on approval or on sale or return the property passes to the buyer:

(a)   when he signifies his approval or acceptance to the seller or adopts the transaction in some other way; or

(b)   if he retains the goods without rejecting them within a fixed or reasonable time: **Poole v Smith's Car Sales** (1962).

Elphick v Barnes (1880):

Seller handed a horse to a buyer on approval for eight days. The horse died on the third day.

Held: Ownership had not passed to the buyer, and the seller had to bear the loss. There was a similar decision in the case of **Re Ferrier** (1944).

Part (a) of Rule 4 can cause inconvenience in practice. Some sellers choose to oust this rule by specifying a contrary intention, eg by specifying that property will not pass until the goods have been paid for: **Weiner v Gill** (1906).

Rule 5 If the contract is for the sale of **unascertained or future goods sold by description**, the property passes when goods of that description and in a deliverable state are unconditionally appropriated to the transaction by one party with the assent of the other.

1.11 Most of the cases on Rule 5 revolve around the words 'unconditionally appropriated' and the decisions are not easy to reconcile. A leading case is that of **Carlos Federspiel v Charles Twigg** (1957).

A contract was made for the sale of bicycles and tricycles. The buyer had paid the price and the seller had crated up and labelled goods (which were thus clearly intended for this contract) ready for shipping. The goods were in his yard when the seller went into liquidation.

Held: There was no unconditional appropriation of the goods under Rule 5. Setting aside goods is not enough; there must be an intention to attach irrevocably to the contract particular goods.

1.12 Part of the reasoning in this case revolved around the question: 'What was to stop the seller changing his mind and delivering the goods elsewhere?'. Moreover appropriation may be said to involve a delivery, actual or constructive, to the buyer. It was difficult to see such a delivery in this case.

1.13 Looking at the intention of the parties, it has been seen that risk *prima facie* ('unless proved otherwise') passes with property. In this case, if one imagines that the crates had been destroyed by fire, the buyers would not have claimed so eagerly that property had passed. Finally, appropriation is usually the last act to be done by the seller: in this case that would be putting the goods on board ship. Thus it was held that property had not passed and that the buyer's claim was as an unsecured creditor.

1.14 Where the seller delivers the goods to the buyer or to a carrier on his behalf without reserving a right of disposal, he is taken to have unconditionally appropriated the goods to the contract. For this to apply the goods must be ascertained: **Healy v Howlett & Sons** (1917).

The seller of fish instructed a railway to deliver fish to the buyer but the particular boxes of fish were not set aside specifically for that buyer until the end of the train journey.

Held: No appropriation occurred until that point, and as the fish had deteriorated prior to that point the seller bore the risk.

1.15 Rule 5 does not apply if, before or on delivery of the goods to the buyer or a carrier, the seller reserves the right of disposal until one or more conditions have been fulfilled: s19(1). We look in more detail at such 'reservation of title' clauses later. Nor will property pass under Rule 5 if the goods appropriated to the transaction are not of the description given in the contract: **Wait v Baker** (1848).

1.16 The 'assent' in Rule 5 may be express or implied and may be given either before or after the appropriation is made: **Pignataro v Gilroy** (1919).

The seller sent a letter to the buyer stating that 15 bags of rice (the relevant contract goods) were ready for delivery from his place of business.

Held: Since the buyer did not object to this he had impliedly assented. The goods were stolen shortly before he came to collect them and it was further held that he still had to pay for them since property, and therefore risk, had already passed to him.

1.17 Since the Sale of Goods (Amendment) Act 1995, where the buyer of unascertained goods forming part of an identifiable bulk pays for the goods, then property passes at the time of payment (now s20A SGA 1979).

1.18 Provided that the buyer has paid the price for all or part of the goods, he becomes an 'owner in common' of the bulk. As an 'owner in common', the 'undivided share' which he owns is 'such share as the quantity of goods paid for and due to the buyer out of the bulk bears to the quantity of goods in the bulk'.

1.19   Thus, if a buyer has agreed to buy 200 tons of coal out of the seller's stockpile which contains 400 tons, the buyer will own an undivided share of 50 per cent in the 400 tons provided that he has made payment. If the seller subsequently reduces the bulk (for example by selling 100 tons to a second buyer), then the undivided share will become a larger proportion of the remaining bulk: 200/300 (or 67 per cent) in this example.

1.20   The advantage to a buyer of the new provision is that he becomes a secured creditor as to his proportionate share in the event of the seller going into bankruptcy or liquidation before the bulk has been reduced to the buyer's specified quantity.

1.21   The section is subject to contrary agreement between the parties, who may stipulate that it is not to apply at all, or that property in the undivided share is to pass at some time after payment.

Bailment of goods

1.22   Bailment occurs where a person has custody but not ownership of another's assets.

1.23   Where the seller retains goods but the property has passed to the buyer, or where the buyer takes delivery of goods but the seller retains the property in them, in each case usually pending payment, ownership and possession of the goods are temporarily separated. During this period the possessor has the status of bailee and thereby has the duty of taking reasonable care of them.

1.24   A seller who retains goods after property in them has passed to the buyer must deliver up the goods at the time agreed (this will normally be on payment of the price) unless prevented from so doing without fault on his or his servant's or agent's part.

1.25   A buyer who has goods delivered to him by a seller but who rejects them, and a seller from whom a buyer has agreed to collect them but has failed to do so, are also bailees, albeit involuntary ones, until such time as the seller or buyer collects.

1.26   In most cases bailment comes about under a contract of bailment. Every time you leave a watch at the jewellers for repair, your car at a garage for service, or your clothes at a dry cleaners, you are entering into a contract whereby you are the bailor and the jeweller, garage or dry cleaner is the bailee. Similarly, a hotel proprietor is bailee of his guests' property.

1.27   A contract of bailment is also entered into when a purchaser receives but then rejects goods, or when a purchaser is lent items by a supplier, such as designs or special tools. In both cases the purchaser is a bailee, and so it is important to note that:

   •   the bailee is liable if he wrongfully fails to return goods to the bailor;

   •   the bailee must take reasonable care of the goods but cannot use them;

   •   the bailee has liability for damage to the goods but may sue a third party in respect of them, holding damages on trust for the bailor;

   •   the bailee may not sell the goods unless he has given reasonable notice to the bailor of his intention to do so, and he holds funds received in trust for the bailor.

1.28   A bailee who seeks to rely on an exclusion clause to escape liability for his negligence will not succeed if the clause is unreasonable: **Woodman v Photo Trade Processing** (1981).

2 The passing of risk

The general rule

2.1 Unless otherwise agreed, the risk remains with the seller until property in the goods has passed to the buyer. As soon as property has passed the goods are at buyer's risk: s20. The principle that risk passes with property applies whether or not the party upon whom the risk is placed has in the case of the seller, made delivery or, in the case of the buyer, obtained delivery. This is the general rule on the passing of risk, but some exceptions will be noted later.

2.2 The effect of the general rule is that after the property has passed, the buyer will be liable to pay the agreed price for the goods even if they are lost or damaged, or if they are stolen, even though they are in the possession of the seller at that time. On the other hand, if the goods are lost, eg while in the possession of the buyer but before the property in the goods has passed to him, the seller must bear the loss and cannot claim the price from the buyer.

2.3 To determine where the risk lies the key criterion is ownership, not possession. It is, however, possible to modify the rule by agreement or by trade custom. Default of either party may also alter the position.

2.4 If the cause of the loss or damage is the possessor's negligence the owner will nevertheless have a counterclaim because a bailee has a duty to take reasonable care of goods in his possession.

Exceptions to the general rule on passing of risk

2.5 In some circumstances the passing of risk does not coincide with the transfer of property, contrary to the general rule. Some of these exceptions are discussed below.

2.6 If passing of property to the buyer is delayed by the buyer, he bears the risk of deterioration during the period of delay: **Stern v Vickers** (1923).

A sale of a quantity of turpentine which was part of a larger bulk. A delivery warrant was issued to the buyer but not presented to the warehouseman.

Held: The goods were unascertained so property could not have passed: s16. However, they were at the risk of the buyer.

2.7 If delivery is delayed by fault of either party, he bears the risk of any loss which would not have occurred but for his fault: s20.

2.8 If one party agrees to hold goods which are owned by the other as the latter's bailee, his duties as bailee prevail over the principle of s20.

2.9 Specific goods which have become the property of the buyer and are in transit to him travel at seller's risk. His risk is limited to abnormal risks of deterioration in transit since the buyer is deemed to accept risks necessarily incident to the course of transit: s33.

2.10   The seller's obligation under s14 to provide goods of satisfactory quality is limited to a reasonable period in transit. If the period in transit is in fact longer than the goods could continue in good condition, the risk of deterioration in the excess period is necessarily incident to the transit and falls on the buyer under s33 – a difficult and doubtful point. However a seller who sends perishable goods in such a state that they arrive in an unsaleable condition is delivering goods which are not of satisfactory quality, and he may not rely on s33.

2.11   If the contract provides for delivery of the goods to the buyer but with passing of property to him deferred until he pays for them, the goods are at his risk after delivery.

2.12   If the goods become the property of the buyer before delivery, the seller's duty is to take reasonable care of them pending delivery and his liability does not extend to loss which he could not reasonably have prevented.

2.13   If goods which are owned by the buyer are sent by sea the seller must give the buyer sufficient advance notice of shipment to enable the buyer to insure them. If the seller fails to do so the goods are at his risk: s32(3).

Perishing of specific goods

2.14   There are two provisions in the 1979 Act which apply in addition to the general rules of passing of property and risk as set out above. Under these provisions, where goods perish, the contract becomes void. There are two such cases.

- Where the goods have, unbeknown to the parties, perished at the time the contract was made: s6. This was more common in former times, before the days of electronic communications, than it is today. The rule reflects the common law rules on common mistake (Chapter 7).

- Where the goods perish between the time the contract is made and before the sale is completed: s7. Here again, the contract is void but only if there has been no fault on the part of buyer or seller.

2.15   In both cases the goods must be **specific**, ie goods identified and agreed upon at the time the contract of sale was made. Thus, a contract for the sale of 'my Ford car' or for 'the five tons of anthracite now lying in my yard' are contracts for the sale of specific goods, but a contract for the sale of 'a Ford car' or for 'five tons of anthracite' are for the sale of unascertained goods. Where specific goods perish the contract becomes void and the price, if paid, can be recovered.

2.16   If the contract is for the sale of unascertained goods and the goods that have been earmarked for the fulfilment of the contract have perished, the seller is under an obligation to obtain and supply other goods of like description and quality.

2.17   Note that the Law Reform (Frustrated Contracts) Act 1943 does not apply to any contract to which s6 or s7 SGA 1979 applies. The practical effect is that the seller who will have to refund any money received, cannot exercise the right granted by the LR(FC)A 1943 to obtain reimbursement of expenses he has incurred. The LR(FC)A 1943 does apply to contracts for the sale of goods which become frustrated for some reason other than that the goods have perished, eg when frustration has been caused by war, embargoes or controls.

Changes in risk

2.18   Under section 32(3) of the Sale of Goods Act 1979 the seller must notify the buyer of any changes of risk, so that the buyer may arrange for insurance to become operative from the moment that the risk passes to him. This would include any extraordinary risk of which the seller may have become aware.

Risk avoidance

2.19   Naturally a prudent buyer will want to minimise the possibility of financial loss. Ideally, he should aim to eliminate risk altogether, or at least to minimise it. If this is not possible, he should at least attempt to cover the risk by means of appropriate insurance.

2.20   We have already seen that the passing of risk may not coincide with the passing of title. The buyer must be alert to the possibility of loss from the moment that the goods are at his own risk, whether or not he has yet acquired title. For example, a contract of sale may state that the property in the goods does not pass to the buyer until he has paid for the goods, whereas risk passes as soon as the goods are delivered to the buyer. In such a case, the buyer must insure the goods from the moment he receives them, because until he later pays for the goods he is effectively holding them as bailee on behalf of the seller.

2.21   Types of insurance that a buyer may consider during his professional work include building insurance (covering damage to property or premises by fire, flooding etc), public liability insurance (covering against claims arising from defective products etc), and insurance against risks such as product recalls, professional negligence etc.

2.22   Buyers may also consider inserting an indemnity clause in the contract to purchase goods. If the buyer faces a claim arising from a customer, and the problem can be traced to goods purchased from a supplier, then the buyer can rely on the indemnity clause to recover from the supplier any costs arising from the customer's complaint.

2.23   You should also refer back to the use of a *force majeure* clause as an instrument for limiting risk.

3   *Transfer of title*

The general rule: *nemo dat quod non habet*

3.1   When ownership is contrasted with mere possession or the bearing of risk, the word property is used as a synonym: we talk of the transfer or passing of the property in goods. But when true ownership is contrasted with a false claim to it, it is customary to use the word title instead: only the true owner has title to goods.

3.2   The general rule is that where there is a sale of goods by a person who does not own them and who is not selling with the authority and consent of the owner, then title in them does not usually pass to the buyer: s21(1). This situation is usually summed up by the Latin phrase *nemo dat quod non habet*, or nobody can give what he does not possess. In other words, if you do not have title to goods then you can not pass on title to anyone who buys the goods from you.

3.3   The true owner can still recover the goods at law without paying any compensation to the buyer, even if the latter has paid the seller for them in all innocence (the buyer may, however, have a claim under s12). This principle applies even if the goods have passed through the hands of several persons before the true owner reclaims them from the final purchaser.

Exceptions to the *nemo dat* rule

3.4   There are exceptions to the *nemo dat* rule, principally framed to protect innocent purchasers and in the interests of commercial expediency. These exceptions may be summarised as follows.

- Estoppel
- Sale under voidable title
- Sale by seller in possession
- Sale by buyer in possession
- Sale by a mercantile agent
- Sale of a motor vehicle on hire-purchase
- Sale under special powers

3.5   These are now discussed in turn.

3.6   **Estoppel**. Where goods are sold by a person who is not their owner and who does not sell them under the authority or with the consent of the owner, the buyer acquires no better title to the goods than the seller had **unless the owner of the goods is by his conduct precluded from denying the seller's authority to sell:** s21(1) SGA 1979. This section confirms the basic principle of *nemo dat* but then introduces the first exception to the rule, ie estoppel.

3.7   For an innocent purchaser to obtain good title by estoppel, three requirements are necessary.

- The original owner must have made a representation (by statement or conduct) that the seller was entitled to sell the goods.
- The representation must have been made intentionally or negligently.
- The representation must have misled the innocent purchaser.

3.8   The situation is illustrated by the case of **Eastern Distributors v Goldring** (1957).

The owner of a van, Murphy, allowed another, a car salesman, to represent to the claimant that he (the salesman) was the owner and could sell the vehicle. The claimants relied on this representation to purchase the van from the salesman. Meanwhile, Murphy sold the van to the defendant. The claimants claimed the vehicle.

Held: The claimants had a good title to the van as Murphy had permitted the salesman to act as the owner and was, therefore, estopped from denying the seller's authority to sell. However, an opposite conclusion was reached in the case of **Mercantile Credit v Hamblin** (1965). The distinction was that the person in Murphy's position was duped into entering the transaction and had not willingly given her permission.

3.9 **Sale under voidable title**. The seller may derive his title from an earlier sale by the true owner. That earlier sale may have been voidable, but if it had not in fact been avoided at the time of the second sale the buyer acquires good title provided he buys in good faith and without notice of any defect in title: s23. The case of **Lewis v Averay** (1972) illustrates the position.

Lewis sold to a rogue, who in turn sold to Averay. Lewis was induced to sell because the rogue told a plausible story and the sale was voidable for misrepresentation. However Lewis did not take steps to recover the car until after Averay had bought it in good faith from the rogue.

Held: Averay had a good title to the car.

3.10 If the sale by Lewis had been avoided (eg by his notifying the police) before the re-sale to Averay, the rogue would have had no title and so Averay also would have had none – **Car & Universal Finance v Caldwell** (1965), **Colwyn Bay Motorcycles v Poole** (2000).

3.11 **Sale by a seller in possession**. A purchaser can obtain a good title to goods when he buys from a seller who has already sold the goods to a previous buyer but retained possession of the goods or documents of title to them, and has then sold them to a second purchaser: s24.

3.12 As long as the second purchaser is acting in good faith and has no notice of the previous sale he obtains good title as against the first purchaser, even though the seller had no title to give him at the time of the second contract of sale: **Worcester Works Finance v Cooden** (1972). The first purchaser can of course sue the seller for breach of contract. This exception to *nemo dat* applies only if the goods have been delivered to the second purchaser: **Nicholson v Harper** (1895). But for this purpose, a **constructive** delivery is sufficient: **Gerson v Wilkinson** (2001).

3.13 **Sale by a buyer in possession**. A purchaser can obtain good title to goods when he buys from a seller who was himself the buyer of the goods on a previous sale and obtained possession (but not yet ownership) of them: s25.

3.14 As long as the second purchaser is acting in good faith and has no notice of the first purchaser's defective title he obtains good title as against the original seller even though the first purchaser had no title to give to him at the time of the second contract of sale. The original seller can sue the first purchaser.

3.15 This exception does not apply where the first purchaser bought under a conditional sale agreement.

3.16 **Sale by a mercantile agent**. An owner may authorise an agent to sell goods on his behalf. A sale by an agent acting within his authority will bind his principal.

3.17 However, a person may purport to have authority to act as an agent when in fact he does not have authority. The purchaser will then not get good title. However, if the agent is a mercantile agent (a person in business selling goods on behalf of others) the purchaser will get good title provided the conditions set out in s2 Factors Act 1889 are complied with.

3.18 Section 2 Factors Act 1889 provides that any sale, pledge or other disposition of goods in the ordinary course of business by a mercantile agent in possession of goods or documents of title to goods with the consent of the owner shall be as valid as if he were expressly authorised by the owner of the goods, provided that the person taking the goods acts in good faith and has no notice that the agent did not have authority.

3.19 A person acts as a mercantile agent where he has an authority either to sell goods or to consign goods for the purpose of sale or to buy goods or to raise money on the security of goods.

3.20 The mercantile agent must be in possession of the goods or documents of title to the goods with the consent of the owner and the goods must be entrusted to him as a mercantile agent. In the case of motor vehicles the registration book is not a document of title. (It merely records the name of the person registered as the holder of the vehicle.)

3.21 The sale must furthermore be in the **ordinary course of business**: **Stadium Finance v Robbins** (1962).

3.22 **Sale of a motor vehicle on hire purchase**. Part III of the Hire Purchase Act 1964 provides one specific exception in respect of certain hire-purchase agreements. The hirer in a hire-purchase agreement does not have ownership of the goods during the lifetime of the agreement and has no right to dispose of them. Where such a disposal occurs the finance company still owns the goods and has the right to recover them.

3.23 The Hire Purchase Act 1964 provides an exception to this rule for motor vehicles. S27 provides that where the hirer of a motor vehicle under a hire-purchase agreement disposes of it before the property is vested in him, the first private purchaser to acquire the vehicle in good faith will acquire good title. This is so whether the private purchaser acquires the car directly from the hirer or obtains it through an intermediate trader or financier.

3.24 This provision clearly is of real benefit to the private purchaser who acquires good title and is able to pass it on to subsequent purchasers. However, the Act is restricted in that it applies only to goods subject to hire-purchase or conditional sale agreements and does not apply, for example, where the car is subject to a lease or is a company car. Further, it applies only to private purchases and thus business purchasers acting in good faith are not protected.

3.25 **Sales under common law or statutory powers**. There are a number of these, under which non-owners are allowed to sell goods in their possession to recover debts due to them.

   • A pawnbroker is allowed to sell goods that have been pledged to him if the loan remains unpaid beyond the agreed time. In these circumstances, the purchaser gets good title.

   • Sale by court order – the High Court has powers to order the sale of goods that are subject to dispute, but for which there is a good reason for immediate disposal, such as where the goods are deteriorating

   • Sales in market overt – an old exception relating to sales in market overt has been abolished by the Sale of Goods (Amendment) Act 1994.

4 Delivery and acceptance

Seller's duty to deliver

4.1   The seller has a duty to deliver, and the buyer a duty to accept and pay for, goods subject to a contract of sale, in accordance with its terms: s27.

4.2   Delivery means the voluntary transfer of possession from one person to another: s61. This may or may not involve a physical delivery of the goods by the seller to the buyer, since delivery may be actual or constructive.

4.3   Constructive delivery can occur in three ways.

- The seller remains in possession but consents to hold the goods for the buyer.

- The buyer was already in possession of them, eg as bailee, and he simply starts to hold them on his own account.

- A third party, such as a warehouseman, is in possession, and he consents to hold for the buyer instead of for the seller.

4.4   There is also **symbolic** delivery, eg where a bill of lading representing the goods is transferred.

4.5   Unless the seller agrees, payment and delivery are concurrent obligations, ie the seller must be ready and willing to give possession of the goods to the buyer in exchange for the price, and the buyer must be ready and willing to pay the price in exchange for the possession of the goods: s28. Frequently, of course, the seller allows the buyer to have possession before any payment is required, the sale then being called a credit sale.

The place of delivery

4.6   Whether it is for the buyer to take possession or for the seller to send the goods to him is dependent on the agreement, but in the absence of agreement the place of delivery is the seller's place of business if he has one, and otherwise his residence, except that if the contract is for specific goods known by the parties to be in some other place, that place is the place of delivery: s29(1).

The time of delivery

4.7   If the seller is bound to send the goods to the buyer but no time is fixed, the seller must send them within a reasonable time: s29(2). Delivery may be treated as ineffectual unless made at a reasonable hour: s29(4). If a delivery time is fixed in the contract, it will normally be regarded as a contract condition. If the deadline is missed, the buyer may then repudiate the contract, though he may choose instead to affirm it (and possibly sue for damages). By doing so he loses his right to treat the term as a contract condition, but may reinstate this right later: **Charles Rickards v Oppenheim** (1950).

A seller agreed to manufacture a motor car for delivery to a buyer on 20 March. It was not ready on time, but the buyer allowed the seller to continue the work. Later, the buyer laid down a new deadline, saying that if the car was not ready in a further four weeks he would reject it. It was not ready in time.

Held: Although the buyer had waived the original deadline he had made time once more 'of the essence' and was entitled to repudiate.

Expenses of delivery

4.8   Any expense needed to put the goods into a deliverable state must be borne by the seller: s29(5).

Delivery of wrong quantity

4.9   If the seller delivers less of the goods than the contractual quantity, the buyer can reject them, but if he accepts them he must pay for them at the contract rate.

4.10   If the seller delivers more than the contractual quantity the buyer may accept the proper quantity and reject the rest or accept the whole, paying for the excess at the contract rate.

4.11   If the seller delivers, in addition to the goods contracted for, goods of a different description the buyer can reject the whole or accept the contractual goods and reject the other goods: s30. The buyer cannot, however, accept any goods of a type not contracted for, except of course under a new contract. Section 30 must be read in the light of **Re Moore & Landauer** (delivery of correct quantity in wrong batch sizes).

4.12   Thus if the seller delivers goods some of which are of the contract description and some of which are not, the buyer may retain those which correspond with the contract and reject those which do not; if, however, he delivers goods all of which correspond to the contract description but some of which are unsatisfactory, the buyer is faced with the stark choice of accepting the whole or rejecting the whole: s30 is of no application.

Delivery by instalments

4.13   There are three distinct types of contract to consider.

4.14   In the first situation, the contract makes no provision for delivery of the goods by instalments nor consequently for payment of the price separately as instalments are delivered. The buyer is **not bound** to accept delivery by instalments: s31(1) SGA 1979.

4.15   In the second situation, the contract provides for delivery by instalments but payment of the price by a single payment. The problem which may arise here is that some instalments of the goods but not others may be defective. The buyer may then treat the contract as repudiated.

4.16   Until enactment of the Sale and Supply of Goods Act 1994, a problem arose for the buyer if he accepted any instalment of goods. He was then held to have lost his right to treat defects in subsequent instalments as grounds for repudiating the contract. He was reduced in that case to suing for damages only. Now, though, the situation is that he does not lose his right to repudiate just because an earlier instalment has been accepted; he may still reject later instalments if defective: s35A (inserted into the 1979 Act by the 1994 Act).

4.17   In the third situation, the contract provides for delivery by instalments with separate payments for instalments. In such a case if the seller makes some defective deliveries or the buyer does not accept instalments or does not pay for them, this fault may be treated either as a repudiation of the entire contract or as a severable breach with a right to compensation for the breach. The terms of the contract and the circumstances of the case will determine which alternative is applicable: s31(2).

4.18   The buyer's failure to pay an instalment of the price would not usually (unless so agreed) be a repudiation of the entire contract: **Maple Flock v Universal Furniture Products (Wembley)** (1934).

The sixteenth out of seventy-five instalment deliveries of rag flock was defective. The buyer sought to treat the whole contract as repudiated.

Held: The court said that it had to have regard to the ratio of the breach to the contract as a whole and the possibility that the breach would be repeated: in this case the buyer could not treat the contract as repudiated.

4.19   In simple terms, in the Maple Flock case not enough had gone wrong, or appeared likely to go wrong, to justify the buyer in repudiating the entire contract. However, if the defective instalments are a higher proportion of the total contract a different conclusion is justified: **Munro v Meyer** (1934).

It was discovered when half the contract quantity had been delivered that all the deliveries to that date had been defective.

Held: The court upheld the buyer's repudiation of the contract.

4.20   The buyer's failure to pay an instalment of the price would not usually, unless so agreed, be a repudiation of the entire contract.

Buyer's duty to accept

4.21   The buyer is deemed to have accepted the goods in any of the following situations: s35.

- When he intimates to the seller that he has accepted them. Mere signature of a storeman on a delivery note may not be sufficient to signify acceptance, but it may be binding if a person of high authority signs and the delivery note contains wording that suggests acceptance.

- When the goods have been delivered to him and he performs any act in relation to them which is inconsistent with the seller's ownership, such as re-selling them. (However, where goods are delivered which the buyer has not previously examined, he is not deemed to have accepted them unless and until he has had a reasonable opportunity of examining them to see if they conform with the contract. Unless otherwise agreed, when the seller tenders delivery of the goods he must on request give the buyer a reasonable opportunity of examining the goods: s34).

- When, after the lapse of a reasonable time, he retains the goods without intimating to the seller that he rejects them. The case of **Bernstein v Pamsons Motors** (1987) is relevant: the car purchased by Bernstein was defective but he did not seek to reject it until three weeks after purchase. He lost his case because he was held to have accepted the car. However, this contrasts with the case of **Rogers v Parish** (1987), where the buyer was allowed to reject the car after using it for six months.

4.22   In the case of goods sold for re-sale onwards, a reasonable time may be the actual time taken to re-sell, plus an additional period where they may be tried out by the sub-purchaser: **Truk v Tokmakidis** (2000).

Chapter summary

- The two main rules governing the transfer of property in goods are contained in s16 (property cannot pass until goods have been ascertained) and s17(1) (property passes when the parties intend it to pass).

- Where the intention of the parties is not clear the five rules of s18 apply instead to determine when property passes.

- Bailment occurs when a person has custody of another's assets but not ownership. A bailee of goods has a duty to take reasonable care of them.

- In general, risk passes at the same time as property: s20. However, there are exceptions to this rule, mostly concerned with delay or fault by either party.

- The general rule on the transfer of title is *nemo dat quod non habet* – nobody can give better title than he possesses. The main exceptions to this rule are: estoppel; sale under voidable title; sale by seller in possession; sale by buyer in possession; and sale by a mercantile agent.

- Delivery from seller to buyer may be actual or constructive. In the absence of contrary agreement, the place of delivery is the seller's place of business.

- In severable contracts the rules in the **Maple Flock** case determine whether a buyer is entitled to repudiate a contract in its entirety as a result of defective instalments.

Self-test questions

Numbers in brackets refer to the paragraphs above where your answers can be checked.

1   Why is it important to determine when the property in goods passes? (1.3)

2   What are the two general principles governing when property passes? (1.4)

3   Explain the five rules of s18. (1.10)

4   What were the facts and the decision in the case of **Carlos Federspiel v Charles Twigg**? (1.11)

5   In what circumstances may a bailment arise? (1.22 –1.27)

6   What is the general rule on the passing of risk? (2.1)

7   What were the facts and the decision in the case of **Stern v Vickers**? (2.6)

8   Explain the meaning of the *nemo dat* rule. (3.2)

9   List the main exceptions to the *nemo dat* rule and explain each of them. (3.4ff)

10   What is meant by sale under voidable title? Name a leading case illustrating this. (3.9)

11   How may constructive delivery occur? (4.3)

12   Explain the facts and the decision in the **Maple Flock** case. (4.18)

CHAPTER 13

Remedies for Breach in Sale of Goods Contracts

Learning objectives and indicative content

1.2 Distinguish between different types of contractual terms and assess the legal validity of specific types of contractual clause

- Retention of title clauses

1.4 Evaluate the different common law methods by which a contract is terminated and the remedies available should a contract be breached.

- Breach

Chapter headings

1 Remedies of the seller

2 Goods sold under retention of title

3 Remedies of the buyer

Introduction

In this chapter we conclude our examination of sale of goods contracts by looking at the remedies available to buyers and sellers in the event of breach. We also discuss the position of goods sold under a contract where the seller retains property until a condition is satisfied (usually receipt of payment from the buyer).

1 Remedies of the seller

Summary of seller's remedies

1.1 A seller is deemed to be an **unpaid seller** when either:

- the whole of the price has not been paid or tendered; or
- a bill of exchange or other negotiable instrument (eg a cheque) has been received as conditional payment, and the condition on which it was received has not been fulfilled by reason of the dishonour of the instrument or otherwise: s38(1).

1.2 An unpaid seller has remedies against the goods and against the buyer.

- Against the goods: lien, stoppage in transit and right of resale
- Against the buyer: action for the price and action for damages for non-acceptance.

1.3   The above are the statutory remedies of the unpaid seller. In addition it is possible for the contract itself to expressly give additional remedies to the seller: the prime example is the 'reservation of title' clause, discussed in the next section of this chapter.

Seller's lien: ss41–43

1.4   A lien is the right of an unpaid seller in possession of goods to retain them until the price has been paid or his debt secured or satisfied. Notice that for lien to operate the seller must have possession but not property.

1.5   The right of retention operates:

- until the seller is paid, if it is a cash sale;
- as from the expiration of the term of credit, if credit has been given; or
- if the buyer becomes insolvent (even if credit has been given): s41. (Insolvent means that the buyer has ceased to pay his debts in the ordinary course of business or he cannot pay his debts as they become due.)

1.6   Where a period of credit has been agreed, the buyer can demand delivery during that period; it is only where the goods are still in the possession of the seller at the expiration of the period of credit (or when the buyer is insolvent), and the price is unpaid, that the lien operates.

1.7   The lien is only enforceable against the goods in respect of which the price is owing, not in respect of any other debt due by the buyer to the seller.

1.8   The unpaid seller loses his lien:

- when he delivers the goods to a carrier without reserving the right of disposal of the goods; or
- when the buyer or his agent lawfully obtains possession of the goods; or
- by waiver: s43.

1.9   In general, a lien is not affected by a sub-sale by the buyer. However it is defeated:

- where the seller assents to the sub-sale; and
- where a **document of title** to the goods has been lawfully transferred to the buyer, and he in turn transfers it to a third party who takes it in good faith and for valuable consideration: s47.

Right of stoppage in transit: ss45–46

1.10   An unpaid seller loses any lien on goods he may have had when he delivers them to a carrier or other bailee to transmit them to the buyer without reserving a right of disposal. However, he may still be able to stop the goods being delivered to the buyer.

1.11   Where the buyer becomes insolvent (as defined above), and the goods are in the hands of a carrier who cannot be regarded as the agent of the buyer, the seller can require the carrier not to deliver to the buyer. This right only applies where the property in the goods has passed to the buyer (if they were still his the seller could recover them merely because he was the owner).

1.12   A seller exercises his right of stoppage by taking actual possession of the goods or by giving notice of his claim to the carrier in possession: s46 (1–3). On being given such notice the carrier must redeliver the goods to, or to the order of, the seller, the latter bearing the extra cost: s46 (4). If, despite this, he delivers them to the buyer, he may be sued in conversion.

1.13   The seller must exercise the right before the transit is completed. It is deemed to be completed if:

- the buyer or his agent obtains delivery before arrival at the appointed destination; or

- after arrival at the appointed destination the carrier acknowledges to the buyer or his agent that he (the carrier) now holds the goods on his behalf; or

- the carrier or other bailee wrongfully refuses to deliver the goods to the buyer or to his agent: ss45 (2), (3) and (6).

1.14   A right of stoppage in transit, like a lien, is not affected by a sub-sale by the buyer except:

- where the seller assents to the sub-sale; or

- where a document of title has been lawfully transferred to the buyer and he has transferred it to a third party taking it in good faith and for valuable consideration.

1.15   Where the seller retains the property in the goods, there can strictly be for him neither a lien nor a right of stoppage in transit. But this is only because by virtue of ownership he has no need of them. He still has the same right of withholding delivery: s39(2). It is then referred to as a right of retention.

Right of resale: s48

1.16   If the buyer expressly or by his conduct repudiates the contract, the seller is free to resell the goods because the buyer no longer has any right to them.

1.17   The mere exercise of a lien or right of stoppage in transit by the seller does not of itself give the seller the right to resell them. (As a trader he will usually wish to do so, especially if the goods would otherwise deteriorate.) However, he will have the right to resell if:

- the goods are of a perishable nature; or

- he gives notice to the buyer of his intention to resell, and the buyer does not tender the price within a reasonable time; or

- he has expressly reserved a right of resale in the contract.

1.18   In the first two cases the seller may in addition to the remedy of resale recover damages from the original buyer for any loss occasioned by the breach of contract. In the third case the contract is rescinded by resale but the seller may claim damages: s48(4). Although the seller cannot sue for the price, his claim to damages is in lieu of that; he may retain any deposit paid by the buyer.

1.19   The second buyer to whom the original seller resells the goods obtains good title to them against the original buyer provided that either:

- the seller had exercised, whether lawfully or not, a right of lien or stoppage in transit; or
- the seller had the right, against the original buyer, to resell: s48(2).

1.20   This protection to a second buyer in some measure overlaps with s25 resale by a seller in possession of the goods. Note that in the first case above it is not necessary that the seller should have title to the goods against the original buyer, ie this is an exception to the *nemo dat* rule.

Action for the price: s49

1.21   The seller may sue the buyer for the price where:

- the property in the goods has passed to the buyer and the buyer fails to pay the price in accordance with the contract; or
- the price is due but unpaid on a date specified in the contract.

1.22   It does not matter in this latter case that:

- the goods have not yet been delivered;
- property in the goods has not yet passed to the buyer; or
- goods have not been appropriated to the contract.

1.23   The price must be tendered in legal tender or, if agreed by the parties, in the form of a cheque or other bill normally operating as a conditional payment.

Action for damages for non-acceptance: s50

1.24   An action for the price is not appropriate where the buyer wrongfully neglects or refuses to accept and pay for the goods and the property has not passed. In such a case the seller can maintain an action against the buyer for damages for non-acceptance: s50(1).

1.25   The measure of the damages is the estimated loss directly and naturally resulting, in the ordinary course of events, from the buyer's breach of contract: s50(2). However, in a suitable case, **special damages** may be available in addition: s54. These two provisions correspond respectively to the first and second rules on the measure of damages for breach of contract in **Hadley v Baxendale** as modified in subsequent cases such as **Victoria Laundry (Windsor) Ltd v Newman Industries Ltd** (see Chapter 9). In addition, the seller's expenses on the care and custody of the goods may be taken into account: s37.

1.26   Where there is an available market for the goods in question the measure of damages is initially the difference between the contract price and the market or current price at the time when the goods ought to have been accepted, or, if no time was fixed for acceptance, at the time of the refusal to accept: s50(3). Thus, unless the market price for the goods of the type sold has fallen since the contract, the seller may recover nothing.

1.27   'Market' is to be understood in the abstract sense of economics, ie buyers must be available. There will not be an available market if conditions in the trade are not such that goods can be freely sold. Moreover, a market cannot be described as available if the seller has no ready access to it.

1.28   Where there is no available market by which to measure the seller's loss he will be able to recover his lost profit margin on a fixed price sale if he can show that by reason of supply exceeding demand he could not readily resell the goods to another buyer.

1.29   A seller has the choice whether to sue for the price under s49 or for damages under s50 where the buyer wrongfully refuses to accept and pay for the goods and the property in them has already passed.

2   *Goods sold under retention of title*

2.1   A retention of title clause (also called reservation of title clause) put into the contract by the seller is becoming an increasingly common commercial practice in the UK. In its simplest form the clause will state that the property in the goods will not pass to the buyer until the seller has been paid in full.

2.2   The aim of such clauses is that although the buyer obtains possession the seller remains owner of the goods until they are paid for so that if the buyer fails to pay then the seller can repossess his goods. This gives an unpaid seller a far more effective remedy against a buyer who becomes insolvent than an action for the price.

2.3   Such a clause is often called a Romalpa clause after the case of **Aluminium Industrie Vaassen BV (AIV) v Romalpa Aluminium Limited** (1976).

The claimants, a Dutch company, supplied aluminium foil to the defendants who were importers based in the UK. The defendants subsequently went into liquidation. The contract stipulated that title to the goods did not pass to the defendants until they had paid in full. The defendants failed to pay for a quantity of goods (some of which they had resold) and the claimants sought an order to recover them.

Held: In accordance with the conditions of the contract the claimants were entitled to the goods belonging to them still in the possession of the defendants. Note that this reflects s17 SGA 1979: property passes when the parties intend it to pass under the contract.

2.4   The **Romalpa** case involved raw aluminium which was not mixed with any other metal or alloy. Indeed, the purchasers specifically contracted to store the aluminium separately so that it remained identifiable as the sellers' property. What would the position be, therefore, where the goods are rendered into other manufactured products? Is reservation of title to goods possible in such circumstances? A leading case is **Re Peachdart Ltd** (1983).

The supplier provided leather under a contract with the usual clause reserving title until full payment. The buyer became insolvent and a receiver was appointed. It was explicitly provided in the contract that ownership was reserved even if the goods were rendered into manufactured items, so that the seller's property would remain in the resultant products, and the seller's rights in the original goods would extend to those products. The receiver found some unused leather, and some partially completed handbags, but the greater part of the buyer's assets consisted of money owing from sale of manufactured handbags.

Held: The title reservation clause was ineffective except in relation to the small quantity of unmarked leather. A similar conclusion was reached in the case of **Borden v Scottish Timber** (1981).

2.5 To summarise, it appears that reservation of title clauses are effective so as to allow the seller to repossess only if:

- • the goods are still in the possession of the buyer, and

- • the goods are identifiable (ie they are not mixed with other goods), and

- • the goods are in their original state (ie they have not been subjected to any manufacturing process).

2.6 In order to give the right of repossession practical effect it is common for the contract to include a provision allowing the seller to enter the buyer's premises to retake possession.

2.7 It is worth noting a slight extension to the Romalpa principle, which has been held to be valid in Scottish law (and presumably also in English law). This is where the seller reserves title in the goods sold until the buyer has settled **all** his liabilities to the seller, and not just the payment for the goods in question: **Armour v Thyssen** (1990). This is sometimes referred to as a '**rolling Romalpa clause**'.

3 *Remedies of the buyer*

Statutory remedies

3.1 The buyer's remedies will depend on the breach by the seller. Apart from actually rejecting the goods (see the previous chapter) the buyer's remedies include:

- • damages for non-delivery
- • order for specific performance
- • damages for breach of warranty
- • special damages
- • suing for wrongful detention of goods.

3.2 The Act has four sections dealing with buyer's remedies: ss51–54.

3.3 If the seller fails to make delivery the buyer may recover damages for non-delivery: s51.

3.4 In a contract for specific or ascertained goods the buyer may seek an order of the court for specific performance: s52. This is, of course, an equitable remedy given at the court's discretion. It would only be available if the goods were of unique value so that damages would be an inadequate remedy.

3.5 Where there is a breach of warranty or the buyer elects or is compelled to treat a breach of condition as a breach of warranty, the buyer may set off the breach of warranty in reduction of the price, or claim damages for breach of warranty: s52.

3.6 In such a case the buyer may claim additional damages for any additional loss: s53(4). Thus a buyer who had accepted goods but later discovered that they were not of satisfactory quality would have to sue for damages, ie he could not reject the goods: s11(1)(c). But he might be able to claim for additional loss of profits on resale.

3.7 Any common law right to special damages, eg under the second part of the rule in **Hadley v Baxendale**, is preserved by s54. This is particularly important to the buyer who is entitled to reject the goods for want of title or other breach of condition, before acceptance. He may recover any part of the price he has paid on a total failure of consideration and also possibly claim special damages for consequential loss.

Remedy in tort

3.8 The buyer has one other remedy where the title to the goods has passed to him. He may sue the seller for the tort of wrongful detention of goods under Torts (Interference with Goods) Act 1977.

Damages

3.9 It will be apparent that the buyer's remedy is normally for damages. Much of ss51–53 is concerned with the measure of damages and incidentally with remoteness, ie the two halves of the rule in **Hadley v Baxendale**.

3.10 Both s51, damages for non-delivery, and s53, damages for breach of warranty, specify as the normal measure of damages the estimated loss directly and naturally resulting in the ordinary course of events from the breach. The two situations are, however, essentially different.

3.11 In an action for damages for **non-delivery** the buyer has received no goods at all. If there is an available market he can purchase substitute supplies at the prevailing price. The *prima facie* measure of damages in this case is the amount, if any, by which the market price at the time when delivery was due exceeds the contract price: s51(3). If, however, the market price at that time is lower than the contract price he has suffered no loss and normally recovers no damages.

3.12 In an action for **breach of warranty** the buyer has accepted goods but they are not in accordance with the contract. One obvious measure of his loss is the difference in value between goods of contract quality and the goods actually delivered. The available market test could determine the amount. But it is not the only relevant test and so, presumably for that reason, it is not specified as the *prima facie* test in s53, nor is any other yardstick provided.

3.13 An alternative measure of the loss to the buyer could be the cost of remedying the defect in the goods by putting them into sound condition.

Chapter summary

- An unpaid seller's remedies against the goods are lien, stoppage in transit and right of resale.

- An unpaid seller's remedies against the buyer are an action for the price and an action for damages for non-acceptance.

- Sellers may also protect their position by means of a retention of title clause, but this will be effective only in limited cases.

- Buyers may reject the goods according to the rules described in the previous chapter. Other remedies include damages and specific performance.

Self-test questions

Numbers in brackets refer to the paragraphs above where your answers can be checked.

I   When is a seller deemed to be an unpaid seller? (1.1)

2   List the possible remedies of an unpaid seller. (1.2)

3   In what circumstances does a seller lose his right of lien? (1.8)

4   When does a seller have a right of reselling the goods? (1.17)

5   Explain the facts and the decision in the **Romalpa** case. (2.3)

6   In what circumstances will a retention of title clause be effective? (2.5)

7   When might a buyer be given the remedy of specific performance? (3.4)

CHAPTER 14

The Supply of Goods and Services

Learning objectives and indicative content

2.1   Define different types of contract and analyse the statutes applicable to each type.

- Contracts for goods and services
- Contracts for work and materials
- Contracts for services
- Contracts of hire
- Supply of Goods and Services Act 1982

Chapter headings

1   Contracts not covered by the Sale of Goods Act 1979

2   The Supply of Goods and Services Act 1982

Introduction

We have already mentioned that not every contract involving transfer of goods falls to be considered as a contract of sale of goods. In this chapter we look at some of the other types of contract that are possible. Mostly we are concerned with contracts for the supply of services, in which goods may also be transferred but only as an incidental part of the overall transaction. However, we also look briefly at contracts of hire and hire purchase.

Statutory references in this chapter are to sections of the Supply of Goods and Services Act 1982, unless otherwise stated.

1   Contracts not covered by the Sale of Goods Act 1979

Contracts of hire

1.1   A contract of hire is a contract for the bailment of goods only. Ownership does not pass to the hirer. For example, if you hire a car for a month you do not become the owner, you merely have the right to possess and use the car for the period agreed. You pay the owner for the right to use the car.

1.2   A contract of hire is covered by the Supply of Goods and Services Act 1982.

Contracts of hire purchase

1.3   These are contracts for the bailment of goods under which ownership may pass to the debtor if he exercises his option to purchase.

1.4   He has not agreed to buy and is therefore not a 'buyer', and the contract is therefore not a contract for the sale of goods. Thus, if you 'buy' something on hire purchase you are hiring it for the period during which you are making the payments and will only become the owner of it if you make the final payment which is identified as the price you pay to exercise your option to purchase the goods.

1.5   A contract of hire purchase is covered by the Supply of Goods (Implied Terms) Act 1973, and may also be regulated by the Consumer Credit Act 1974.

Contracts for work and materials

1.6   Where the substance of the contract is the buying of a skill rather than the buying of a product there is not a sale of goods: **Robinson v Graves** (1935).

There was a contract to have a portrait painted.

Held: This was a contract which was not a contract for the sale of goods and would therefore not be covered by the Sale of Goods Act 1979.

1.7   It is difficult to distinguish between a contract for the sale of goods and a contract for work and materials. Thus, a contract for the sale of a fur coat made to the customer's requirements was a contract for the sale of goods (**Marcel Furriers v Tapper**) but a contract for the repair and supply of parts for a car was not (**Stewart v Reavell's**).

1.8   A contract for work and materials is covered by the Supply of Goods and Services Act 1982.

Exchanges

1.9   A sale of goods presupposes a price which is money consideration, not goods. Thus, contracts where the whole of the consideration for the goods is in the form of other goods will not come within the definition. However, where the consideration for the goods is part money and part exchange the contract will come within the definition of a contract for the sale of goods: **Dawson v Dutfield** (1936).

There was a sale of two lorries for £475 which were paid for by £250 cash and the exchange of two other lorries which were valued at £225.

Held: There was a contract for the sale of goods covered by SGA 1979.

1.10   A contract of exchange is governed by the Supply of Goods and Services Act 1982.

Sale of Goods Act 1979

1.11 The Sale of Goods Act 1979 does not cover any of these types of contract. Although common law implied certain terms into such contracts about the quality etc of the goods these implied terms were not as stringent nor as clear as those under the Sale of Goods Act 1979. In addition, the uncertainty about whether a contract was or was not covered by the Act, eg whether a contract was for the sale of goods or for work and materials, was unsatisfactory. Thus, statutes were enacted to rectify the situation.

2 *The Supply of Goods and Services Act 1982*

Contracts for the transfer of goods

2.1 'Contracts for the transfer of goods' includes contracts by way of exchange and contracts for work and materials.

2.2 Section 2 implies undertakings as to **title** similar to those in s12 SGA 1979.

2.3 Section 3 implies terms where the transfer is by description and s5 implies terms where the transfer is by sample similar to those in ss13 and 15 SGA 1979.

2.4 Section 4 implies undertakings as to **satisfactory quality** and **fitness for purpose** similar to those in s14 SGA 1979.

Contracts for the hire of goods

2.5 Section 7 implies undertakings as to title similar to those in s12 SGA 1979, ie that the owner or bailor has the right to transfer possession of the goods to the bailee.

2.6 Section 8 implies terms where the hire is by **description** and s10 implies terms where the hire is by sample similar to those in ss13 and 15 SGA 1979.

2.7 Section 9 implies undertakings as to **satisfactory quality** and **fitness for purpose** similar to those in s14 SGA 1979.

Exclusion of liability

2.8 This is covered by s11 Unfair Contract Terms Act 1977 in the same way as for contracts governed by SGA 1979.

Contracts for the supply of services

2.9 The second part of the Act deals with contracts for the supply of services, which have been the subject of much complaint over the last twenty years, particularly about the quality of services, delay in performance and cost. The problems arise because in many service industries the consumer has little idea of what is involved in providing the service and is therefore not in a good position to judge whether a good service has been provided or whether a reasonable charge has been made.

2.10 In addition, there is the problem that many people who provide services do not quote the price for providing the service at the commencement of the contract: it depends on the amount of time they clock up in providing the service.

2.11   The service industries have expanded greatly and a review of the complaints made by the National Consumer Council highlighted these areas of complaint. The 1982 Act therefore attempts to codify the existing law and take into account the recommendations made by the National Consumer Council, in particular, to deal with the three main areas of complaint of quality, delay and cost.

2.12   The Act covers 'contracts for the supply of a service' under which a person 'the supplier' agrees to carry out a service. The Act does not cover contracts of employment, apprenticeship, services of an advocate in a court or tribunal or of a company director to his company.

Implied terms

2.13   Section 13 implies a term into a contract for the supply of a service, where the supplier is acting in the course of business, that the supplier will carry out the service with **reasonable care and skill**.

2.14   This idea was clarified by Lord Denning in the case of **Greaves & Co v Baynham Meikle and Partners** (1975): 'The law does not usually imply a warranty that the professional man will achieve the desired result, but only a term that he will use reasonable care and skill. The surgeon does not warrant that he will cure the patient. Nor does the solicitor warrant that he will win the case. But when a dentist agrees to make a set of false teeth for a patient, there is an implied warranty that they will fit his gums'.

2.15   Section 14 implies a term into a contract for the supply of a service, where the supplier is acting in the course of business and where the time for the service to be carried out is not fixed by the contract, but is left to be fixed in a manner agreed by the parties or by a course of dealing, that the supplier will carry out the service within a **reasonable time**.

2.16   Section 15 implies a term into a contract for the supply of a service where the consideration for the service is not determined by the contract, but is left to be determined in a manner agreed by the parties or a course of dealings, that the party contracting with the supplier will pay a **reasonable charge**.

Exclusion of implied terms

2.17   Section 16 provides that exclusion or limitation of liability for breach of any of these implied terms is subject to the Unfair Contract Terms Act 1977. Note that s13 imposes liability for negligence which means that under UCTA 1977 any liability for death or personal injury caused by negligence cannot be excluded and liability for any other loss caused by negligence can only be excluded if it is reasonable.

2.18   Consumer contracts for the supply of services are subject to the Unfair Terms in Consumer Contracts Regulations 1999 (see Chapter 6). The regulations expressly invalidate terms purporting to exclude liability for death or personal injury arising from act or omission of the supplier of services. Other terms (apart from 'core terms') are subject to the fairness test imposed by the regulations. Even 'core terms' may be caught if they are not in 'plain intelligible language'.

2.19   To summarise, the Supply of Goods and Services Act 1982 implies similar terms to those in the Sale of Goods Act for contracts of hire, contracts for work and materials, and contracts by way of exchange. In contracts for the supply of a service, the SGSA implies three terms as to reasonable care and skill, reasonable time and reasonable charge.

Chapter summary

- The Sale of Goods Act 1979 does not apply to contracts of hire, contracts of hire purchase, contracts for work and materials, exchanges, or contracts for the supply of services.

- The Supply of Goods and Services Act 1982 fills some of the gaps left by SGA 1979. In particular, it covers contracts for work and materials and contracts for the supply of services.

- In relation to contracts for work and materials, the 1982 Act implies terms similar to those of SGA 1979 on title, quality, fitness for purpose, sample and description.

- In relation to contracts for the supply of services, the 1982 Act implies terms on reasonable care and skill, reasonable time for completion, and payment of a reasonable charge.

Self-test questions

Numbers in brackets refer to the paragraphs above where your answers can be checked.

1   What legislation applies to contracts for hire purchase? (1.5)

2   What was decided in the case of **Dawson v Dutfield**? (1.9)

3   How did Lord Denning clarify the idea of 'reasonable care and skill' in carrying out a service? (2.14)

CHAPTER 15

Third-party Rights

Learning objectives and indicative content

2.5   Evaluate the various methods for circumventing the problems created by privity of contract.

- •   Collateral contracts and warranties
- •   Contract (Rights of Third Parties) Act 1999
- •   Assignment and novation of rights and obligations to a third party

Chapter headings

1   Privity of contract

2   Assignment of contractual rights

Introduction

An important feature of contract law is that rights and obligations under a contract only apply to the parties actually contracting together. This is what is known as the doctrine of privity of contract. In this chapter we look at some of the consequences of privity, particularly in cases where innocent third parties are denied redress because they are not parties to the contract.

The basic rule of privity of contract is subject to a number of exceptions, and its importance has been substantially reduced by the Contracts (Rights of Third Parties) Act 1999.

We also look at the limited circumstances where rights under a contract may be transferred ('assigned') to others.

1   Privity of contract

The doctrine of privity

1.1   A contract creates a personal obligation and only the original contracting parties can acquire enforceable rights or be subject to legal liabilities under it. The leading case in this area is that of **Dunlop Pneumatic Tyre Co v Selfridge** (1915).

Dunlop made and sold tyres to a distributor on condition that he would not resell the tyres at less than the list price (the Resale Prices Act 1976 would now invalidate such terms) nor resell them to a retailer without imposing the same condition. The distributor resold to Selfridge who offered the tyres at less than Dunlop's list price.

Held: Dunlop could not enforce the contract between the distributor and Selfridge because Dunlop was not a party to it.

1.2   The doctrine of privity of contract is closely related to, but not the same as, the rule which requires consideration to be provided by each party to the contract. (This rule was discussed in Chapter 4.) Often both matters will be relevant in the same question.

The Contracts (Rights of Third Parties) Act 1999

1.3   The doctrine of privity is now subject to the Contracts (Rights of Third Parties) Act 1999. The Act applies to contracts entered into on or after 11 May 2000.

1.4   The principal objective of the Act is to allow third parties to enforce their rights under contracts, thus bringing English law into line with the law in Scotland and in certain European Union countries. It should be noted that the Act is intended to confer benefits on third parties. It does not operate to impose burdens or liabilities on them. The Act will only operate with the consent of the parties, either express or implied.

1.5   Under s1 of the Act, a third party may in his own right enforce a term of the contract if:

    •   the contract expressly states that he may; or

    •   the contract purports to confer a benefit on him.

However, the latter will not apply if, on proper construction of the contract, it appears that the parties did not intend the contract to be enforceable by the third party.

1.6   For a third party to enforce a term of the contract in his own right he must be expressly identified in the contract by name, as a member of a class, or answering a particular description.

1.7   Under s1(3) the third party does not have to be in existence at the time the contract is made. However, he must be expressly identified in the contract in a way referred to in s(1)3. This allows contracting parties to confer enforceable rights on, for example, a company that has not yet been incorporated.

1.8   Third parties may take advantage of exclusion and limitation clauses, provided such clauses are worded to cover particular classes of third party, such as employees. The Act confers the benefit of the clause on them as they are identified as a member of a class.

1.9   The Act affects the contracting parties' rights to vary or cancel the contract by providing that the parties may not without the consent of the third party vary the contract or cancel the contract if:

    •   the third party has communicated his assent on the term to the promisor; or

    •   the promisor is aware that the third party has relied on the term; or

    •   the promisor can reasonably be expected to have foreseen that the third party would rely on the term and the third party has in fact relied on it (s2(1)).

However, s2(3) states that the parties can expressly provide that the contract may be cancelled or varied without the consent of the third party, or otherwise expressly agree circumstances (different to those in the Act) in which the third party's consent is required.

1.10   A contracting party will generally have the same defences and set-offs against the third party that it would have had if the other contracting party had brought the proceedings (s3(2)), as well as those that would have been available had the third party been a party to the contract (s3(4)). However, these can be extended or limited by express terms in the contract.

1.11 Section 5 protects the promisor from double liability to the promisee and the third party by providing that if the promisee has recovered from the promisor a sum in respect of:

- the third party's loss; or
- the expense to the promisee of making good to the third party the default of the promisor.

The court shall reduce an award to the third party to such extent as it thinks appropriate to take account of the sum recovered by the promisee.

1.12 The Act does seem to deal successfully with the problems caused by the doctrine of privity.

1.13 Where a contract is clearly intended to benefit a third party, the court can give effect to the intentions of the parties without having to rely on the artificial devices (eg collateral contracts, see later) which have been used in the past. As the right given by a third party to enforce a benefit would be of limited value if the parties could change their minds and remove the benefit at any time, the Act also contains certain restrictions on their right to cancel or vary the contract without the consent of the third party. These restrictions will apply unless the contract contains an express provision to the contrary (s2).

Contracts under seal (deeds)

1.14 There is one decisive method of ensuring that any benefit conferred by the terms of a contract will be legally enforceable at the instance of the person intended to benefit, and that is by joining him as a party to a contract under seal (a deed). To meet the requirements of the doctrine of privity, the intended beneficiary is now a party to the contract, and further, his failure to provide consideration will not bar any attempt to enforce the agreement since it is a specialty contract which need not be supported by consideration.

Exceptions and limitations to the doctrine of privity

1.15 There are a number of exceptions to the general rule of privity, but mostly they are of little relevance to purchasing and are ignored here. For example, certain exceptions arise through the operation of trust law, and others arise under various statutes such as the Married Women's Property Act 1882. There are also cases where a contracting party is clearly operating on behalf of a group of people: **Jackson v Horizon Holidays** (1975). (In this case the claimant had booked a holiday for his whole family and was entitled to compensation for all of them when the holiday was unsatisfactory.)

1.16 Two more important exceptions will be discussed below: collateral contracts and assignment of rights and benefits.

Collateral contracts or warranties

1.17 The court may find a collateral contract, for example, where there is a contract between A and B which in some way relates to C although C is not a party. There may be another contract between A and C in which C can sue. The leading case is that of **Shanklin Pier Ltd v Detel Products Ltd** (1951).

The claimants owned a pier which needed painting. They were told by the defendants that the paint which they manufactured would last for seven to ten years. The claimants employed a contractor to paint the pier and told him to use paint manufactured by the defendants. The contractor purchased the paint from the defendants and painted the pier with it. After three months it began to flake. The claimants sued the defendants, who argued that the claimants were not a party to the contract under which the paint was sold.

Held: That there was a separate – collateral – contract between the claimants and the defendants, which contained a warranty by the defendants that the paint would last for seven to ten years. The claimants had provided consideration by requiring the contractor to use the paint.

1.18 Note that the defendants made firm representations about the quality of the paint, on which the plaintiffs acted reasonably in relying. If the representations had merely appeared in advertising literature, for example, the courts would probably not imply a collateral contract: **Lambert v Lewis** (1980).

1.19 This admittance of collateral contracts and warranties by the courts is a welcome step to assist aggrieved parties in overcoming the restrictive doctrine of privity. Another avenue open to such parties lies in an action for negligence, and this will be examined in Chapter 16. You should note that this is an area where change is to be expected.

Other exceptions to privity of contract

1.20 You should also look at two further areas of law related to the doctrine of privity. In Chapter 6 (section 5) we looked at indemnities and their use in commercial contracts to provide a primary liability, for example, by a parent company against a subsidiary company becoming insolvent. In Chapter 17 we will study the law of agency and consider the relationship between principal and agent, and the liability of the agent, in certain circumstances, to third parties in discharging the agent's obligations to the principal.

2 Assignment of contractual rights

Voluntary assignment of rights (benefits)

2.1 A person entitled to the benefit of a contract may assign it (ie transfer it) to a third party, who will then be entitled to sue the other party to the contract. For example, suppose S and B make a contract under which S supplies goods to B who will pay S £500 for them. S's right to receive the £500 may be assigned to C who then has the right to sue B for the money.

2.2 Compare this with the situation where S and B have a similar contract except that the payment by B was to be made to C and not to S. C could not sue for the money as he is not party to the contract.

2.3 Most contractual rights in intangible property, such as debts and obligations, can be assigned unless otherwise agreed. However, there are exceptions. For example, rights which are personal cannot be assigned; an employer cannot assign his right to his employees' services. Also, public policy may forbid assignment. For example, salaries and pensions of public office may not be assigned.

2.4 The right to receive payment of a debt, like the benefit of any other contract, may be transferred or assigned. To remove difficulties of earlier procedure, s136 Law of Property Act 1925 gives a statutory right to assign provided that:

- the assignment is in writing

- written notice is given to the debtor

- the assignment is absolute (ie of the whole debt).

2.5 If all of these conditions are satisfied then the assignee can sue in his own name to enforce payment of the debt, and his receipt discharges the debtor from his liability to the original creditor.

2.6 Where these conditions are not wholly satisfied the assignee must sue in the name of the original creditor or owner to whom in law the debt is still due.

2.7 Even the statutory assignment procedure is inadequate for some commercial needs. One major disadvantage arises from the doctrine of *nemo dat* (which is discussed in detail in Chapter 12). The transferor of a debt can only give to his transferee the same title to the debt as he has – nothing more. Thus, if the assignor's title is defective, so is that of the assignee.

2.8 For example, suppose P sells a car to D for £600, the money to be paid in a month's time, and P then assigns the debt (ie the right to claim the £600 from D) to Q. D now discovers that the car is defective and has in consequence a counterclaim against P for £100. The effect of the *nemo dat* rule is that Q owns a debt only worth £500. The assignment is said to be 'subject to equities', ie subject to any rights of set-off or counterclaim that the debtor may have against the original creditor. In short, Q obtained no better rights to the debt than P had.

Novation

2.9 A novation clause is commonly used in business contracts. Novation occurs when a contract is replaced by a new one either between the same parties or introducing a new party. The parties specify the circumstances in which and the manner in which a new contract arises as a result of the discharge of the obligation under the original one. Such provisions take effect as subsequent independently drafted variations of the original contract.

Assignment by operation of law

2.10 When a person dies, the law automatically transfers his rights and duties to his personal representative: **Beswick v Beswick** (1968).

By written agreement, Peter Beswick, a coal merchant, sold his business to his nephew, John Beswick. In return John promised to pay £6.50 per week to Peter during his lifetime and thereafter a payment of £5 per week to his widow. On Peter's death his widow became administratrix of his estate. John made only one payment of £5 and refused to make further payments. The widow sued John for arrears and specific performance of the contract in her capacity as administratrix.

Held: John's failure to pay the annuity did not result in any loss to the deceased's estate; nevertheless the administratrix, standing in the shoes of the deceased and taking over his rights in relation to the contract, could enforce it by way of specific performance.

2.11 Note that the widow could not sue in her personal capacity to enforce the contractual promise to pay the annuity since she was not a party to the agreement. If someone other than the widow had been appointed administrator, her only remedy would have been through an action by the administrator on her behalf, with accountability to her for any benefit secured as the result of a successful action.

2.12 The same involuntary assignment occurs of a bankrupt's rights and duties to his trustee in bankruptcy.

Chapter summary

- The rights and obligations arising under a contract accrue only to the parties to that contract. This is the doctrine of privity of contract.

- The effects of this doctrine have sometimes been to leave an injured party without redress, and the courts have been ready to admit ways around it. One way in particular is to admit the existence of a contract collateral to the main contract.

- The problems caused by the doctrine of privity are now covered by the statutory provisions in the Contracts (Rights of Third Parties) Act 1999.

- In general, the rights and benefits accruing under a contract may be assigned to a party not involved in the contract.

Self-test questions

Numbers in brackets refer to the paragraphs above where your answers can be checked.

1   Explain the doctrine of privity of contract. What is the leading case illustrating this doctrine? (1.1)

2   Under s1 of the Contracts (Rights of Third Parties) Act 1999, how may a third party enforce a term of a contract in his own right? (1.5)

3   State the three conditions which must be fulfilled in order to effect a legal assignment of a debt. (2.4)

4   What is the meaning of the phrase 'subject to equities'? (2.8)

CHAPTER 16

Liability in Negligence

Learning objectives and indicative content

2.5 Evaluate the various methods for circumventing the problems created by privity of contract.

- Negligence
- Consumer Protection Act 1987 Part One

Chapter headings

1	General principles of tort
3	Defences and remedies in tort
3	The tort of negligence
4	Product liability and defective goods

Introduction

So far in this study text we have been looking at the law of contract. However, we saw in the previous chapter that an injured party may sometimes find no redress in contract because of the rules on privity. In such cases the law relating to tort may come to his aid.

'Tort' is a Norman French word meaning harm or wrong. The claimant's case, generally, is that he has suffered loss, eg personal injury or damage to property, as a result of a wrong which was done to him by the defendant and the defendant should pay him money compensation (damages) for the loss suffered. In certain circumstances the claimant may also ask the court to order the defendant not to cause him harm (ie grant an injunction).

The tort which we look at in this chapter is that of negligence: one party's failure to exercise due care leads to another party suffering loss. There is extensive case law on this subject, but in addition there is protection from statute in cases of product liability.

1 General principles of tort

The nature of tort

1.1 The law of tort is the set of rules which determine when one person must pay another person compensation for harm wrongfully caused. Over the years a number of 'torts' have been recognised and rules established for determining whether the claimant's action will succeed or not.

1.2 A 'tort' can be defined as a breach of a legal duty or infringement of a legal right arising independently of contract which gives rise to a claim for unliquidated damages.

- **Breach of legal duty or infringement of legal right** – there is no liability in tort unless the law recognises that a legal duty or right exists which has been breached.

- **Arising independently of contract** – no contractual relationship need exist for a claim to be made.

- **Claim for unliquidated damages** – the compensation to be paid for the loss suffered is not a set amount, but is determined by the court.

1.3   Both contract and tort are largely based on case law and their development has resulted in rather complicated rules for both. However, there are basic differences between them.

1.4   A **contract** is an agreement between two or more persons that can be enforced in the courts. A breach of contract is an infringement of rights which the injured party acquired through the agreement (contract) with the wrongdoer.

1.5   A **tort** is an infringement of a right which exists under general principles of law. It gives rise to an action for **unliquidated damages**. The development of various torts has been piecemeal. Thus, there are many cases where a person is injured or has suffered loss and there is no remedy in tort.

1.6   Certain situations may give rise to an action both for breach of contract and for tort. If A employs B to decorate his house and B carelessly leaves a ladder lying around which causes A injury, A may sue for breach of contract. B is obliged to carry out his work with reasonable care (a term implied by the Supply of Goods and Services Act 1982).

1.7   Alternatively, A could sue in tort for negligence. A cannot claim double damages but it is common to plead both breaches as alternatives.

1.8   Only the parties to a contract may sue. In tort any person injured may sue if he can prove that he has suffered. In the above example, if A and B had made the contract but C, A's daughter, had been injured by the negligence of B, C could not sue B in contract as she was not a party to the contract; she may, however, have an action in tort.

Liability in tort

1.9   Not all 'wrongs' give rise to liability in tort: only those which are recognised by the law. If there is no infringement of a legal right or breach of a legal duty there is no tortious liability even if damage is caused. This situation is sometimes referred to by the Latin phrase *damnum sine injuria* – loss without wrong.

1.10   Each individual tort has rules governing liability but, in general, liability is based on fault. The defendant's conduct must have been:

- either **intentional** – the state of mind of one who both foresees and desires the consequences of his conduct

- or **reckless** – the state of mind of one who foresees the consequences of his conduct and is indifferent to them

- or **negligent** – the state of mind of one who fails to pay attention to the consequences of his conduct as a reasonable man would do.

1.11 In some torts intention must be proved (not merely negligence). In other torts negligence (carelessness) is sufficient. In torts of **strict liability** the defendant is liable for the consequences of his acts or omissions even though his conduct was neither intentional nor negligent. Some breaches of duty imposed by statute come into this category.

1.12 The claimant must establish a causal link between the defendant's conduct and the damage which was incurred. The defendant's conduct must have been an effective cause of the claimant's loss. It need not be the sole cause. The test used to decide liability is referred to as the 'but for' test. If the claimant's loss would not have occurred 'but for' the defendant's conduct then the defendant has caused the loss. If, however, the claimant would have suffered the loss regardless of the defendant's conduct then he has not caused the loss: **McWilliams v Sir William Arrol Ltd** (1962).

An experienced steel erector fell 70 feet to his death. His employers had not provided him with a safety harness, but at the trial there was evidence that he would not have worn one even if it had been made available.

Held: The employers were not liable. The cause of the injury was not the employer's breach but the employee's failure to wear the safety harness.

Vicarious liability

1.13 The person who committed the tort (the **tortfeasor**) is always liable because it was his wrongful act. The injured person can always sue him. His liability is said to be **personal**. In certain circumstances the injured person may sue someone else, even though he took no part in the wrongful act: this other person is said to be **vicariously** liable. The most important application of vicarious liability is the case of an employer's liability for the acts of his employees.

1.14 An employer will be liable for a tort of a worker if it is shown that:

- he is an employee (under a contract of service) and not an independent contractor (under a contract for services); and

- the tort was committed by the employee in the course of his employment, and not while the employee was on a 'frolic of his own'.

1.15 Unless the employer has expressly authorised the conduct, he is vicariously liable only for those torts committed by his employee 'in the course of his employment'. In determining this difficult question, the courts pay regard to several factors.

1.16 A distinction is drawn between a wrongful way of doing something which the employee is authorised to do, and an act which the servant is not authorised to perform at all. The first case is exemplified in **Limpus v London General Omnibus Co** (1862).

The defendants' driver was forbidden to race with or obstruct other buses. He disobeyed these instructions and the claimant was injured.

Held: The company were held to be vicariously liable for his tort since he had merely done what he was authorised to do (drive buses) albeit in an improper and unauthorised manner.

1.17   By contrast, in the case of **Beard v London General Omnibus Co** (1900) a bus conductor, acting on his own initiative, turned round a bus at a terminus and injured a bystander. It was held that he was not acting in the course of his employment, and the employer was not liable.

1.18   Where an employer is sued and pays the damages under the vicarious liability principle he has a right of full indemnity against the employee: **Lister v Romford Ice and Cold Storage Co Ltd** (1957).

A company employed S to drive a lorry and he negligently injured his father who also worked for the company. The employers were held liable to the father; they paid him compensation and then sued S for reimbursement.

Held: They were entitled to a full reimbursement.

1.19   An employer is never vicariously liable for the torts of independent contractors. The employer may, however, be personally liable in tort if he is in breach of his own primary duty. If a person is under a duty to ensure that care is taken, the fact that he has engaged an independent contractor is immaterial.

1.20   Where an employee commits a tort the injured party may be able to sue two persons: the employee, who will be personally liable, and the employer, who will be vicariously liable if the employee was acting within the scope of his employment.

2   Defences and remedies in tort

Defences

2.1   The claimant must first prove that the defendant has committed a tort. The defendant's first line of argument will therefore be that no tort was committed (eg he was not negligent). Only if the claimant proves that the defendant committed a tort need the defendant actually plead a defence.

2.2   One defence is characterised by the Latin phrase *volenti non fit injuria* – 'to him who consents no injury is done'. In this defence (sometimes simply called 'consent') the defendant is claiming that the claimant was aware of risk of harm and consented to that risk. For example, a patient under the surgeon's knife has consented to the operation.

2.3   This defence is never available as a defence to strict liability, such as the absolute duty to fence dangerous machinery under the Factories Act 1961.

2.4   Another defence is 'inevitable accident'. This is an accident which could not have been foreseen nor avoided by any reasonable precautions. This is strictly not a defence, rather a plea to the effect that no tort has been committed. It is not available as a defence in torts of strict liability where fault is immaterial.

2.5   Another defence is statutory authority – a plea to the effect that the defendant had the backing of statute to perform the act complained of. Where the authority is absolute (ie where the law compels the defendant to act in that way) he has no liability.

2.6 However, modern statutes generally require persons acting under their authority to do so reasonably: their authority is therefore **conditional**. If injury arises from unreasonable exercise of conditional authority, liability will arise.

2.7 At common law, the claimant recovered nothing if he was guilty of any negligence which contributed to the cause of his injury. A claim of contributory negligence was, therefore, a complete defence. The Law Reform (Contributory Negligence) Act 1945 reformed the law so that contributory negligence no longer absolves the defendant but merely reduces the damages which he has to pay.

Remedies

2.8 The usual remedy is unliquidated damages (ie which cannot be predetermined by the parties). Generally the amount of damages awarded by the court is based on the principle of compensating the claimant for the loss he has suffered. The basis of assessment in the law of tort is to put the claimant in the position he would have been had the tort not occurred. Tort rules on remoteness are different from contract rules and are covered in relation to the tort of negligence below.

3 The tort of negligence

Introduction

3.1 The tort of negligence is a developing area of the law and has become the most common tort. As a tort, negligence is the breach of a legal duty to take care which results in damage. In order to establish negligence the claimant must prove that the defendant owed him a duty of care, that there was a breach of that duty and that the claimant thereby suffered loss or damage.

3.2 In this section of the chapter each of these three areas – duty of care, breach of duty and damage – will be considered. This area of the law is still developing and is therefore very dependent upon case law.

The duty of care – the 'neighbour' principle

3.3 'You must take reasonable care to avoid acts or omissions which you can reasonably foresee would be likely to injure your neighbour. Who then is my neighbour? The answer seems to be persons who are so closely and directly affected by my act that I ought reasonably to have them in contemplation as being so affected when I am directing my mind to the acts or omissions which are called in question.' These are remarks made by Lord Atkin in the leading case of **Donoghue v Stevenson** (1932).

Mrs Donoghue went to a cafe with a friend. The friend bought her a bottle of ginger beer which Mrs Donoghue drank and then discovered that there was a decomposed snail in the bottom of the opaque bottle. Mrs Donoghue found this sight so upsetting that she suffered physical illness. She sued the manufacturer, claiming that they were under a duty to see that such outside bodies did not get into the beer.

Held: There was a duty on the part of the manufacturer to take reasonable care in the manufacture of products. The manufacturer owes a duty to the consumer to take reasonable care to prevent injury.

3.4   Note that the word 'reasonable' appears twice in the quoted passage from Lord Atkin's judgement. In general, it denotes the objective standard of an ordinary person (as distinct from any personal standard of the individual involved). Certainly a duty of care is owed by an employer to his employees: **Wilsons and Clyde Coal v English** (1938). The employer must provide safe plant, appliances, premises and systems of work. The standard of 'reasonable' care may be affected by the physical capacity of the person concerned. In **Mansfield v Weetabix** (1998), a driver was unaware that he suffered from a physical impairment which was likely to affect his driving, and would not have driven had he known about it. In this case, liability was **not** established.

3.5   The importance of the neighbour principle is that it can impose a duty of care towards persons with whom the party at fault has no contractual relationship and of whose identity he was previously unaware. In the **Donoghue** case, the soft-drink manufacturer was held to owe a duty of care towards any person who might consume his product. This was because he could foresee that if he put his product on the market in an impure state and in a closed and opaque container, injury to the consumer was likely to result. He had no contractual relationship with Mrs Donoghue.

3.6   The neighbour principle underlies the considerable extension of the tort of negligence in recent times. There are, however, exceptions to it and limitations on it. The court is not prepared to find that a duty of care exists in all situations. Thus, there are situations where the claimant has suffered damage as a consequence of the defendant's behaviour but the courts are not willing to impose liability on the defendant.

3.7   One example is the case of making statements (as opposed to doing or failing to do physical acts). In **Donoghue v Stevenson** damage was caused by a negligent omission (failure to check that there was no extraneous matter in the ginger beer). It was once thought that there was no liability for loss caused by the production of inaccurate information through lack of care.

3.8   This situation changed following the case of **Hedley Byrne & Co Ltd v Heller & Partners Ltd** (1963). This case concerned a company that, relying on a banker's reference, laid money out on behalf of a client company who subsequently went into liquidation. The money could not be recovered and the banker's reference was claimed to have been negligent.

3.9   The House of Lords recognised liability for negligent **statements** causing **economic** loss made in circumstances where there exists a **special relationship** between the parties, where it is reasonable for the claimant to rely on the statement, and where the party making the statement has not expressly disclaimed responsibility. Previously, damages for pecuniary loss were recoverable only if the loss arose from a wilful or reckless false statement, ie the tort of deceit.

3.10   In fact, the case was decided in favour of the bank, but only because they had included a clause in their reference disclaiming responsibility in the matter. Meanwhile, the principle had been established that a duty of care was owed in such circumstances.

3.11   Note that a company obtaining services from its own professional advisers – solicitors, bankers, accountants etc – will not need to rely on the neighbour principle, because a contractual relationship is present. The importance of the principle is in cases where no such relationship exists.

Breach of duty of care

3.12   The second element of negligence is that there has been a **breach of the duty of care**.

3.13   'Negligence is the omission to do something which a reasonable man, guided upon the considerations which ordinarily regulate the conduct of human affairs, would do, or doing something which a prudent and reasonable man would not do.'

3.14   The claimant generally must show that the defendant failed to take the degree of care which a 'reasonable man' would have taken in the circumstances. The reasonable man is sometimes described as 'the man in the street' or 'the man on the Clapham omnibus'.

3.15   There are some general rules on the standard applied to determine whether a person has acted as a 'reasonable man'. The reasonable man is not expected to be skilled in any particular trade or profession. However, if he acts or purports to act in a professional capacity he must show the care and skill of an ordinary man of that profession. This is sometimes referred to as the **Bolam test** after the case of **Bolam v Friern Hospital** (1957). The higher standard of care expected from a professional, such as a medical practitioner, was also illustrated in the case of **Bolitho v City and Hackney Health Authority** (1998).

3.16   The skill of an ordinary man of that profession will depend on the profession and the standards and practices existing at the time, and not those applied with more advanced knowledge: **Roe v Minister of Health** (1954).

The claimant was injured when contaminated anaesthetic was administered to him during an operation. This contamination occurred because of invisible cracks in the container, the possibility of which was not known to the medical profession at that time.

Held: The defendant was not liable in negligence as his behaviour was to be judged in the light of medical knowledge current at the time of the incident.

3.17   In general, the burden of proving breach of duty rests on the claimant. However, there may be cases where the facts speak for themselves (***res ipsa loquitur***) and raise a presumption of negligence. In this situation the burden of proof shifts to the defendant to prove he did exercise reasonable care.

3.18   In **Scott v London and St Katherine Docks Co** (1865) *res ipsa loquitur* was defined as follows: 'There must be reasonable evidence of negligence. But where the thing is shown to be under the management of the defendant or his servants, and the accident is such as in the ordinary course of things does not happen if those who have the management use proper care, it affords reasonable evidence, in the absence of explanation by the defendants, that the accident arose from want of care.'

3.19   Unless the doctrine of *res ipsa loquitur* applies it is for the claimant to prove that the defendant did not exercise the degree of care of a reasonable man in the circumstances.

Resultant loss

3.20   In negligence there is no liability unless damage is shown to have resulted from the breach of the duty of care. The claimant must establish a causal link between the defendant's conduct and the damage which he has incurred. The defendant's conduct must have been an effective cause of the claimant's loss.

3.21 Once causation has been proved the claimant must then prove that the loss is not too remote. A number of cases on alleged psychiatric damage suffered by claimants illustrate how tricky an area this can be. In the case of **White v Chief Constable of South Yorkshire Police** (1999) Lord Steyn commented: 'the law on the recovery of compensation for pure psychiatric harm is a patchwork quilt of distinctions which are difficult to justify'.

3.22 The test used to describe liability is referred to as the 'but for' test. If the claimant's loss would not have occurred but for the defendant's conduct then the defendant has caused the loss. If, however, the claimant would have suffered the loss regardless of the defendant's conduct then he has not caused the loss: **McWilliams v Sir William Arrol Ltd** (1962) – see earlier.

3.23 This point is also illustrated in **Barnett v Chelsea and Kensington Hospital** (1969).

A doctor in casualty failed to examine three men who had been vomiting for hours. One of them subsequently died from arsenic poisoning.

Held: Causation was **not** established because the dose of arsenic was so great that the man would probably have died anyway.

3.24 The court will have to determine the extent of the loss for which the claimant is entitled to recover damages. The defendant will not be liable for damage which, legally, is too remote a consequence of his conduct. Whether other damage is too remote or not depends on the 'reasonable foreseeability' test. A loss is not too remote if a reasonable man would have foreseen the type of injury: **The Wagon Mound** (1961).

Owing to the defendants' negligence, oil was spilled overboard and accumulated around the claimant's wharf. Somehow, the oil ignited and the wharf suffered fire damage.

Held: The defendants were held not liable since, while damage to the wharf by oil pollution was foreseeable, damage by fire was not.

Economic loss

3.25 Except in cases of negligent misstatement pure economic loss is too remote to be recoverable in tort. Pure economic loss is economic loss which is not consequent on physical damage: **Spartan Steel and Alloys Ltd v Martin & Co Ltd** (1973).

In excavating a trench in a public road workmen damaged an electric cable (belonging to the local electricity company) which they knew lay under the road and which supplied power to the claimant's factory. As a result of the interruption of power supply one batch of molten metal in furnaces was spoilt and the factory was out of action for fourteen hours.

Held: Damages would be awarded for the value of the spoilt metal and the loss of profit allocated to that melt. But the claimant's claim for loss of profits for the entire period of interruption of their operations was dismissed on the ground that this pure economic loss was too remote.

3.26 The case of **Junior Books v Veitchi** (1982) appears to offer an exception to the general rule on economic loss in certain circumstances, but many commentators have criticised the judgement in this case and it appears to be exceptional.

Liability of subcontractors

3.27 This is an area of the law which has often been tested in examination questions. Another relevant case is that of **Simaan General Contracting Co v Pilkington Glass Ltd** (1988).

A claim for economic loss was made by a purchaser against subcontractors, because the goods supplied by the subcontractors to the main contractors were not up to specification.

Held: The House of Lords dismissed the claim. In the judgement it was emphasised that the situations which could give rise to a claim for pure economic loss were limited.

3.28 The general issue here is the limit on a buyer's powers to obtain redress when the fault is caused by a subcontractor. In the usual case the buyer has a contractual relationship only with the main contractor, who in turn has contractual relationships with subcontractors. If things go wrong, and it is the subcontractor who is at fault, then it is difficult for the buyer to bring an action for breach of contract.

3.29 A possible way out of this problem is the existence of a collateral warranty or contract (see the **Shanklin Pier** case in the previous chapter). Another possibility is direct action against the main contractor, in effect holding him liable for the shortcomings of the subcontractor. This is preferable to reliance on an action in tort, because as has been seen the buyer will rarely if ever be able to recover damages in tort for the pure economic loss he has suffered.

4 Product liability and defective goods

Civil liability

4.1 Liability for products involves a mixture of approaches, both civil and criminal.

4.2 **Civil liability** includes a possible breach of contract under the Sale of Goods Act 1979. This contract-based liability covers goods which are not of satisfactory quality or not fit for their purpose. We examined this in Chapter 11.

4.3 Civil liability may also arise in tort:

- for negligence
- for breach of statutory duty
- under the Consumer Protection Act 1987 – Part I for defective goods.

4.4 These possibilities are examined below.

4.5 **Criminal liability** is covered by Part II Consumer Protection Act 1987 for unsafe goods (see below). There may also be criminal liability under other statutory provisions.

The tort of negligence

4.6 The basic elements which the claimant needs to prove to establish liability for dangerous goods in the tort of negligence are:

- a duty of care owed by the defendant to the claimant
- a breach of the duty
- damage suffered by the claimant as a result.

4.7   Prior to 1932 a duty only existed if either the thing causing the damage was of a class of dangerous things or if it was dangerous for some reason known to the defendant. However, the duty of care owed by manufacturers was set out by the House of Lords in the case of **Donoghue v Stevenson** where Lord Atkin described the 'narrow principle' of manufacturer's negligence in the following terms.

4.8   'A manufacturer of products, which he sells in such a form as to show that he intends them to reach the ultimate consumer in the form in which they left him with no reasonable possibility of intermediate examination, and with the knowledge that the absence of reasonable care in the preparation or putting up of the products will result in an injury to the consumer's life or property, owes a duty to the consumer to take that reasonable care.'

4.9   This classic statement of the liability of manufacturers in negligence (which is independent of any right of action in contract), has been extended in several respects by subsequent case law. The principle has been extended beyond the manufacturer so that it can encompass anyone in the chain of distribution, from manufacturer through assembler, distributors and possibly repairers.

4.10   A good illustration is the case of **Andrews v Hopkinson** (1957).

The defendant sold an eighteen-year-old car to a finance company which was providing HP for the claimant, the person who had agreed to buy the car from the defendant. The defendant had not checked the car, and it had a defective steering mechanism which caused the claimant to have an accident. The claimant sued the defendant in tort (remember there was no contract between the claimant and the defendant).

Held: The defendant was held liable since he was a supplier, and should have known that the car was likely to be dangerous.

4.11   The claimant generally must show that the defendant failed to take the degree of care which a 'reasonable man' would have taken in the circumstances.

4.12   Fault (lack of reasonable care) may arise in a variety of ways.

- Miscarriage in the production and assembly process. The manufacturer may fail to take reasonable care to ensure that foreign substances do not find their way into the product or the manufacturer may use weak or unsuitable materials. The product may alternatively be poorly assembled or constructed.

- Inadequate warnings or directions for use. A failure to warn adequately or give directions will lead to liability in some circumstances.

4.13   In deciding whether the defendant has been negligent the courts will take into consideration (although these may not be decisive), the safety record of the product and industry standards and practices. Moreover, the manufacturer may argue that the product was not defective when put into circulation: it had been interfered with, or it should have been inspected or tested before use or sale, or finally it has been misused.

4.14   In negligence there is no liability unless damage is shown to have resulted from the breach of the duty of care. The claimant must establish a causal link between the defendant's conduct and the damage which he has incurred. Thus, a product not working may mean it is not fit for its purpose but there is no liability in negligence. For example, in the case of **Daniels v White & Sons** (1938) the manufacturers were held to have proved that the presence of carbolic acid in their lemonade was **not** the result of negligence.

4.15 If a manufacturer produces and sells a thing which is defective, rendering it dangerous to people or property, the manufacturer will be liable for any injury to persons or property caused by it. However, if the manufacturer produces and sells a thing which is merely defective in quality even to the extent that it is useless, the manufacturer's liability is in contract only and he will not be liable to persons who, having no contract with him, suffer purely economic loss due to the defect. This has already been illustrated in the **Simaan v Pilkington** case, and is reinforced by the similar decision in **Murphy v Brentwood DC** (1990).

Part I of the Consumer Protection Act

4.16 Part I of the Consumer Protection Act 1987 was enacted to implement the provisions in an EC Directive to harmonise the laws on product liability.

4.17 The Act imposes strict civil liability on certain people which they cannot exclude or limit, for damage caused by defective products. It is intended to fill a gap in the law to protect consumers who cannot claim breach of contract (because the person damaged did not buy it) or negligence (because the producer cannot be shown to have been negligent). However the common law claims are preserved – see above.

4.18 Where any damage is caused wholly or partly by a defect in a product **primary liability** rests with:

- the producer
- any person who by putting his name or brand or trade mark on the product holds himself out as being the producer (eg a supermarket offering own-brand products)
- any person who imported the product from outside the EC.

4.19 **Secondary liability** lies on the supplier of the product if he has been requested to identify the producer, brand or importer and fails to do so. Thus, he may avoid liability by disclosing on request the name of his supplier. The purpose of this provision is to ensure that as far as possible the product is traced back to the producer or some other person who is deemed responsible.

4.20 This secondary responsibility also applies to an assembler who uses unsafe parts. Thus, a car manufacturer who uses another's components which are unsafe will only be liable as a supplier of the finished product.

4.21 Section 1 of the Act defines 'product' widely to include any goods, electricity, component parts and raw materials which have been abstracted (eg minerals) or agricultural products which have been subject to an industrial or other process.

4.22 'Goods' are defined as including substances, growing crops and things attached to the land, ships, aircraft or vehicles. Buildings are not products but a supplier of bricks, cement, etc will be liable as supplier of the constituent parts.

4.23 Section 3 of the Act provides that there is a defect in a product if its safety is not such as people generally are entitled to expect. Lack of safety includes risk of damage to property, death or personal injury.

- In the case of **Abouzaid v Mothercare** (2001) one of the defendant's products had an elasticated strap, which recoiled and struck the claimant in the eye. The product was held to be defective, even though the defendant was held **not** to have been negligent.

- In the case of **Worsley v Tambrands** (2000) the product's packaging, which gave notice of possible adverse effects of use, was regarded as part of the product.

- In the case of **St Albans CDC v ICL** (1996) the product was a standard software package. It was stated (*obiter*) that this must include the software, not just the disk on which it was contained.

4.24 Liability is strict. The producer cannot plead that he took all reasonable care. Once it is shown that the product was unsafe when it was supplied (subject to the defences below) the producer is liable. There is a shift of emphasis from the nature of the defendant's conduct or lack of it to the nature of the product. Was it unsafe when marketed?

4.25 Section 5 of the Act defines the damage which will give rise to liability: death, personal injury, loss or damage to any property including land. It does not include:

- loss or damage to the product itself

- loss or damage to a product which is not ordinarily intended for private use, occupation or consumption and was not actually used privately by the persons suffering the loss or damage. Thus for damage to property by reason of defective products, in a commercial context, the common law alone will still apply

- loss or damage of £275 or less.

4.26 Section 8 provides that liability under the Act cannot be excluded or limited.

4.27 Section 4 provides the following defences.

- The defect is attributable to compliance with any requirement imposed by EC obligations.

- The defendant did not supply the product.

- The defendant did not supply in the course of business nor with a view of profit.

- The defect did not exist in the product at the relevant time (the time it was supplied).

- The state of scientific and technical knowledge at the relevant time was not such that the producer of such products might be expected to have discovered the defect.

- The product was comprised in another product and the defect was wholly attributable to the design of the other product or compliance with instructions given by the manufacturer of the other product.

Part II of the Consumer Protection Act

4.28 The Consumer Protection Act 1987 (Part II) imposes a general duty to ensure that goods comply with general safety requirements, and failure to do so is a criminal offence. In addition it empowers the Secretary of State to make more specific regulations and failure to comply with any such regulation is also an offence.

Food safety legislation

4.29 The Food Safety Act 1990 introduced a strict liability concept in respect of the provision of unfit food. There are four offences.

- Section 7 – rendering food injurious to health
- Section 8 – providing food which fails to meet safety requirements

- Section 14 – providing food which is not of a required quality (this is very wide-reaching and is something of a 'catch-all')
- Section 15 – falsely describing food.

4.30 All of these are criminal offences for which no **mens rea** (guilty intent) is required. However, the Act does provide two defences, as follows.

- Section 20 – fault of some other person. Where the offence is due to an act or default of another person, that other person may be charged with the offence.
- Section 21 – reasonable precautions and due diligence defence. It is a defence for a person charged to prove that he took all reasonable precautions to avoid the commission of the offence, either by himself or by some other person.

Enterprise Act 2002

4.31 This Act, which primarily makes changes to competition law as we shall see in Chapter 19, also contains two provisions to improve consumer protection.

- Individuals can obtain a Stop Now Order against traders who do not meet their legal obligations under consumer protection legislation, such as failing to carry out building work to a reasonable standard.
- Consumer bodies, such as the Consumers Association, are able to being claims for damages on behalf of identifiable individuals who have suffered due to anti-competitive behaviour.

4.32 A Stop Now Order is an injunction preventing the trader from further breaches of legislation, including that regulating services provided under a contract for the supply of goods to be manufactured or produced, and that regulating the installation of goods under a sale or supply of goods contract.

Chapter summary

- The law of tort provides an additional possibility of redress to injured parties who have no claim under contract law.

- A tort is an infringement of a right which exists under general principles of law. It gives rise to an action for unliquidated damages.

- Liability in tort is usually personal, but may in some cases be vicarious – eg the liability of an employer for acts of his employees.

- Defences in tort include consent (*volenti non fit injuria*), inevitable accident, statutory authority and contributory negligence.

- To establish a tort of negligence three things must be proved: existence of a duty of care; breach of that duty; and resultant loss.

- Except in cases of negligent misstatement pure economic loss is too remote to be recoverable in tort.

- Product liability can arise both at common law and in statute. Both civil and criminal liability are possible.

Self-test questions

Numbers in brackets refer to the paragraphs above where your answers can be checked.

1   Explain the differences between contract and tort. (1.4, 1.5)

2   What is meant by *damnum sine injuria*, and what are its consequences? (1.9)

3   What is meant by strict liability? (1.11)

4   In what circumstances is an employer liable for torts committed by his employees? (1.14)

5   What are the consequences of a claim for contributory negligence? (2.7)

6   What three matters must be proved to establish a tort of negligence? (3.1)

7   Describe the facts and the *ratio* in the **Hedley Byrne** case. (3.8–3.10)

8   What standard of care is expected in the tort of negligence? (3.15)

9   Describe the facts and the *ratio* in the **Spartan Steel** case. (3.25)

10   With whom does the primary liability rest in the case of product liability? (4.18)

11   What statutory defences are available in a case of product liability? (4.27)

12   What are the four offences under the Food Safety Act 1990, and what defences are available? (4.29, 4.30)

CHAPTER 17

The Law of Agency

Learning objectives and indicative content

2.4   Evaluate the various methods for circumventing the problems created by privity of contract.

- Agency arrangements

2.5   Identify and analyse the legal principles that apply to agency and bailment.

- Creation of agency
- Rights and duties of agents and principals
- Relationship of principal/agent with third parties

Chapter headings

1   Formation of an agency

2   Types of agent

3   The authority of an agent

4   Liability to third parties

5   The relationship between principal and agent

6   Termination of an agency

Introduction

An agent is a person empowered by a principal to enter into legal relations with a third party on the principal's behalf. In this chapter consideration will be given to how an agency relationship is created and terminated, the authority and liability of an agent and the relationship between the principal and the agent.

1   Formation of an agency

The nature of agency

1.1   Agency is the relationship which arises when one person, the agent (often referred to in legal texts as A), is authorised to act as the representative of another, the principal (P), and to effect the principal's legal rights and obligations.

1.2   The agent is the instrument for entering into legal relations between his principal and the third party (T). As long as the agent acts within the scope of the authority delegated to him the principal is bound by the transactions made by the agent with the third party.

1.3   Although agents may commit their principals in a variety of ways (eg a principal may be liable for torts such as negligence committed by his agent in the course of his agency), the following discussion is limited to agents entering into contracts on behalf of their principals. The contract is made between the principal and third party and generally the agent has no rights or liabilities in the contract.

1.4   As the contract is between the principal and the third party the principal must have capacity to make the contract but the agent need not.

How an agency is formed

1.5   In deciding whether one person has acted as an agent for another (the principal) and affected that principal's legal position it is necessary to consider whether an agency has been created and whether the agent has acted within the scope of his authority.

1.6   An agency may be created by agreement (express or implied) between the principal and agent, or by ratification; or, in the absence of any agreement, by estoppel, or by necessity.

1.7   The terms used to describe an agent's authority are derived to a degree from the way in which the agency is created. However, there is an overlap of types of authority and some disagreement as to the terms used to describe the different types of authority. The five ways in which an agency may be created are set out in the paragraphs below. The terminology used to describe the agent's authority is discussed later in the chapter.

Formation by express agreement

1.8   The principal expressly appoints the agent to act for him. Apart from one exception, no formality is required. The appointment may be oral, in writing or by deed. The one exception is that if the agent is to be empowered to execute deeds on behalf of the principal his appointment must be by deed and is referred to as a power of attorney. The agreement appointing the agent will usually set out the extent of the agent's authority (express authority) although this may be extended by implication (implied or usual authority) or by estoppel (apparent/ostensible authority).

1.9   The agreement may, but will not necessarily, be a contract. If the appointment is by contract all the rules of contract will apply to its formation and termination. An agreement will not be a contract where, for example, no consideration is paid to the agent.

Formation by implied agreement

1.10   Even where there is no express agreement whereby the principal appoints the agent an agreement may be implied from their conduct towards each other or their relationship.

1.11   Where one person (the principal) places another in a position in which it would usually be accepted, either by general custom or by the custom in a particular trade, that the person in that position would have the authority to act for the principal, that person will be impliedly appointed to act as agent for the principal.

1.12   For example, an auctioneer of land will become the agent for the buyer when he accepts the buyer's bid by banging the hammer. The auctioneer will have been expressly appointed by the seller. On the fall of the hammer he will also become the agent of the buyer for the purpose of signing the memorandum of sale and purchase. When he signs, both parties are bound.

1.13   The agency is derived from the implied mutual consent of the principal and agent to an agency relationship. This should not be confused with agency by estoppel which is created by representations by the principal to a third party that a person is his agent, and the third party relies on it (see later).

Formation by ratification

1.14   A person may purport to enter into a contract as an agent although he has no authority to do so either because no agency exists or because he is acting beyond the scope of his authority. If the person for whom he purports to act, the principal, ratifies or adopts the contract it becomes binding on the principal and third party as if the principal had been the original contracting party.

1.15   The ratification is effective even if the third party has given notice to the principal that he wishes to withdraw, unless the agent made the contract subject to ratification, either expressly or impliedly. In that case the offer or acceptance may be withdrawn at any time before ratification: **Bolton Partners v Lambert** (1888).

1.16   For example, on 1 January T offers to sell goods to A who accepts on behalf of P even though he has no actual or apparent authority to act for P and does not make his acceptance subject to ratification. On 3 January T states that he is revoking his offer and on 4 January P ratifies A's acceptance. Provided all the conditions set out below are fulfilled there is a binding contract between P and T and T's attempted revocation is ineffective.

1.17   The ratification validates the agent's actions and relieves him of any liability to the third party for breach of warranty of authority. It will not confer authority on the agent for future transactions.

1.18   The doctrine has been criticised mainly because of the possible oppressive effect on the third party and ratification is therefore only possible under conditions described below.

1.19   First, the agent, in making the contract, must purport to act as an agent and must name or clearly identify his principal: **Keighley, Maxted v Durant** (1901).

An agent purchased wheat at a price which was higher than that which he had been authorised to pay. The agent had not revealed that he was acting as an agent when he bought the wheat. The principal refused to accept delivery of the wheat, even though he had purported to ratify the contract of sale.

Held: The principal was not liable for breach of contract.

1.20   Second, the principal must be in existence and competent to contract when the contract is made and ratified: **Kelner v Baxter** (1866).

The claimant sold wine to the defendant who purported to act as agent for a company which was about to be formed. When it was formed, the company attempted to ratify the contract made by the defendant.

Held: The company could not do so, since it was not in existence when the contract was made.

1.21   However, s36C Companies Act 1985 provides that where a contract purports to be made by a company, or by a person as agent for a company, at a time when the company has not been formed, then subject to any agreement to the contrary the contract shall have effect as a contract entered into by the person purporting to act for the company or as agent for it and he shall be personally liable on the contract accordingly: **Phonogram Ltd v Lane** (1981).

Prior to the formation of F Ltd, which was to manage a pop group, the defendant, their manager, reached an agreement with the claimants regarding finance. The defendant signed an undertaking for and on behalf of F Ltd to repay the monies advanced if the contract was not completed within a certain period. The claimants sued for the money advanced, and the defendant denied that he was personally liable to repay the sum.

Held: A contract was purported to be made on behalf of an unformed company, even though both parties to the contract knew that the company had not been formed and was only about to be formed. Section 36C applies whatever formula is adopted for signing a contract on behalf of an unformed company. An agreement contrary to s 36C cannot be inferred by the fact that the contract is signed by that person as agent for the company.

1.22   In the circumstances, the simplest and safest course for a company promoter is to bring the negotiations to the point of agreement but to postpone any binding contract until the company is formed and can enter into the contract for itself. However, if it is essential to commit the other party before the company exists, the promoter can try to persuade the other party to some formula of assignment or novation (by which the company is to take over his obligations as a new contract) to be made after incorporation and when it does so, or if it does not within a specified time, he is then to be released.

1.23   Third, at the time of ratification the principal must either have full knowledge of what has been done on his behalf or be willing to adopt the agent's acts whatever they might prove to be.

1.24   Fourth, the principal cannot ratify the contract in part only. Any such attempt will operate as ratification of the whole contract.

1.25   Fifth, the principal must ratify in time, either before the time fixed for performance of the contract or, if no time is fixed, within a reasonable time. This rule was laid down in **Metropolitan Asylums v Kingham** (1890), but later cases have cast doubt upon it: **Bedford Insurance v Instituto de Resseguros** (1984).

1.26   Finally, the principal must signify his intention to ratify. This may be by express affirmation of the contract, or it may be by conduct, although mere inactivity is insufficient.

1.27   The principal cannot, of course, ratify a void or illegal contract.

Formation by estoppel

1.28   Estoppel is the doctrine which 'estops', or prevents, a person from denying representations he has made to others either by word or conduct. The concept has been discussed in relation to contracts generally earlier in this text.

1.29   In the law of agency it arises when a person (the principal) by words or conduct holds out another as having authority to make contracts on his behalf (ie to act as his agent). The principal is estopped or prevented from denying that the person has this authority and is bound by such contracts as if he had expressly authorised them.

1.30   The authority which the agent appears to have rests on the representations (or 'holding out') by the principal that the agent has authority, and is called **apparent** or **ostensible authority**. There is not necessarily any agreement between the principal and agent and the agent need not be, although he generally is, aware of the existence of the representation.

1.31   The doctrine operates where a person allows another who is not his agent at all to appear as his agent. For example, P tells T that he has taken A into partnership and A orders goods from T for the firm. P will be liable for the goods even if the firm is a sham.

1.32   Another example is where a board of directors of a company allow one of the directors to act as a managing director even though he has not been properly appointed. A managing director will usually have extensive actual authority to act as agent for the company. By allowing the person to act as managing director the board will be estopped from denying that he has the usual authority of a managing director.

1.33   Apparent authority also arises where a principal fails to notify third parties who have dealt with his agent that the agent's authority has been terminated.

1.34   Finally there is the case where the principal allows his agent to appear to have (or 'holds him out' as having) more authority than he actually has by agreement. This can be done by appointing someone to a position which usually carries with it the authority to make certain contracts but specifically forbidding him to make such contracts.

1.35   For example, a company might appoint a person as managing director but forbid him to enter into contracts of more than £100 without the board's consent. If he orders goods worth £1,000 the board may be estopped from denying his apparent authority as it is usually within such a managing director's authority to make such contracts for the company.

1.36   An important case in this area is that of **Freeman and Lockyer v Buckhurst Park Properties** (1964).

Kapoor, a property developer, and Hoon formed a private company which purchased Buckhurst Park Estate. The board of directors consisted of Kapoor and Hoon and a nominee of each. The company's articles gave the company power to appoint a managing director but none was appointed. Kapoor, however, acted as such with the board's knowledge and consent. He instructed the claimants, a firm of architects, to do work for the company which was completed. The company refused to pay, claiming that Kapoor had no authority to bind the company to this type of transaction.

Held: Kapoor had been held out as having apparent authority to enter into this transaction by those having actual authority to commit the company in this way, ie the board. The company was therefore estopped from denying that he had authority to contract on behalf of the company.

Formation by necessity

1.37 If one person, A, is entrusted with another's property and an emergency arises requiring action to preserve that property then the person holding the property may take the necessary action on behalf of the owner. Because of the necessity such authority is implied: **G N Railway v Swaffield** (1874).

A horse was sent by rail and on its arrival at its destination there was no one to collect it. The railway incurred the expense of stabling the horse for the night, and sought to recover the stabling costs from the owner.

Held: The railway was an agent of necessity which had implied authority to incur the expense in question, and also therefore the right to recover expenses.

1.38 Agency of necessity is confined within narrow limits. All four of the following conditions must be satisfied.

- P's property is entrusted to A. It seems that there is no agency of necessity where a person who has no existing responsibility for the other's property takes charge of it. The most usual examples of agency of necessity are perishable goods entrusted to a carrier such as a ship or railway company.

- An emergency arises, making it necessary for 'A' to act in the way he did.

- 'A' is unable to communicate with 'P' to obtain his instructions.

- The action 'A' took was in good faith in the sense of being in P's interests and not merely for A's own convenience.

2 *Types of agent*

General and special agents

2.1 A **general agent** is a person who has the authority to act in the ordinary course of his trade or profession or to act in all matters of a particular trade or nature; an example might be the managing director of a limited liability company.

2.2 A **special agent** is one whose authority is limited to perform a particular act which is not in the ordinary course of his trade or profession as an agent. The distinction, therefore, depends on the continuity of employment and the nature of the employment in each individual case. The distinction is important in determining the extent of the agent's authority. A special agent has no usual authority.

Types of agent

2.3 In commercial practice there are various types of agent carrying on business as such. Their special powers and responsibilities are defined by the practice of each type of agency.

2.4 A **factor** is defined in s1(1) Factors Act 1889 as a mercantile agent having, in the customary course of his business, usual authority:

- to sell goods or to consign goods for the purpose of sale; or

- to buy goods; or

- to raise money on the security of goods.

2.5   He is normally given possession of the goods by the principal, contracts in his own name and receives payment for the goods himself.

2.6   A person can be a mercantile agent even if it is not normally his business to be a mercantile agent – provided he is entrusted with goods as set out in s1 Factors Act 1889, even if it is for one occasion and for one principal. However, the term does not include a shop assistant or other employees who have no discretionary powers, or agents who merely obtain orders but have no power to buy or sell.

2.7   One of the reasons it may be important to establish whether a person is a factor or not is that s2 Factors Act 1889 provides an exception to the *nemo dat* rule. A purchaser from a factor who was in possession of goods with the owner's consent and sold them in the ordinary course of business may acquire good title to them, even if the factor acted without authority to sell, provided the buyer acted in good faith and had no notice of lack of authority on the part of the agent.

2.8   A **broker** is a mercantile agent who in the ordinary course of his business is employed to make contracts for the buying and selling of property (not limited to goods – for example, a stockbroker) and receives compensation known as brokerage. He is a negotiator. A broker is distinguished from a factor in that:

•   he does not usually have possession of the goods or documents of title

•   he does not buy or sell in his own name

•   he has no power to pledge goods.

2.9   **Commercial** agents are a relatively new kind of agent introduced by the Commercial Agents (Council Directive) Regulations 1993. They define a commercial agent as:

'A self-employed intermediary who has continuing authority to negotiate the sale or purchase of goods on behalf of another person ('the principal') or to negotiate and conclude sale and purchase of goods on behalf of and in the name of the principal.'

2.10   The regulations are discussed in more detail later in this chapter. In brief, they confer rights and impose duties on both principal and agent. Both must act dutifully and in good faith.

2.11   Obligations are imposed on the principal regarding the agent's right to remuneration, commission and compensation.

2.12   Officers of a company and partners are expressly excluded from the regulations.

2.13   A ***del credere* agent** is similar to a mercantile agent in that he is employed to sell goods usually in international trade. However, for an additional commission, he also agrees to indemnify the principal if purchasers whom he has introduced do not pay.

2.14   His agreement to indemnify the principal is a secondary liability for the debt so that the principal must first try to obtain payment from the third party before recourse to the *del credere* agent.

2.15   A *del credere* agent only guarantees payment and does not generally guarantee any other liability of the purchaser, eg performance of other aspects of the contract.

2.16   A **banker** is an agent of his customer in two ways.

- A banker acts as an agent of the customer when he makes payment on a cheque drawn by the customer. The cheque is an instruction by the customer to the banker to pay the payee and the banker must obey those instructions provided there are sufficient funds in the account (or an agreed overdraft).

- A banker acts as an agent of the customer when he collects payment on a cheque made out in favour of the customer.

2.17   **Company directors and officers** act as agents for the company. We have seen that there are certain circumstances in which a company may incur liability (for contracts). Most likely, an act will be done on behalf of the company by a servant or agent. Whether or not such an act will make the company liable depends on the power of the company to act in such a situation and on whether or not the person acting is capable of binding the company.

2.18   A **partner** in a partnership is an agent for the firm and all his partners. The Partnership Act 1890 provides that every partner is an agent of the firm and his co-partners, and will bind them by acts done in the ordinary course of the firm's business.

2.19   The test of what is carrying on the firm's business **in the usual way** has been developed into a list of transactions which are or are not within the limits of a partner's apparent authority. The general test is one of normal practice – which is not the same for all firms nor for all types of business.

2.20   If one appoints an agent for business purposes, that is an implied authorisation to do acts which are usually or normally done in the transaction of the relevant type of business. For example, if one appoints a manager of a public house he has apparent authority to make those trade purchases of goods which are usually made by those who are in charge of a public house: **Watteau v Fenwick** (1891), discussed below.

3   *The authority of an agent*

Actual authority

3.1   The ability of the agent to bind the principal depends on his having the authority to act. As long as the agent acts within the scope of his authority the principal will be bound.

3.2   Actual authority is the authority which the principal has agreed the agent shall have. It may be express actual authority or implied actual authority. Implied actual authority may be given:

- either to do everything necessarily and ordinarily incidental to the carrying out of the activity expressly authorised

- or to do whatever an agent in that trade, profession or business would usually have the authority to do. For example, a managing director of a company has usual authority to act for a company in all commercial matters connected with managing the business.

Apparent or ostensible authority

3.3 Apparent or ostensible authority is the authority of an agent as it appears to others, based on representations by the principal (eg by estoppel). A leading case is **Watteau v Fenwick** (1891).

Humble owned a hotel which he sold to Fenwick who employed Humble as manager. Humble's name remained over the door of the hotel. Fenwick specifically forbade Humble from ordering cigars on credit. However, Humble did order cigars from Watteau on credit. Watteau gave credit to Humble and had never heard of Fenwick. It was usual to supply cigars to such hotels. Watteau discovered Fenwick's existence and sued him for the price of the cigars.

Held: The real principal Fenwick was liable for all acts of his agent, Humble, which were within the authority usually conferred on an agent of that particular kind, even though Humble had never been held out by Fenwick as his agent and the actual authority given to Humble by Fenwick had been exceeded.

Actual and apparent authority

3.4 Modern discussions, such as that in **Freeman & Lockyer v Buckhurst Park Properties** above, state the principles of agency based on actual and apparent authority. In that case Diplock LJ, in restating the agency principle, said: 'It is necessary at the outset to distinguish between an 'actual' authority of an agent on the one hand, and an 'apparent' or 'ostensible' authority on the other. Actual and apparent authority are quite independent of one another. Generally, they coexist and coincide, but either may exist without the other and their relative scopes may be different.'

3.5 An agent's apparent authority may be greater than his actual authority, eg where restrictions have been placed on his authority but the principal has not notified third parties of these restrictions. For example, in the case of **Hely Hutchinson v Brayhead** (1968) the chairman of the defendant company acted as though he had the powers of a managing director, even though he had not formally been appointed as such. On the other hand, the agent's actual authority may exceed his apparent authority, eg where the principal specifically gives him more authority than an agent in his position would usually have, but third parties are unaware of this.

Agent acting without authority

3.6 If an agent acts without any authority and purports to negotiate a contract on behalf of an alleged principal with a third party, then:

- the alleged principal will not be bound
- there is no contract between the agent and the third party as the third party did not intend to contract with the agent personally
- the agent will have impliedly warranted to the third party that he had authority and he will be liable to the third party for breach of warranty of authority.

3.7 If an agent acts in excess of his actual authority the principal will be bound if he has acted within his apparent authority but the agent may be liable to the principal for breach of their agreement.

4   *Liability to third parties*

Principal disclosed

4.1   When ascertaining the liability of an agent or his principal it is important to distinguish between situations where the principal is disclosed and situations where the principal is not disclosed.

4.2   In the normal case the agent discloses to the third party that he is acting as an agent for a named principal or at least for some principal even if not named. The general rule is that the agent is not then liable on the contract nor can he enforce it. The contract is between the principal and the third party.

4.3   There are however certain exceptions.

•   The agent may in signing the contract for his principal accept personal liability. In particular the agent is liable on a deed or bill of exchange if he signs it in his own name.

•   Where by custom of the trade the agent is liable.

•   If the agent purports to act for a named principal who does not exist, ie is fictitious.

•   If the agent, when required, refuses to disclose the identity of the principal.

•   If a person purports to act on behalf of a company which is not yet incorporated – s36C Companies Act 1985.

4.4   Where the agent purports to act for an unnamed principal he can subsequently declare himself the true principal if it is consistent with the description of the supposed unnamed principal and the third party cannot show that he was not willing to contract with the agent.

Principal not disclosed

4.5   The agent may, of course, make a contract without disclosing that he has a principal for whom he is acting. The agent will then appear to be the principal. When the other party discovers the true position he may at his option hold the agent bound by the contract or treat the principal as bound. However, if he obtains judgement against one then he is barred from suing the other.

4.6   The undisclosed principal can usually intervene and claim against the third party provided the following conditions are satisfied.

•   The terms of the contract are consistent with agency: **Humble v Hunter** (1948) (an agent entered into a contract to charter his principal's ship and signed as owner; this was not consistent with him acting as an agent and the principal could not sue on the contract).

•   The agent had the authority to act for the principal when he made the contract.

•   The third party cannot show that he had wanted to deal with the agent and no-one else, eg the agent was well known as possessing certain skills which were necessary for performance of the contract. This is similar to the rules on unilateral mistake of identity in contract law.

4.7 If the principal does intervene and claims against the third party he thereby makes himself liable. The agent remains liable to be sued and entitled to sue on the contract.

4.8 If an agent discloses that he is an agent then generally the agent is not liable on the contract. If an agent does not disclose that he has a principal then the third party has a choice: he may sue either the principal or the agent on the contract, but not both.

5   The relationship between principal and agent

Introduction

5.1 Agency is a relationship between the principal and the agent. This may be a contractual relationship and the rights and duties of agent and principal will depend on the terms of the contract. However, where there is no contract (eg an agent undertakes to act without pay), or where there is a contract but the terms are not clear, the rights and duties of agent and principal will be implied by the common law. These general rules are set out below as the common law duties of the agent and the common law duties of the principal. These have been added to by the Commercial Agents (Council Directive) Regulations 1993, which are discussed later.

Common law duties of an agent to his principal

5.2 The agent must perform the agency by obeying his principal's lawful instructions – unless he is acting gratuitously, an agent is liable in damages if he fails to carry out his instructions: **Turpin v Bilton** (1843).

An insurance broker, in return for a fee, agreed to arrange insurance for P's ship. He failed to do so. The ship was lost at sea.

Held: The broker had failed to perform the agency and was liable to P in damages for the loss.

5.3 Note that an agent will not be liable if he fails to perform an act which is illegal or void: **Cohen v Kittell** (1889). But it is no excuse for an agent to claim that, even if the contract had been made, the other party could have escaped liability under it if in fact he would have been unlikely to do so: **Fraser v Furnam** (1967).

5.4 The agent must perform the agency with reasonable care and skill. What is reasonable will depend on the circumstances. In general a professional and paid agent would be expected to show a greater degree of care and skill than an unpaid amateur. However, even an unpaid agent is expected to exercise such care and skill as the circumstances require: **Chaudry v Prabhakar** (1988).

5.5 The agent must render an account when required (monetary and factual).

5.6 The agent must act personally and not delegate his authority, except:

- when expressly or impliedly authorised by the principal to delegate
- where delegation is customary
- in case of necessity, or
- where the acts delegated are purely ministerial eg simple clerical tasks.

5.7 The duty of the agent is one of utmost good faith (*uberrimae fidei* in the Latin expression). He has a fiduciary duty to his principal. This duty has a number of different, but overlapping, aspects.

5.8 First, an agent must not allow his personal interests to conflict with those of his principal. An agent who sells his own property to his principal (or vice versa) breaches this duty: **Armstrong v Jackson** (1917).

A stockbroker, who was appointed to buy shares for his principal, sold the principal his own shares without disclosing this fact.

Held: This was a breach of fiduciary duty and the principal could avoid the contract and recover his money. (Similarly, an agent appointed to sell property must not purchase the property himself: **McPherson v Watt** (1877).)

5.9 Second, an agent must not make a secret profit. Thus, for example, he must disclose to his principal the receipt of any gift or commission. Where the secret profit takes the form of a payment from a third party who is aware that he is dealing with an agent, it is called a 'bribe'. An agent employed to make wagering contracts must hand over any winnings to his principal: **DeMattos v Benjamin** (1894).

5.10 Finally, an agent must maintain confidentiality about his principal's affairs.

Remedies for breach of duty

5.11 Every breach of duty is a breach of the agency agreement and renders the agent liable in damages to the principal for any loss. See for example **Turpin v Bilton** (1843).

5.12 The principal may have an action for damages against the third party where he is party to the breach and the breach is fraudulent (as is the case with a bribe).

5.13 Where the breach is serious (as is always the situation where the agent is dishonest) the principal may dismiss the agent and refuse to pay him his remuneration: **Boston Deep Sea Fishing v Ansell** (1888).

A (a managing director of a company) agreed with suppliers that he would receive a commission on any of their goods which he arranged for the company to order.

Held: The company was entitled to dismiss him (and to recover the commissions from him).

5.14 The principal may recover any benefit from the agent. See **Boston Deep Sea Fishing v Ansell** (1888).

5.15 Where the agent sells his own property to the principal (or vice versa) the principal may avoid the contract. See **Armstrong v Jackson** (1917).

Common law duties of a principal to his agent

5.16 The principal is under a duty to indemnify the agent for all acts performed, expenses incurred and liability arising from the proper performance by the agent of his duties. This does not include any liability incurred solely by the agent's negligence, breach of duty or insolvency: **Duncan v Hill** (1873).

5.17 The other duty of the principal is to pay the agent his agreed remuneration. Where there is no formal agreement on renumeration, the agent will not be able to enforce it: **Re Richmond Gate Property** (1965). The case law on this duty relates almost entirely to claims by estate agents for their commission on the sale of property. Where the sale goes through to a purchaser found by the estate agent there is usually no difficulty. He has performed his duty and is clearly entitled to commission out of the proceeds of the sale.

5.18 However, an estate agent is not entitled to commission unless a purchaser introduced by him signs a contract and completes the purchase or the agent's appointment states in explicit terms that the mere introduction of a person willing to purchase is sufficient and he introduces such a person. The presumption is that commission is to be payable only on completion of the sale and very clear words are needed to establish entitlement for anything else.

5.19 If, however, the house owner signs the contract and then refuses to complete the sale the agent is usually entitled to commission. It is not his fault if the sale is not completed.

5.20 The principal's duties to pay agreed remuneration and to indemnify the agent are accompanied by one other common law right of an agent: the right to retain lawfully held goods of another person in order to secure payment of a debt. This right ceases when and if the agent ceases to possess the goods, unless he was induced to relinquish the goods by fraud. An obvious application of these rights is where an agency agreement has been terminated, but the principal still owes the agent some remuneration and the agent still holds some of the principal's goods.

The Commercial Agents (Council Directive) Regulations 1993

5.21 These regulations extend the duties owed between principal and agent.

5.22 For the purposes of the regulations, a commercial agent is a self-employed intermediary who has continuing authority to negotiate the sale or purchase of goods on behalf of another person (the principal), or to negotiate and conclude the sale and purchase of goods on behalf of and in the name of that principal.

5.23 Either principal or agent has the right to receive from the other, on request, a signed written document setting out the full terms of the agency contract.

5.24 The regulations impose detailed duties as to when, where and in what circumstances commission is payable, including in particular the duty of the principal to supply written information, so as to enable the agent to check the amount, not later than the end of the month following the quarter in which the commission becomes due.

5.25 If the agency is for an indefinite period, the agent has a right to defined minimum periods of notice depending on the duration of the agreement.

5.26 The agent has a right to compensation if the agency is terminated for reasons not involving failings on his own part.

5.27 The principal is permitted, subject to certain restrictions, to limit the agent's right to compete after termination of the agency agreement.

6 Termination of an agency

Termination by complete performance

6.1 A contract of agency may be terminated in the same way as any other contract: by performance, agreement (expressly, or by lapse of an agreed period of time), breach or frustration. In addition, there are certain rules which apply to termination of agency.

6.2 Termination can be by complete performance: in an agency for a particular transaction where the agent completes the transaction; or by expiration of time where the agency was for a fixed period and the period expires.

Termination by unilateral revocation or renunciation

6.3 Termination can be by unilateral revocation (by the principal) or renunciation (by the agent). If the principal and agent are contractually bound there may be an action for breach of contract if the terms of the contract (eg as to notice of termination) are not followed. The revocation or renunciation will terminate the agency even if there is a breach of contract, unless the agency is one which is irrevocable.

6.4 Where the agent's authority is **coupled with an interest** it is irrevocable during the subsistence of that interest because the agency has been created to protect that interest. For example, P owes A money and appoints A as his agent to sell some of P's property to pay the debt.

6.5 Where the agent has started to perform his duties and incurred liabilities (eg to pay a third party), the agency is irrevocable in that the agent is entitled to be reimbursed for the payments due to the third party even if the principal forbids them.

6.6 In certain cases statute provides that the agent's authority cannot be revoked. For example, the Powers of Attorney Act 1971 provides that certain powers of attorney are irrevocable while the donee of the power retains an interest to be protected.

Termination by operation of law

6.7 Agency will be terminated by operation of law in the following circumstances.

- Death of the agent or principal, even if the agent is unaware of the principal's death

- Insanity of the agent or principal. However, the Enduring Powers of Attorney Act 1985 provides that powers of attorney created in the manner prescribed by the Act may endure after the donor becomes insane

- Bankruptcy of the principal (or of the agent if it makes the agent unfit to carry out his duties)

- Frustration, eg where the agency becomes unlawful because the principal becomes an enemy alien, or military service makes it impossible for the agent to perform his duties.

The effect of termination

6.8   Termination of agency ends the agent's actual authority. However, he may still appear to have authority to third parties who have not had notice of the termination of his actual authority. The principal will be bound by acts of the agent within this apparent/ostensible authority unless the agent's authority was terminated by the death or bankruptcy of the principal. There are conflicting cases on termination by insanity.

Chapter summary

*   An agency can be created by express or implied agreement, by estoppel, by ratification or by necessity.

*   Once created an agent's authority may be actual or apparent.

*   In general terms if an agent does not disclose the existence of a principal then the agent himself may be liable, whereas if he does disclose that a principal exists, then the agent will not be liable on the contract.

*   An agent must carry out his agreed duties in good faith and disclose or account for any secret profit.

*   In a company the directors will act on behalf of the company and make contracts in the name of the company. The law of agency will often determine whether or not the company is liable on such contracts and whether the person acting is capable of binding the company.

*   A partner is an agent both of the firm and of the other partners. Therefore the other partners may be bound by one partner's contracts and be liable for them.

*   An agency can be terminated by performance, agreement or operation of law.

Self-test questions

Numbers in brackets refer to the paragraphs above where your answers can be checked.

1 What is agency? (1.1)

2 What are the five ways in which an agency may be created? (1.6)

3 What are the conditions necessary for ratification of a contract made by an agent? (1.19–1.27)

4 What is the doctrine of estoppel in agency law? (1.28)

5 What is a general agent? (2.1)

6 What is a special agent? (2.2)

7 What is a factor? (2.4)

8 What is an agent's actual authority? (3.2)

9 What is an agent's apparent authority? (3.3)

10 What is the effect of an agent acting without authority? (3.6)

11 What is the liability of an agent if he discloses a principal but does not name the principal? (4.2)

12 What are a principal's rights where an agent has received a bribe? (5.9)

13 What are the duties of a principal to his agent? (5.16–5.20)

14 In what ways may an agency terminate? (6.1, 6.2)

CHAPTER 18

Tendering and the EU Procurement Directives

Learning objectives and indicative content

3.1   Determine the collateral legal obligations that arise from a tendering process (including e-tendering).

- Tendering processes
- Legal status of the tender bid
- Open and closed tenders
- Duty to consider all compliant tenders
- Equal and timely access to information
- Fair treatment and good faith
- Post-award negotiations
- Avoidance of the battle of the forms

3.2   Analyse the main provisions of the Public Contract Regulations 2006 and explain how it affects the purchasing function.

- Thresholds, time limits, advertising
- Evaluation criteria
- Right to feedback
- Framework agreements
- Open, restricted, negotiated and competitive dialogue procedure
- E-procurement mechanisms
- Central purchasing bodies
- Social and environmental considerations
- Standstill procedure
- Common vocabulary

Chapter headings

1   Pre-tender undertakings

2   Post-tender negotiation

3   Letters of comfort

4   EU procurement directives

5   Recent developments in public procurement

Introduction

This chapter aims to introduce you to some more of the legal issues surrounding tendering and outsourcing. You have already seen how to distinguish between invitations to treat and contractual offers. For example, is a tender a definite offer capable of acceptance leading to a contract, or is a tender merely a device by which a company invites offers from interested parties? Refer back to Chapter 3 on this. You must understand the legal status of post-tender negotiation, pre-tender undertakings, and letters of comfort. You must also gain an understanding of the effects of European Union Procurement Directives.

1 Pre-tender undertakings

An offer or an invitation to treat?

1.1 Firstly we have to establish the legal status of a tender. It is vital to distinguish, in respect of tenders, whether they are invitations to treat or definite offers capable of acceptance.

1.2 An invitation to treat is a device whereby an interested party invites offers, and it is up to that party whether or not to accept any offers that may be received.

1.3 The party who invites the tender is under a contractual duty to contemplate all tenders received within any time limit laid down and that comply with any important conditions: **Blackpool & Fylde Aero Club Ltd v Blackpool BC** (1990).

The council invited tenders from interested parties to run certain services. The invitation stated that tenders had to be received before 12 noon on a particular date. Furthermore, the tender had to be placed in an envelope provided by the council. The claimant's tender met with all the council requirements. The claimant had placed the envelope in the council's letter box one hour before the deadline. The council staff did not forward the tender and therefore the claimant was regarded as being in breach of the council's instructions. The claimant's tender was not considered by the council.

Held. The council had a contractual duty to consider the claimant's tender and this it had failed to do.

1.4 So all tenders received that comply with any requirements laid down must be at least considered by the party that invited them, but this does not mean that the party making the invitation to treat, ie inviting the tender, is duty bound to accept the most favourable bid, or any bid at all for that matter. There may be a variety of definite offers (tenders) on the table but ultimately it is up to the party that initiated the tender whether it decides to accept them or not.

1.5 Merely because someone makes you an offer that you solicited does not mean that you are obliged to accept that offer. There can be many reasons why you would not be willing to proceed to a contract.

1.6　In summary, therefore, a tender document is an invitation to treat. It is not an offer that can be accepted: **Spencer v Harding** (1870).

The defendants had been given responsibility for selling a business and all its stock. To this end the defendants issued a circular which invited tenders from interested parties. The claimants submitted a tender which turned out to be the highest bid but the defendants refused to accept it. The issue centred around whether the circular had been a definite offer capable of acceptance or whether it was merely an invitation to treat.

Held. The circular was just an invitation to treat. It was the claimants who had made the offer which the defendants were not compelled to accept.

Collateral obligations

1.7　The precedent established in the *Blackpool* case – namely that the person inviting tenders is required to give due consideration to all tenders received on time and in compliance with the terms – has sometimes been referred to as a **collateral obligation**. There are three other collateral obligations that may arise in this context.

1.8　First, if the invitation to tender states that the contract will be awarded to the lowest bidder, then the person issuing the invitation is obliged to do exactly that. If instead he awards the contract to someone else, the lowest bidder will be able to insist on compliance with what was stated in the invitation to tender. To avoid placing this restraint on his own actions, the person inviting tenders will usually state that the contract will not necessarily be awarded to the lowest bidder.

1.9　Second, the normal rule on contractual offers is that they may be withdrawn at any time prior to being accepted. However, the person inviting tenders needs a period of time in which to consider the offers made, and this period is usually stated in the invitation to tender. A person making a tender is under an implied obligation not to withdraw his offer during that period. Unlike the other collateral obligations discussed here, this obligation binds the bidder rather than the person issuing the invitation to tender. If there have been delays and the period of time is soon to expire, it can be extended by the person running the tender sending a letter of intent to the bidder who is most likely to be awarded the tender. This letter does not constitute acceptance of the bid, and is a risky procedure, as we saw in Chapter 5.

1.10　Third, the case of **R v The National Lottery Commission (ex parte Camelot plc)** (2000) appears to establish an obligation on the person inviting tenders to treat all unsuccessful bidders on equal terms. The case arose because a government agency rejected the only two bids received for a contract to run the UK national lottery, but then entered into discussions with one of the unsuccessful bidders with a view to awarding them the contract after all. Since no similar discussions were proposed with the other unsuccessful bidder the court decided that the process was fundamentally flawed, and the agency should treat both bidders in the same way.

2 *Post-tender negotiation*

2.1 Even when a preferred offer has been received following a tender, there may still be post-tender negotiation to deal with. Particular problems arise in situations of referential bidding. This occurs when one party has not made the highest bid but agrees or states that they will 'top' the highest bid by a specified amount of money.

2.2 For example, someone might offer to buy shares 'for £200,000, or £50,000 more than any other higher bid'.

Tenders and standing offers

2.3 What is the legal status of a rolling series of offers? An example of this type of arrangement can be seen in the case of **Great Northern Railway v Witham** (1873).

The company advertised for tenders for the supply for one year of such stores as they might require from time to time. W submitted a tender to supply certain specified quantities of goods for the period. The company accepted the tender and gave orders to W which were carried out. Eventually, W refused to carry out an order made by the company and a court action was brought.

Held. W was in breach of contract. The tender was a standing offer which was converted into a series of contracts as the company placed an order. W could revoke his offer for the remainder of the period covered by the tender, but he must supply the goods already ordered by the company.

3 *Letters of comfort*

3.1 Letters of comfort (which we saw in Chapter 6) are just statements of fact concerning a defendant's present intentions. They are not contractual promises about how a defendant may behave in the future.

3.2 Anyone issuing a letter of comfort would do well to state that it is not their intention to enter into a legal relationship as a matter of course: **Kleinwort Benson Ltd v Malaysia Corporation Berhad** (1989).

The defendant company refused to give a formal guarantee in relation to its subsidiary company's debts but did state in writing a policy to ensure that the subsidiary was at all times in a position to meet its liabilities.

Held. These words of assurance amounted to a policy statement only and not a promise by which the defendant was contractually bound.

3.3 It has become a well established business practice that holding companies are asked to issue comfort letters by the creditors of their subsidiaries. This in effect means that the holding company is stating that its subsidiary will probably be able to meet its liabilities. However, comfort letters are perhaps not as valuable as they at first seem as they are presumed not to be legally binding.

4 EU procurement directives

4.1 The need for a simplified legal framework adapted to modern procurement methods and best practice was highlighted in the response to the European Commission's 1996 Green Paper. The subsequent consultation process culminated in the publication of the new public procurement directives in the *Official Journal of the European Union* (OJEU) on 30 April 2004. Provisions of the new directives were transposed into UK national legislation on 31 January 2006 and were implemented by regulations made under s2(2) of the European Communities Act 1972.

4.2 The principal objective of the directives is to promote free, open and non-discriminatory competition within the EU.

Public Sector Directive

4.3 The new Public Sector Directive (2004/18/EC) simplifies and consolidates the three existing directives for public works, supplies and services into a single text. Many of the basic provisions remain the same as in the existing directives. The Directive was implemented into UK law by virtue of the Public Contracts Regulations 2006 on 31 January 2006.

Financial thresholds

4.4 Once a buyer has specified the goods, services or works he requires, and if he is purchasing on behalf of a public body, he must ensure compliance with the Regulations. The Regulations do not apply to the private sector unless, for example, a private sector company is purchasing on behalf of a public body (perhaps as result of outsourcing). The Regulations apply to all purchases above certain financial thresholds that are reviewed every two years. The current thresholds apply from 1 January 2010 until 31 December 2011 and are set out below.

Supplies – £101,323

Services – £101,323

Works – £3,927,260

For non-central government bodies (eg local authorities, education) the thresholds are as follows.

Supplies – £156,442

Services – £156,442

Works – £3,927,260

All figures exclude VAT.

Advertising the requirement

4.5 Subject to certain exceptions, the Regulations require public bodies to use open tendering procedures. They must **advertise** the invitation to tender according to certain rules designed to secure maximum publicity across member states. The contract notice advertising the requirement must be published in the Supplement to the European Journal (available in electronic form only) before it may be published in any other media. To avoid ambiguity the public body should use the **common procurement vocabulary** (CPV) in specifying the requirement. The CPV aims to standardise the description of goods and services required by providing a comprehensive list, each item being described by a numerical code of up to nine digits.

Procedures and time limits

4.6   Contracting authorities now have the choice of four contract award procedures: open, restricted, negotiated (with or without contract notice) and competitive dialogue.

4.7   For the **open procedure** there is no requirement for pre-qualification of suppliers. Tenders must be issued within six days of request by a prospective bidder. The contracting authority must set the closing date for receipt of tenders no less than 52 days from the publication of the contract notice.

4.8   For the **restricted procedure**, pre-qualification of suppliers is permitted but the contracting authority must indicate in the contract notice a predetermined range of suppliers to whom tenders will be sent. This must comprise not fewer than 5 and not more than 20 suppliers. The contract notice must allow a minimum of 37 days for prospective bidders to register an interest and submit the required information for pre-qualification. Suppliers who are pre-qualified must be allowed a minimum of 40 days to submit their tenders in response to the invitation issued by the contracting authority.

4.9   The **negotiated procedure** takes two forms: with publication of a contract notice, and without publication. In the latter case other formalities are dispensed with as well. The procedure without publication may be used for a number of reasons including when:

- the open or restricted procedure was discontinued, but only if the contracting authority invites to negotiate the contract every supplier who submitted a tender (not being an excluded tender) under the other procedures;
- there were inappropriate or no tenders under the other procedures;
- for technical or artistic reasons, or because of exclusive rights;
- because of urgency the time limits in the other procedures cannot be met;
- additional and/or repetitive goods/services/works are required.

4.10   Under the negotiated procedure where a contract notice is required, prospective bidders must be given a minimum of 37 days to register their interest to negotiate. Where there is a sufficient number of persons who are suitable to be selected to negotiate, the number selected must not be less than three.

4.11   Where contract notices are drawn up and transmitted by electronic means in accordance with the format and modes of transmission stipulated, the Regulations allow for the time limits for the receipt of tenders in open procedures, and the time limit for the receipt of requests to participate in restricted and negotiated procedures and competitive dialogue, to be shortened by seven days.

4.12   The time limit for receipt of tenders may be reduced by a further five days where the contracting authority offers unrestricted and full direct access by electronic means to the contract documents and any supplementary documents from the date of publication of the notice, by specifying in the text of the notice the internet address at which this documentation is accessible.

4.13   Where contracting authorities seek to take advantage of the above opportunity to shorten the time limits for the receipt of tenders on the basis of the electronic availability of their contract documents, they must publish the specifications and the additional documents in their entirety on the internet.

4.14   In general, buyers are obliged to award the contract on the basis of the lowest quoted price, or on the basis of the economically most advantageous tender. If they choose the latter alternative, they must make the fact known to candidates, and must explain by what criteria, and their relative importance, they mean to assess 'economically advantageous'. The buyer is allowed, in certain circumstances, to exclude bidders if they fail to meet defined criteria relating to general suitability, financial and economic standing and technical competence. This is discussed in more detail later in this section.

Evaluation and award criteria

4.15   The Regulations set out criteria designed to ensure that all suppliers or contractors established in countries covered by the rules are treated on equal terms, to avoid discrimination on the grounds of origin in a particular Member State.

4.16   At the specification stage requirements must be specified, avoiding brand names and other references which would have the effect of favouring or eliminating particular providers, products or services. The Regulations now make it clear that authorities may use performance specifications rather than technical specifications. They also provide clarification on the scope to reflect environmental and social issues in specifications. We will look at this aspect later in this section.

4.17   Where the procedures permit pre-qualification of candidates (eg when using the restricted procedure) the selection of candidates must be based upon general criteria including their economic and financial standing (eg they are judged to be financially sound on the basis of their annual accounts) and their technical capacity and ability (eg they will be adequately equipped to do the job and their track record is satisfactory). There are also a number of grounds for exclusion, including bankruptcy, professional misconduct and non-payment of taxes.

4.18   After the tenders have been received by the public body, the contract should be awarded on the basis of objective award criteria which ensure compliance with the principles of transparency, non discrimination and equal treatment and which guarantee that tenders are assessed in conditions of effective competition. The Regulations allow the application of two award criteria only: either lowest price or various criteria for determining which is the 'most economically advantageous tender (MEAT)' to the purchaser. Government policy is to use the latter criterion, as this is consistent with the obligation to achieve value for money.

4.19   On 24 January 2008 the European Court of Justice (ECJ) ruled on the award criteria under the procurement rules in a case concerning the interpretation of the EU procurement directives: **EMM G Lianarkis and Others v Dimos Alexandroupolis and Others (2008)** (the Lianarkis case). In its ruling the ECJ made two important findings.

- A contracting authority cannot apply weightings and sub-criteria to award criteria set out in tender documentation unless those weightings and sub-criteria have been previously brought to the attention of tenderers. Moreover, contracting authorities are bound to place tenderers on an equal footing throughout the tender procedure by adequately publishing the criteria and conditions governing the award of a contract.

- A contracting authority cannot take account of a tenderer's experience, manpower, equipment or ability to perform the contract by an anticipated deadline as part of the award criteria. Such criteria can only be taken into account at selection stage (pre-qualification).

4.20 The ECJ affirmed the basic principle that there are two procedures and they are distinct and governed by different rules: the selection procedure, where qualitative selection criteria are to be evaluated on the basis of economic and financial standing and technical capacity; and the award procedure, where award criteria are limited to the lowest price or most economically advantageous tender. The evaluation of the most economically advantageous tender should exclude criteria linked to evaluating a tenderer's capacity to perform the contract.

4.21 To ensure compliance with the principle of equal treatment in the award of contracts, it is appropriate to lay down an obligation – established by case law – to ensure the necessary transparency to enable all tenderers to be reasonably informed of the criteria and arrangements which will be applied to identify the most economically advantageous tender. It is therefore the responsibility of contracting authorities to indicate the criteria for the award of the contract and the relative weightings given to each of those criteria in sufficient time for tenderers to be aware of them when preparing their tenders.

4.22 Contracting authorities may omit to indicate the weightings of the criteria for the award in duly justified cases for which they must be able to give reasons, where the weighting cannot be established in advance, in particular on account of the complexity of the contract. In such cases, they must indicate the descending order of importance in the criteria.

4.23 The contracting authority must specify in the contract notice or in the contract documents or, in the case of a competitive dialogue, in the descriptive document, the relative weighting which it gives to each of the criteria chosen to determine the most economically advantageous tender.

4.24 Where the contracting authorities choose to award a contract to the most economically advantageous tender, they shall assess the tenders to determine which one offers the best value for money. To do this, they shall determine the economic and quality criteria which, taken as a whole, must make it possible to determine the most economically advantageous tender for the contracting authority. The determination of these criteria depends on the object of the contract since they must allow the level of performance offered by each tender to be assessed in the light of the object of the contract, as defined in the technical specifications, and the value for money of each tender to be measured.

4.25 In the case of public service contracts, the award criteria should not affect the application of national provisions on the remuneration of certain services, such as, for example, the services performed by architects, engineers or lawyers.

4.26 There are restrictions on the use of post-tender negotiation under the open and restricted procedures. The European Commission has issued a statement on post-tender negotiations in which it specifically rules out any negotiation on price.

In open and restricted procedures all negotiations with candidates or tenderers on fundamental aspects of contracts, variations in which are likely to distort competition, and in particular on prices, shall be ruled out; however, discussions with candidates or tenderers may be held only for the purpose of clarifying or supplementing the content of their tenders or the requirements of the contracting authorities, and provided this does not involve discrimination.

Debriefing

4.27 The Regulations now contain a requirement to debrief prospective bidders, upon request, after any pre-qualification process. This will, of course, be on a more limited basis than the debriefing undertaken after the tendering process has concluded, and will focus on their general economic and financial standing and technical capability as required under the Regulations. This type of debrief is most commonly used under the restricted procedure which permits pre-qualification of prospective bidders.

4.28 It is important to understand the purpose of debriefing as it takes time and effort to conduct effectively. Therefore subject to EU procurement rules, public bodies need to consider the benefits in each particular case. Likely benefits include the following.

- Establishing a reputation as a fair, honest, 'open' and ethical client, Such a reputation encourages good suppliers and contractors to seek government business and submit tenders
- Offering unsuccessful tenderers some benefit from the time and money spent in preparing their tenders
- Assisting suppliers to improve their performance.

4.29 It is important for candidates and tenderers to understand either why they were not selected for the bid list, or why they failed to win the contract. This will help them to improve in future competitions. Effective debriefing will therefore promote better value for money in the longer term.

4.30 The requirement for public bodies to provide a debrief to unsuccessful bidders is now subject to a mandatory process termed the 'standstill period'. This is discussed in more detail later in this chapter.

5 Recent developments in public procurement

Framework agreements

5.1 New provisions have been added to take account of modern procurement methods and developments in best practice. These include specific provisions on **framework agreements, central purchasing bodies** (eg consortia purchasing), **dynamic purchasing systems** (eg electronic frameworks, electronic auctions), and **electronic auctions**.

5.2 The regulations define a framework agreement as follows.

A framework agreement is an agreement between one or more contracting authorities and one or more economic operators, the purpose of which is to establish the terms governing contracts to be awarded during a given period, in particular with regard to price and, where appropriate, the quantity envisaged.

5.3 Under the new provisions in the Regulations, when a contracting authority enters into a framework agreement in accordance with the Regulations, it may enter into contracts based on such a framework agreement during its term of validity by applying the terms set forth in the framework agreement or, if all terms have not been fixed in advance in the framework agreement, by reopening competition between the parties to the framework agreement in relation to those terms.

5.4 The reopening of competition should comply with certain rules, the aim of which is to guarantee the required flexibility and respect for the general principles, in particular the principle of equal treatment. For the same reasons, the term of the framework agreements should not exceed four years, except in cases duly justified by contracting authorities.

Central purchasing bodies

5.5 The Regulations define a central purchasing body as follows.

A central purchasing body is a contracting authority which acquires supplies and/or services intended for contracting authorities or awards public contracts or concludes framework agreements for works, supplies or services intended for contracting authorities.

5.6 Certain centralised purchasing techniques have been developed in most Member States. Under these arrangements various contracting authorities are responsible for making acquisitions for resale to other contracting authorities or for awarding public contracts/framework agreements for other contracting authorities to use. In view of the large volumes purchased, these techniques help to increase competition and streamline public purchasing.

5.7 Provisions are therefore included in the Regulations for a definition of central purchasing bodies dedicated to contracting authorities. A definition is also given of the conditions under which, in accordance with the principles of non-discrimination and equal treatment, contracting authorities purchasing works, supplies and/or services through a central purchasing body may be deemed to have complied with the Regulations.

Dynamic (electronic) purchasing systems

5.8 The Regulations define a dynamic purchasing system as follows.

A dynamic purchasing system is a completely electronic process for making commonly used purchases, the characteristics of which, as generally available on the market, meet the requirements of the contracting authority, which is limited in duration and open throughout its validity to any economic operator which satisfies the selection criteria and has submitted an indicative tender that complies with the specification.

5.9 In view of the rapid expansion of electronic purchasing systems, appropriate rules have now been introduced to enable contracting authorities to take full advantage of the possibilities afforded by these systems. Against this background, it is necessary to define a completely electronic dynamic purchasing system for commonly used purchases, and to lay down specific rules for setting up and operating such a system to ensure the fair treatment of any economic operator who wishes to take part therein.

5.10 Any economic operator who submits an indicative tender in accordance with the specification and meets the selection criteria should be allowed to join such a system. This purchasing technique allows the contracting authority, through the establishment of a list of tenderers already selected and the opportunity given to new tenderers to take part, to receive a particularly broad range of tenders as a result of the electronic facilities available, and hence to ensure the optimum use of public funds through broad competition. A dynamic purchasing system may not last for more than four years, except in duly justified exceptional cases.

Electronic auctions

5.11   The Regulations define an electronic auction as follows.

An electronic auction is a repetitive process involving an electronic device for the presentation of new prices, revised downwards, and/or new values concerning certain elements of tenders, which occurs after an initial full evaluation of the tenders, enabling them to be ranked using automatic evaluation methods.

5.12   Since the use of electronic auctions is likely to increase, such auctions are given a definition in the Regulations (shown above) and are governed by specific rules to ensure that they operate in full accordance with the principles of equal treatment, non-discrimination and transparency. To that end, provision is made for such electronic auctions to deal only with contracts for works, supplies or services for which the specifications can be determined with precision.

5.13   With the same objective, it must be also be possible to establish the respective ranking of the tenderers at any stage of the electronic auction. Recourse to electronic auctions enables contracting authorities to ask tenderers to submit new prices, revised downwards, and when the contract is awarded to the most economically advantageous tender, also to improve elements of the tender other than price.

5.14   However, to guarantee compliance with the principle of transparency, only the elements suitable for automatic evaluation by electronic means, without intervention by the contracting authority, may be improved. To this end, such elements must be quantifiable so that they can be expressed in figures or percentages.

The standstill period

5.15   In another major new change, the Regulations give effect to the European Court of Justice judgement in the **Alcatel** case, which decided that an unsuccessful tenderer should have a real chance of being awarded a contract if there have been procedural irregularities. The regulations provide for a 10 day 'stand still' period between contract award and execution, in order to allow for a legal challenge. The contracting authority must notify unsuccessful tenderers promptly, and provide a 'debrief' if requested. Should a challenge emerge, the contract will be suspended for court proceedings.

Competitive dialogue

5.16   A new procedure, the **competitive dialogue**, has been introduced to complement the existing open, restricted and negotiated procedures. It is intended to be used for large complex projects in circumstances where, currently, the use of the negotiated procedure might be considered. The Commission's view of the negotiated procedure (as a fallback in circumstances where other procedures are not workable) remains unchanged.

5.17   In the competitive dialogue (and with the negotiated procedure with contract notice), in view of the flexibility which may be required and the high level of costs associated with such methods of procurement, contracting authorities are entitled to make provision for the procedure to be conducted in successive stages to gradually reduce, on the basis of the previously indicated contract award criteria, the number of tenders which they will go on to discuss or negotiate. This reduction should, in so far as the number of appropriate solutions or candidates allows, ensure that there is a genuine competition.

Environmental and social considerations

5.18 Awareness of the need to take account of **environmental and social impacts** in the procurement process has grown substantially since the publication of the existing directives. The new directive makes explicit provision for sustainability issues. Areas affected are technical specifications, selection of tenderers and **award criteria**.

5.19 Contracts should be let on the basis of objective **award criteria** which ensure compliance with the principles of transparency, non discrimination and equal treatment and which guarantee that tenders are assessed in conditions of effective competition. As a result, it is appropriate to allow the application of two award criteria only: 'lowest price' and 'most economically advantageous tender'.

5.20 To guarantee equal treatment, the criteria for the award of the contract should enable tenders to be compared and assessed objectively. If these conditions are fulfilled, economic and qualitative criteria for the award of the contract, such as meeting environmental requirements, may enable the contracting authority to meet the needs of the public concerned, as expressed in the specifications of the contract.

5.21 Under the same conditions, a contracting authority may use criteria aiming to meet social requirements, or in response to particular needs as defined in the specifications of the contract, or relating to particularly disadvantaged groups of people to which those receiving/using the works, supplies or services which are the object of the contract belong.

5.22 Examples of procurement requirements where environmental and social issues might be considered are given below.

- Inclusion of recognised environmental and social performance standards and systems, eg Fairtrade or EMAS (the Eco-Management and Audit Scheme)

- Inclusion of any new or evolving legislation concerning environmental standards or social initiatives

- Taking account of stakeholders, including any environmental managers, potential suppliers and consultants who can advise on objectives, constraints and new initiatives that could be applicable to the procurement

- Requiring bidders, as part of their plans, to explain how they will comply with the environmental and social requirements. This might involve preparation of an environmental and/or social impact assessment by bidders of their proposed work

- The EU Eco label scheme assists consumers to identify products which are up to the standard of formally approved criteria, based on lifecycle environmental impact.

5.23 For procurements where the award criterion is the most economically advantageous tender, environmental and social factors may be incorporated as part of the award criteria that determine selection of the most advantageous tender.

Utilities Directive

5.24   Changes introduced by the new Utilities Directive (2004/17/EC) are much less extensive, mainly because arrangements such as framework agreements are addressed by the existing Utilities Directive and these have not changed. The Directive was implemented into UK law by virtue of the Public Utilities Regulations 2006 on 31 January 2006. New provisions concerning electronic auctions and dynamic purchasing systems are identical to those contained in the new Public Sector Directive, as are the provisions concerning sustainability issues. The financial threshold for Utilities is £313,694 for supplies and for services contracts, and £3,927,260 in respect of works contracts (all effective from 1 January 2010).

5.25   A competitive dialogue procedure has not been included in the Utilities Directive because utilities already have greater scope to make use of the negotiated procedure than is allowable under the Public Services Directive.

5.26   The major change which is unique to the Utilities Directive is the opportunity to take advantage of an exemption mechanism (Article 30). This enables removal of the need to comply with the directive for utility activity which is subject to competition in this sector in recent years.

Enforcement of the directives

5.27   On 12 November 2009, the UK Government adopted the Public Contracts (Amendment) Regulations 2009, which introduce important new remedies for breach of the EU public procurement rules. The most significant change is the introduction of a new remedy of **contract ineffectiveness**. To date, the general rule has been that, once a contract has been entered into, it cannot be set aside pursuant to a challenge under the procurement regulations. Under the new Regulations, which came into force on 20 December 2009, the High Court may declare ineffective a contract awarded without prior competition and, if it does so, must also impose a civil fine on the authority.

5.28   In the UK, before a contract is concluded, interested third parties who allege a breach may apply to the High Court for an order to set aside or suspend the contract award procedure in question. However, if the contract has already been entered into, the Regulations provide that the contract cannot be disturbed and the complainant's potential remedy is confined to financial damages (which can be hard to establish). This makes it difficult for interested parties to challenge a contract once it has been signed, even if that contract was awarded without any prior publicity or competition, in flagrant breach of the procurement Regulations. The problem was only partly addressed by the introduction of the so-called standstill period in 2006.

5.29   The new Regulations implement an EC directive which amends the Remedies Directives. They will maintain in force all of the existing remedies provisions described above. However, alongside the existing provisions, they add a new remedy under which a claimant may ask the High Court to declare a contract to be ineffective. A claim for contract ineffectiveness may be brought where a public authority:

   •   awards a contract directly to its preferred supplier, without prior publication of a contract notice in the *Official Journal of the European Union*, in circumstances where this omission was not permitted by a derogation; or

- enters into the contract after an action to suspend the award procedure has been lodged, or before expiry of the 10-day standstill period, in circumstances where the authority has also committed a breach of the substantive rules which affected the complainant's chances of obtaining the contract; or

- has breached the rules regarding call-offs under a framework agreement or dynamic purchasing system and has not allowed for the 10-day standstill period before concluding the called-off contract.

5.30 Any claim for a declaration of contract ineffectiveness must be brought within six months of the day following the conclusion of the contract. Where the awarding authority has published a contract award notice in the OJEU (after contract signature), or sent a standstill notice to the losing bidders, the deadline for any challenge is reduced to 30 calendar days from the notice in question, instead of the usual six months.

5.31 Where a declaration of ineffectiveness is made, the High Court must also order the contracting authority to pay a civil financial penalty (fine) in an amount to be decided by the Court in the case. The Regulations do not give any guidance figures or ranges for the amount of the fine. They simply state that the penalty must be 'effective, proportionate and dissuasive', taking into account the seriousness of the breach and the authority's conduct.

5.32 The new Regulations greatly raise the stakes regarding any breach of the procurement rules. They are bound to make public authorities and utilities, as well as their private sector developers, contractors, subcontractors and financiers, even more cautious regarding compliance with the procurement rules.

Chapter summary

- The legal status of a tender is an invitation to treat. The successful bid is an offer that can be, but need not necessarily be, accepted.

- A party that invites a tender is duty bound to consider all tenders submitted which meet the criteria laid down.

- Merely because one party submits a tender does not mean that the other party is duty bound to accept it.

- Letters of comfort are merely statements of fact concerning present intentions of a party. They are not contractual promises.

- EU directives make competitive tendering compulsory in the public sector.

- The two most important directives are the Public Sector Directive and the Utilities Directive. The Public Sector Directive replaces the former Public Works Directive, Public Supply Directive and Public Services Directive.

- These directives are designed to ensure that public bodies advertise for tenders as widely as possible.

Self-test questions

Numbers in brackets refer to the paragraphs above where your answers can be checked.

1 Why is the legal status of a tender important? (1.1)

2 What is meant by a collateral obligation? Give examples. (1.7ff)

3 What is referential bidding? (2.1)

4 What is a letter of comfort and what is its legal status? (3.1)

5 What is the effect of a letter of comfort? (3.3)

6 What is the principal objective of the EU procurement directives? (4.2)

7 List the four contract award procedures available under the EU directives. (4.6)

8 What were the two main findings in the Lianarkis case? (4.19)

9 What benefits may a contracting authority derive from debriefing? (4.28)

10 What is a dynamic purchasing system? (5.8)

11 Give examples of procurement requirements where environmental and social issues may be considered. (5.22)

12 Explain the remedy of 'contract ineffectiveness'. (5.27ff)

CHAPTER 19

Outsourcing and Redundancy

Learning objectives and indicative content

3.3   Analyse the main provisions of the Freedom of Information Act 2000 and explain how it affects the purchasing function.

- Publication scheme
- Right to request information
- Absolute exemptions
- Qualified exemptions
- Partial disclosure

3.4   Assess whether outsourcing a service or operation is compliant with legal requirements.

- TUPE
- Consultation
- Redundancy law
- Alternatives to redundancy

Chapter headings

1   Transfer of undertakings

2   Outsourcing of services and redundancy

3   Resolving employment disputes

4   The Freedom of Information Act 2000

Introduction

In this chapter we examine the situation where a business or an activity is outsourced, paying particular attention to the issue of potential redundancies. There is an extensive legal framework governing this area, including the so-called TUPE regulations, the Employment Act 1996 and the Trades Unions and Labour Relations (Consolidation) Act 1992.

Finally in this chapter we pick up the rather isolated topic of the Freedom of Information Act.

1   *Transfer of undertakings*

The TUPE regulations

1.1   A very popular approach to the need for specialisation and technological currency is to outsource. This involves 'buying in' the expertise of an outside body in replacement of an internal department. Often, this means that the outsourcing organisation has to make staff redundant, although sometimes they are transferred to the external body. Both redundancy and transfer have legal implications.

1.2   The Transfer of Undertakings (Protection of Employment) Regulations 2006 (referred to below as TUPE 2006) is the main piece of legislation governing the transfer of an undertaking, or part of one, to another. The Regulations are designed to protect the rights of employees in a transfer situation, enabling them to enjoy the same terms and conditions as formerly, with continuity of employment. TUPE 2006 entirely replaces the Transfer of Undertakings (Protection of Employment) Regulations 1981. The regulations were introduced to comply with relevant EC Directives concerning transfers of undertakings. In doing so, there have been various amendments to the UK regulations and a great deal of case law.

Transfer of undertakings

1.3   The Regulations apply to situations where an undertaking has a change of owner. This type of transfer is referred to as a 'business transfer' and it means that the staff are also transferred. The relevant issue here is that the staff will have their contracts of employment or service transferred to the new owner of the undertaking. The effect of this transfer under the Regulations is that the new owner of the undertaking must honour the existing terms and conditions of the workers' contracts. This will mean, in effect, that the workers will serve their new employer on the terms and conditions of employment that they enjoyed with their previous employer. In other words, the workers will have continuity of service.

1.4   Both outsourcing and insourcing are covered by TUPE 2006. These situations are described as 'service provision changes' and examples include contracts that provide services such as office cleaning, catering and security. The Regulations do not apply where the service provision is on a one-off basis of short-term duration.

1.5   As a broad guide TUPE has been found to apply to:

- mergers
- sales of businesses by sale of assets
- a change of licensee or franchisee
- the gift of a business through the execution of a will
- contracting out of services
- changing contractors
- bringing previously outsourced services 'in house'
- where all or part of a sole trader's business or partnership is sold or otherwise transferred.

1.6   However, TUPE does not usually apply to:

- transfers by share takeover

- transfers of assets only (for example, the sale of equipment alone would not be covered, but the sale of a going concern including equipment would be covered)

- transfers of a contract to provide goods or services where this does not involve the transfer of a business or part of a business

- the supply of goods for the client's use (for example, supplying food to a client to sell in its staff canteen, rather than a situation where the contractor runs the canteen for the client)

- transfers of undertakings situated outside the United Kingdom (although in some cases these may be covered if certain of the employer's staff are situated abroad).

1.7   Problems may arise in situations where employees are made redundant and they are hired by the new owner of the undertaking under new terms of employment. We shall look at redundancy later in this chapter.

1.8   It is essential to appreciate that the TUPE Regulations do not apply just to employees. They apply to workers generally – a much broader legal term. Potentially, casual workers could also be covered by the Regulations.

Relevant transfers

1.9   One of the first things to consider is whether the transfer falls into the category of a 'relevant transfer'. A 'relevant transfer' will involve situations where the ownership of the undertaking changes (eg where the undertaking is sold, or is the subject of a merger transaction or a change of contractor). If in doubt as to whether the Regulations apply to a given situation, the transferor (seller or incumbent contractor) should, to be on the safe side, assume that they do.

1.10   The ambiguities are well illustrated by the case of **Süzen v Zehnacker Gebäudereinigung** (1997). In this case, a school cleaning contract was awarded to a new external contractor, having previously been held by a different external contractor. This was held to be the transfer of an activity only, not an undertaking, which meant that the employees were not protected.

1.11   The law on relevant transfers in the case of contracting out and changes of contractors for labour intensive activities, such as security, catering, refuse collection and cleaning has given rise to confusion in the past. Many of these difficulties have been resolved by TUPE 2006. However TUPE 2006 applies in many situations where an organisation such as an advertising agency or a law firm takes over a client from another firm following a tender process. The new firm may be under an obligation to also take on the staff who were working on the client account for the previous firm. Case law on this issue is starting to emerge.

Consultation

1.12   The transferor (seller or incumbent contractor) has to initiate a consultation process with the affected workers. This consultation process should address the time of the transfer, reasons for the transfer and how it will be implemented. The process will involve the input of 'appropriate representatives' of the workers who, in the main, will be trade union officials, employee representatives or the workers themselves.

1.13   These consultations should take place ideally 28 days before the exchange of contracts, ie the acquisition of the undertaking or its disposal. However, there is no statutory period for consultation. Failure to consult affected employees or workers may mean that the seller could be liable to pay these individuals up to 13 weeks pay. The employee or worker does not have to demonstrate financial loss.

1.14   Special care should be taken to ensure that all employees or workers are consulted. This includes workers on maternity leave, sick leave and secondment. Failure to consult in such situations may invite liability under the Sex Discrimination Act 1975, the Disability Discrimination Act 1995 and other legislation designed to prevent discrimination.

Other provisions of TUPE 2006

1.15   Dismissals connected with the transfer can be justified only on economic, technical or organisational (ETO) grounds. If a dismissal cannot be justified on these grounds then it may be potentially unfair, leading to a damaging and costly claim for unfair dismissal. At all times, however, the transferor must ensure that it has acted fairly in relation to the dismissal. Any such dismissal should be accompanied by a compromise agreement. If a dismissal on ETO grounds immediately precedes the transfer of undertaking, any liability remains with the transferor: this is the rule in **Secretary of State v Spence** (1986).

1.16   If a TUPE transfer applies, all terms and conditions of work and continuity of employment should be preserved. This principle applies to all employees who were employed in the entity transferred immediately before the transfer; and those who would have been so employed if they had not been unfairly dismissed for a reason connected with the transfer.

1.17   There is a duty imposed upon the transferor to provide information, preferably in writing, to the transferee (the new employer/contractor) about the transferring employees before the relevant transfer takes place. This includes the following details.

   •   The identity and age of all the employees who will transfer; the information contained in their 'statements of employment particulars'

   •   Details of any disciplinary action or grievances in the previous two years

   •   Details of actual or potential legal actions brought by the employees in the previous two years.

1.18   The requirement is for the above information to be provided 'at least two weeks before the completion of the transfer'. The transferee can make a complaint to an Employment Tribunal if the transferor fails to provide this information and the Tribunal may award compensation for any loss which the transferee has incurred as a result of the failure by the transferor. The level of compensation must be no less than £500 per employee unless it is unjust to award this default minimum payment.

1.19   Provision of information to the transferee will have to take into account issues raised by the Data Protection Act 1998 or the Human Rights Act 1998. It is essential to obtain the consent of the individuals affected by any exchange of information between the transferor and transferee. Employees or workers have the right to object to the transfer in writing.

1.20   The Regulations contain special provisions which make it easier for insolvent businesses to be transferred to new employers. For instance, the provisions require that some of the transferor's pre-existing debts to employees do not pass to the transferee, such as statutory redundancy pay, arrears of pay, payment in lieu of notice and holiday pay.

1.21   The Regulations provide some freedom for the transferor or transferee to agree variations to contracts of employment before or after a transfer where the sole or principal reason for the variation is a reason unconnected with the transfer (eg the unexpected loss of a large order), or a reason connected with the transfer which is an 'economic, technical or organisational (ETO) reason entailing changes in the workforce'.

1.22   Strictly speaking, obligations relating to benefits for old age, invalidity or survivors in employees' occupational pension schemes do not transfer under TUPE. However, the provisions of the Pensions Act 2004 does apply to transfers taking place after 6 April 2005. In effect, this means that provisions equivalent to the TUPE regulations apply to pension rights from that date. In essence, if the previous employer provided a pension scheme then the new employer has to provide some form of pension arrangement for employees who were eligible for, or members, of the old employer's scheme. It will not have to be the same as the arrangement provided by the previous employer but will have to be of a certain minimum standard specified under the Pensions Act.

2 Outsourcing of services and redundancy

The Employment Rights Act 1996

2.1   In the previous section we considered the main provisions of the TUPE Regulations which cover the transfer of staff from one organisation to another and provide continuity of employment for the staff involved. There may well be situations where an organisation wishes to outsource without using existing staff. In such cases it must consider and comply with redundancy law. The existing employer will need to ensure that the cost of redeployment or redundancy of staff is included in the contract price.

2.2   Under the Employment Rights Act 1996 a person will be redundant, ie their dismissal will be taken to be by way of redundancy, if it was attributable wholly or mainly to the fact that:

- the employer has ceased or intends to cease to carry on the business for the purposes of which or in the place where the employee was employed, permanently or temporarily; or

- the requirements of that business for employees to carry out work of a particular kind, or in a place where they were so employed, have ceased or diminished or are expected to cease or diminish, permanently or temporarily.

2.3   Redundancy covered by the Employment Rights Act 1996 is usually termed 'compulsory redundancy'.

2.4   The selection of employees for redundancy must be undertaken in a fair, reasonable and consistent manner. It must also be based upon objective criteria. Many employers use a points system, whereby points are awarded according to, for example, length of service, skills and performance reviews. Points will be subtracted in cases of, for example, poor performance reviews.

2.5 In this context, the practice of 'bumping' gives rise to redundancy: **Safeway v Burrell** (1997). Bumping occurs when an individual's job may continue, but there is a reduction in the number of staff required to carry out that job, and that individual is made redundant. In this case the Employment Tribunal decided that the correct approach for determining what is a dismissal by reason of redundancy in terms of s139(1)(b) of the Employment Rights Act 1996 involves a three stage process.

- Was the employee dismissed?
- Has the work of the kind carried out by the employee ceased or diminished?
- Was the dismissal to cease or diminish the work of the kind carried out by the employee?

2.6 If the answer to all three questions above is yes, then the employee has been dismissed by reason of redundancy.

2.7 Some criteria for selecting employees for redundancy are considered to be automatically unfair. An employer cannot select an employee for redundancy in any of the following situations.

- Pregnancy, childbirth, maternity leave
- Employee representatives (eg trade union)
- Protected shop workers
- Trustees of an occupational pension scheme

2.8 In addition to the Employment Rights Act 1996, two more recent pieces of legislation affect redundancy law and the calculation of redundancy payments.

2.9 The Employment Act 2002 updates the law relating to statutory maternity pay and introduces provision for statutory rights to paternity and adoption leave and pay.

2.10 The Employment Equality (Age) Regulations 2006 provide protection against age discrimination in employment and education for people of all ages. The Regulations affect how redundancy payments are calculated. The employer must ensure that its redundancy policies do not directly or indirectly discriminate against older workers. An example of indirect discrimination might be if the employer selected only part-time workers for redundancy when a high proportion of these employees were over 50. The only exception is where the employer can objectively justify the age requirement.

2.11 In proceedings before a tribunal, an employee who has been dismissed by their employer is presumed to have been so dismissed by reason of redundancy, unless the contrary is proved: the employer can only rebut the presumption of redundancy by proving some other main reason for dismissal.

2.12 If the employer wishes to alter the terms on which the work is done, that is not a case of redundancy unless there is a fundamental change in the type of work which becomes the reason for the dismissal of the employee.

2.13 The place where a person is employed means in this context the place where they are habitually employed and any place where under their contract they can be required to work. There will not, therefore, be a redundancy situation where the transfer of location is reasonable or where the contract gives the employer an express or implied right to move the employee in question from one place to another. This is not the case, though, if the employer has no such right.

2.14 A redundant employee will be disqualified from receiving a redundancy payment if he unreasonably refuses an offer made by his employer before the end of the previous contract to renew his contract or to re-engage him on the same terms as before. In addition, if the employer makes an offer to renew the contract or to re-engage the employee but on terms which differ from the previous contract, the employee will lose his right to a redundancy payment if he unreasonably refuses the offer, provided that it constitutes an offer of suitable employment in relation to that employee.

2.15 Whether the alternative employment is suitable, or the offer was unreasonably refused, are both questions of fact to be determined by reference to such matters as the employee's skill and working conditions, the requirements of their family, change in earnings, age, health, sex, etc. Any dispute arising in this respect is for the tribunal to determine and the onus of proof is on the employer: **Taylor v Kent County Council** (1969).

T was headmaster of a school. The school was amalgamated with another school and a new head appointed to the combined school. T was offered employment in a pool of teachers, standing in for short periods in understaffed schools. He would retain his current salary.

Held: T was entitled to reject this offer and claim a redundancy payment: the new offer was substantially different, particularly in regard to status.

2.16 An employee who is dismissed by reason of misconduct has no right to a redundancy payment.

Redundancy payments

2.17 There are two categories of redundancy pay.

- Statutory redundancy pay, which is set down in law
- Contractual redundancy pay, which may be payable if the employer has a redundancy scheme in operation. This information will be set out in the contract of employment.

2.18 Statutory redundancy pay is the minimum amount that must be paid by the employer to the employee being made redundant. If the contractual statutory payment is less than the statutory amount, then the employer must still pay the statutory amount.

2.19 The amount of redundancy pay is calculated by reference to age, length of service and final remuneration. The employer must calculate the amount due and (except where the amount has been specified in a tribunal decision) must give to the employee a written statement indicating how the amount of payment has been calculated.

2.20 Statutory redundancy payments are calculated as follows.

- For each complete year of employment below the age of 22, half a week's pay
- For each complete year of employment between the age of 22 and 40, a full week's pay
- For each complete year of employment above the age of 41, one and a half week's pay
- The maximum statutory payment is based on 20 years' employment. The employment period runs up to the expiry of the employee's notice period. If no notice was served by the employer, it is taken as the date that the notice should have expired by law. The employee may also qualify for pay in lieu of notice in addition to the redundancy payment

2.21 Under the statutory scheme the calculation of redundancy pay is based upon continuous service with a maximum cap on weekly earnings of £350. The amount is reviewed annually by the government.

2.22 The basic award on redundancy will be set against the basic award for unfair dismissal or an 'unfair redundancy claim'. However, damages awarded for wrongful dismissal do not affect and are not affected by a redundancy payment. Wrongful dismissal should not be confused with unfair dismissal. Wrongful dismissal is based on contract law. Any claim for wrongful dismissal will therefore mean looking at the employee's employment contract to see if the employer has broken the contract.

2.23 There is no automatic right to a redundancy payment. The employer must pay a lump sum if all of the following conditions are satisfied.

- The employee is made redundant.
- The employee has at least two years' continuous service since the age of 18 years.
- The employee meets the other conditions set out in redundancy legislation.

2.24 There is no upper or lower age limit on the entitlement to statutory redundancy pay. The employer is required to pay the statutory minimum redundancy payment to employees who are under 18 and also to those who are over 65 (or after the employee's normal retirement age if this is lower).

3 Resolving employment disputes

3.1 Until recently, all employers have had to comply with legally binding procedures known as the Dispute Resolution Regulations (2004), brought in under the Employment Act 2002. They were introduced to set minimum fair standards for the conduct of internal disciplinary, dismissal and grievance procedures in the workplace.

3.2 The aim was to encourage more informal resolution of workplace disputes and reduce the number of claims being taken to Employment Tribunals. The procedures imposed new legal obligations on both employers and employees. A three-step procedure had to be followed.

- Put disciplinary allegations or grievances in writing.
- Hold a meeting to discuss.
- Give a right of appeal against the decision.

3.3 In addition, there were other obligations during the process for both the employer and employee.

3.4 The Regulations were repealed from 6 April 2009, but much remains the same on the basic procedures. The three-step process mentioned above is still a required bare minimum plus appropriate investigation at the start, but there are a number of very important changes.

3.5 Employers must now comply with the Advisory, Conciliation and Arbitration Service (ACAS) *Code of Practice 2009* and the ACAS *Guide on Discipline and Grievances At Work*. Breach of the *Guide* alone does not lead to sanctions but unreasonable breach of the *Code* does. These have been developed as a result of measures contained within the Employment Act 2008.

3.6   The Code's language and emphasis are noteworthy: employers are told they 'should', not that they 'must', or 'will' do something. This indicates a major change in approach. Now it is only an unreasonable failure to comply which may lead to penalties being imposed in a Tribunal. Employers will now have the chance to explain non-compliance and the Tribunal must take the size and resources of an employer into account when deciding relevant cases.

3.7   The new core principles are as follows.

- Prompt action, no unreasonable delay
- Consistency
- Appropriate investigations
- Provide information on the problem and an opportunity for the employee to respond
- The right for the employee to be accompanied at any formal meeting
- The opportunity to appeal

3.8   Where there are economic, technical or organisational (ETO) reasons for the dismissal of an employee, the dismissal will be deemed to be fair. If there are no ETO reasons, the dismissal will be treated as unfair. The onus is on the employer to show that the dismissal falls within the ETO criteria. If the dismissal occurred for reason of redundancy then the usual redundancy arrangements will apply.

Constructive dismissal

3.9   A constructive dismissal occurs where an employee terminates his employment in response to his employer's treatment. Although there has been no actual dismissal, the treatment is sufficiently bad that the employee is entitled to regard himself as having been dismissed.

3.10   Constructive dismissal is a form of unfair dismissal. It entails the termination of employment by an employee in response to a fundamental breach of contract by the employer. It occurs when an employee resigns because of an action by an employer. That action must makes the employee believe that continuation of employment is impossible. That is, the employee leaves his job because of the employer's behaviour. When this happens the employee's resignation is treated as an actual dismissal by the employer, so the employee can claim unfair dismissal.

3.11   The components of constructive dismissal are as follows.

- The employer committed a serious breach of contract.
- The employee did not accept the breach.
- The employee felt forced to resign because of that breach.

3.12   The breach of contract can result from either a single serious event or the last in a series of less serious events.

3.13   A constructive dismissal is not necessarily an unfair one – an employee still needs to go on and prove that the dismissal was unfair – but in practical terms, once a breach of contract by the employer is established, it is difficult to show that the dismissal was in fact fair.

Employment tribunals

3.14 An Employment Tribunal is a judicial body designed to determine arguments between employees and employers over rights. Both employees and employers may submit claims through the Tribunal. The claim must be made within three months of the date when their employment ended. The Tribunal can extend this period if it considers that it was not reasonably practicable for the complaint to be made within the usual time limit. The limit may also be extended where an employee wishes to claim a redundancy payment. In this case, the employee must claim within six months of the dismissal.

3.15 The complaints that Employment Tribunals deal with include the following.

- Unfair dismissal (including 'constructive dismissal')
- Discrimination on the grounds of disability, race, sex, age, sexual orientation, religion or belief
- Not being allowed to have someone accompany you to a disciplinary or grievance hearing;
- Not being consulted in a redundancy situation
- Breach of contract

The employer's duty to consult

3.16 Where the employer is proposing to dismiss any employee as redundant and there is a recognised trade union the employer must consult representatives of the union about the dismissal. The procedures for handling redundancies originate under EC directive 75/129. These procedures were brought into UK law by virtue of the Trades Union and Labour Relations (Consolidation) Act 1992 (TULRA) (as amended). TULRA places a duty upon the employer to consult with representatives of the affected employees. This may include recognised trade unions or elected representatives.

3.17 The consultation must include such matters as the following.

- Reasons for the proposed redundancies
- Number of employees involved
- Proposed methods of selecting those to be made redundant
- Timing of the dismissals
- Ways of avoiding redundancy (eg offers of alternative employment)

3.18 The employer must consult with the union at the earliest opportunity and, in any event:

- at least 90 days before the first of the dismissals take effect if there are to be 100 or more redundancies within a period of 90 days or less;
- at least 30 days before the first of the dismissals take effect if there are to be 20– 99 redundancies within a period of 30 days or less.

3.19 If the employer fails to consult, the trade union may complain to the Employment Tribunal which may make a protective award to the redundant employees. A protective award is a sum of money calculated in accordance with a statutory formula.

3.20 Consultation does not mean negotiation, and the unions and other representatives have no rights to insist on negotiation over the numbers of employees that are to be made redundant or the selection process.

Employer's duty to notify

3.21   Where the employer is proposing to dismiss as redundant ten or more employees it must notify the Secretary of State. The notice must include such matters as the following.

- Numbers to be made redundant
- Proposed date(s) of the dismissals
- Identification of any trade union with which consultation is necessary

3.22   The employer must notify the Secretary of State:

- at least 90 days before the first of the dismissals take effect if there are to be 100 or more redundancies within a period of 90 days or less
- at least 30 days before the first of the dismissals take effect if there are to be 20–99 redundancies within a period of 30 days or less.

3.23   The period of notice must commence as soon as possible and consultation by the employer with the parties must take place within this period. The period runs from the date on which notice was given by the employer to the Secretary of State until the effective date of dismissal.

3.24   For all redundancies covered by the Employment Rights Act 1996, the employer has a duty to disclose certain information to the affected employee. If notice is not given to any employee being made redundant, then the employee is entitled to a protective award representing the notice they should have been given. This is in addition to any compensation award made by the employment tribunal for possible unfair dismissal.

Voluntary redundancy

3.25   In many organisations there are formalised procedures for voluntary redundancy, often with employees being asked to volunteer even though another (often cheaper) person will be taken on to do the job. In fact this is not redundancy at all, although it may come about because the employee's role is now redundant. Instead, it is a procedure whereby the employer asks the employee to agree, in return for severance pay, to being dismissed. The employee neither resigns nor is made redundant, and so the rules on compulsory redundancy outlined above need not be complied with.

Alternatives to redundancy

3.26   Redundancies cost time, money, face and morale. According to the Chartered Institute of Personnel and Development (CIPD), an average redundancy costs £10,000. In addition to this real cost is the time and resource required to pursue a redundancy, the resulting impact on operations and staff morale, and the potential cost of re-recruiting should the business situation improve.

3.27   Redundancy by an employer should always be a last resort after other potential avenues have been explored. We will now consider some of the options that an organisation might consider as alternatives to redundancy. There are advantages and disadvantages to all these measures, and they will need to be considered by an organisation in the context of the issues being faced at the time.

3.28 A **recruitment freeze** forces business functions to re-train and re-recruit existing employees into new job roles. This approach could be impractical for some skilled roles and is likely to require significant training. Even so, a recruitment freeze could serve to limit financial difficulties.

3.29 **Capping overtime expenditure** is a simple measure which could minimise labour costs but may also limit productivity.

3.30 **Pay cuts** may be sensitive to manage but could nevertheless be less damaging than redundancy.

3.31 **Natural wastage** is effective when reductions are needed across the workforce over a prolonged period. Such an approach takes time and areas of wastage may not match areas of redundancy, leading to a requirement to re-train employees into new roles.

3.32 **Unpaid sabbaticals** could save money in the short to medium term and offer willing employees the chance to take a career break. The complexities of covering a departing employee will depend on the job role.

3.33 **Loaning an employee** may be possible, either to a different part of an organisation, or to a completely different organisation, for a period of time usually up to 12 months. If handled strategically such an approach could coincide with cross-training to help fill organisational or individual skills gaps.

3.34 Some employees may be looking to move on, and thus react positively to an invitation to take **voluntary redundancy**. This could also help to minimise the negative effects of compulsory redundancy.

3.35 **Identifying alternative job roles** which could add value and revenue to a business could help to re-task potentially redundant employees into new roles of higher strategic worth to the business. The employee can, of course, choose not to accept any alternative offer. If the employee unreasonably refuses the offer then the employer may avoid paying that employee a redundancy settlement. The refusal by an employee is considered from the employee's point of view. The job offered may be identical to the current job or may be one where similar skills are required. The job must have similar pay. conditions and skills requirements.

3.36 The alternative offer must be made by the employer before the current job terminates and the commencement date for the new job must be within four weeks of the termination of the previous job. The first four weeks in the new job are on a trial basis and the employee can still leave and claim dismissal on grounds of redundancy and redundancy pay. If retraining is required then the trial period can be extended by written agreement to consider the retraining requirements.

3.37 If the organisation operates across multiple locations a potentially redundant employee could be asked to **move to a location which is understaffed**.

3.38 Employees could be invited to take **early retirement**. Caution must be exercised by the employer to ensure compliance with discrimination laws.

3.39 **Revised working arrangements,** such as a shorter working day or three-day week, could offer flexibility to employees in suitable job roles and help to trim costs.

3.40 Though not suitable for all individuals or job roles, those looking for a significant cut in hours could agree to **share a job role**.

3.41 Depending on employment terms, some casual or contract workers may become candidates for dismissal before redundancies are considered.

3.42 If redundancy is solely a financial consideration, and such a move could harm the operational capacity of the organisation, the most viable alternative to redundancy could be to raise finance to keep employees. If the employer can demonstrate how keeping an employee will provide a greater return than losing one, lenders may reconsider financing.

4 *The Freedom of Information Act 2000*

4.1 For the first time in the UK, the Freedom of Information (FOI) Act 2000 gives the public extensive rights of access to information held by public authorities.

4.2 The Act, which came into force on 1 January 2005, gives any individual, company or organisation the right to request recorded information held by a public authority (provided it is not covered by one of 23 exemptions). All types of information are covered: contracts, letters, faxes, e-mail and even scribbles in the margin.

4.3 The Act covers local authorities, government departments, NHS trusts, educational institutions, police authorities, and companies owned by a public authority. The appropriate Secretary of State has power to extend the act to bodies exercising functions of a public nature, which could potentially include suppliers that provide goods or services on behalf of a public authority.

4.4 On receipt of a request, the public authority must confirm or deny whether it holds the information and then make a disclosure. This must usually be completed within 20 working days of receipt of the request.

4.5 Regulations issued under the Act set rules as to when the public authority can charge a fee for responding, but the intention is that most requests will be free of charge.

4.6 The exemptions, divided into 'absolute' and 'qualified' exemptions, will ensure that sensitive information remains confidential. With an absolute exemption, the public authority need not confirm or deny that it holds the information nor make a disclosure. With a qualified exemption, disclosure must only be made if this is in the 'public interest'.

4.7 Although the act does not define it, the Commissioner's definition of the public interest is 'something that serves the interests of the public. When applying the test, the public authority is simply deciding whether it serves the interests of the public better in each case to withhold or disclose information'.

4.8 The exemptions likely to be relevant for suppliers include the confidence exemption (an absolute exemption) and the commercial interests exemption (a qualified exemption).

4.9 The confidence exemption will apply where a supplier provides information to a public authority in confidence and disclosure of the information would give the supplier an 'actionable breach' against the authority. The information must be confidential, so not in the public domain and of some value.

4.10   The commercial interests exemption will apply where a supplier provides information whose disclosure would be prejudicial to the supplier's or another's commercial interests.

4.11   Public authorities cannot 'contract out' of FOI: confidentiality clauses are acceptable only where they can be justified. Public authorities can, however, agree with suppliers that certain information is commercially sensitive and therefore likely to be exempt.

4.12   Suppliers that tender to public authorities should be aware that all information submitted as part of a tender is potentially subject to disclosure. They should carefully consider what to disclose and identify commercially sensitive information.

4.13   In order to protect their interests, suppliers should agree a list of potentially exempt information to attach as a schedule to the contract. This is likely to cover pricing, financial information about the supplier and innovative or original processes or products.

4.14   Contracts should also require public authorities to notify suppliers of information requests. Suppliers will then have the opportunity to make a submission if they are concerned that commercially sensitive information might be disclosed.

4.15   Every public authority must adopt a publication scheme setting out the kinds of information that the authority will make routinely available. The information should be easy to access for both the authority and any individual. Public authorities must adopt a scheme approved by the Information Commissioner and will normally adopt the model scheme published by the Information Commissioner's Office (ICO).

Chapter summary

- The Transfer of Undertakings (Protection of Employment) Regulations 2006 apply to situations where an undertaking undergoes a change of ownership.

- TUPE Regulations do not just apply to employees but rather to workers in general.

- Transfer of undertakings can be fraught with problems. This is because they can potentially involve redundancy situations.

- The TUPE Regulations apply only to 'relevant transfers'.

- There should be a proper consultation process with 'appropriate representatives' of the individuals concerned.

- Failure to consult affected employees or workers may mean that the seller could be liable to pay these individuals up to 13 weeks' pay. The employee or worker does not have to demonstrate financial loss.

- Employees made redundant have a claim for redundancy pay.

- An employer imposing redundancies must follow legal regulations in relation to selection criteria and consultation.

- In the last resort, disputes over employment issues, including redundancy, may have to be resolved by Employment Tribunals.

- Employers should explore all possible alternatives before imposing redundancies.

- The Freedom of Information (FOI) Act 2000 gives the public extensive rights of access to information held by public authorities, including commercial matters.

Self-test questions

Numbers in brackets refer to the paragraphs above where your answers can be checked.

1   In what situations do the TUPE Regulations apply? (1.3–1.6)

2   What is a 'relevant transfer'? (1.9)

3   Obligations for pension benefits are covered by the TUPE Regulations. True or false? (1.22)

4   How is redundancy defined in the Employment Rights Act 1996? (2.2)

5   List criteria that are automatically unfair in selection for redundancy. (2.7)

6   What are the two categories of redundancy pay? (2.17)

7   What are the three steps that must be followed to resolve an employment dispute? (3.2)

8   What is meant by constructive dismissal? (3.9ff)

9   Outline the employer's duty to consult in relation to proposed redundancies. (3.16ff)

10   List alternatives to redundancy. (3.26ff)

11   What rights are given to members of the public by the Freedom of Information Act? (4.2)

CHAPTER 20

The Law Relating to Competition

Learning objectives and indicative content

3.5   Analyse and explain the circumstances when anti-competitive behaviour and abuse of a dominant market position can be a breach of legal requirements in the UK and EU.

- • Competition Act 1998
- • Article 81 EC Treaty
- • Article 82 EC Treaty
- • Enterprise Act 2002

Chapter headings

1   UK competition law

2   EU rules on free competition

Introduction

Free competition between commercial enterprises is an important element in a market economy such as that of the UK and most developed nations. Governments attempt to foster such competition by means of legislation which restricts any attempt to limit competition.

Competition may be stifled if companies enter into arrangements which deliberately or incidentally keep prices high, restrict entry into the market etc. Equally, competition may be damaged if one company, or a small number of companies, enjoy a dominant position in a particular market. Both of these situations – the use of restrictive trade practices and the abuse of a monopoly position – are tackled in UK law, which has recently come very much into line with EC law, although there are still differences.

The law relating to restrictive trade practices, monopolies and mergers recently underwent radical revision in the form of the Competition Act 1998. This Act replaces the Restrictive Trade Practices Act 1976, the Resale Prices Act 1976, and the majority of the Competition Act 1980. The Restrictive Practices Court is to be run down.

However, transitional arrangements will apply for some time for agreements registered under the Restrictive Trade Practices Act 1976 so that an outline knowledge of the 1976 Act, as described in this chapter, will still be required.

The Enterprise Act 2002 adds further reforms to competition law, and consumer protection.

1   UK competition law

Introduction

1.1   In general terms, the Competition Act 1998 outlaws any agreements, business practices and conduct which have a damaging effect on competition in the UK.

1.2   More specifically, the Act prohibits:

*   those agreements between undertakings, decisions by associations of undertakings (such as trade associations), and concerted practices which prevent, restrict or distort competition, or are intended to do so, and which may affect trade within the UK. This is known as the Chapter 1 prohibition.

*   the abuse by one or more undertakings of a dominant position in a market which may affect trade within the UK. This is known as the Chapter 2 prohibition.

1.3   Under the Act, the UK regulatory authorities have powers to investigate undertakings believed to be involved in anti-competitive activities and to impose financial penalties where appropriate. Third parties may be able to claim for damages in the courts.

1.4   The Act is modelled on European competition law, set out in Articles 81 and 82 of the EC Treaty, under which the European Commission examines agreements, business practices and conduct which may affect trade between member states of the European Union. The UK authorities must deal with cases under the Act in a way that ensures consistency with European law.

1.5   The main responsibility for administering the Act lies with the Director General of Fair Trading supported by the Office of Fair Trading (OFT), although the regulators for electricity, gas, water, telecommunications, and railways have responsibility for the cases in the sector they regulate.

Chapter 1 prohibition

1.6   The Chapter 1 prohibition applies to both informal and formal arrangements (that is, agreements, decisions, or practices), whether or not they are set out in writing. So an informal understanding where Companies A and B agree to match the prices of Company C will be caught in the same way as a formal agreement between competitors to set prices.

1.7   Although many different types of arrangements may be caught by the prohibition, the Act lists specific examples to which the prohibition is applicable. These include:

*   agreeing to fix purchase or selling prices or other trading conditions;
*   agreeing to limit or control production, markets, technical development or investment;
*   agreeing to share markets or supply sources;
*   agreeing to apply different trading conditions to equivalent transactions, thereby placing some parties at a competitive disadvantage;
*   agreeing to make contracts subject to unrelated conditions.

1.8   Those agreements that do not have any appreciable effect on competition will not be caught by the prohibition.

1.9   The guideline on Chapter 1 sets out how this will be determined. Although there will be circumstances in which this is not the case, an agreement is unlikely to be considered as having an appreciable effect where the combined market share of the parties involved does not exceed 25 per cent. However, agreements to fix prices, impose minimum resale prices or share markets will generally be seen as capable of having an appreciable effect even where the parties' combined market share falls below 25 per cent. This applies also where an agreement is one of a network of similar agreements that have a cumulative effect on the market in question.

Cases brought under the Competition Act

1.10   Among many cases brought under the Competition Act 1988, you may like to note the following examples.

1.11   **Hasbro UK Ltd/Argos Ltd/Littlewoods Ltd** (December 2003). The OFT concluded that Hasbro (one of the largest toy and games suppliers in the UK), Argos and Littlewoods had entered into price-fixing agreements that infringed Section 2 (the Chapter 1 prohibition) of the Competition Act. The companies entered into an overall agreement and/or concerted practice to fix the price of certain Hasbro toys and games from 199 to 2001. The OFT took the view that these agreements may have affected trade within the UK and had, as their object and effect, the prevention, restriction or distortion of competition in the supply of the toys and games in the UK.

Hasbro was granted 100% leniency for co-operating fully with the (then) Director General of Fair Trading, but Argos and Littlewoods suffered financial penalties (a decision upheld by the Competition Appeal Tribunal in 2004).

1.12   The **'duplicate kit cartel'** (August 2003). The OFT found that a group of ten undertakings had entered price-fixing agreements in breach of Chapter 1 in relation to the sale of replica football kit around the time of the Euro 2000 Championship.

- The Competition Appeal Tribunal subsequently rejected appeals by two of the undertakings, finding evidence that the largest sportswear retailers JJB Sports plc and Allsports Ltd had both complained to the manufacturer Umbro in relation to proposed discounting of England replica kit by a third retailer (Sports Soccer), which eventually agreed not to discount on the understanding that JJB and Allsports would not do so either. This amounted to an agreement or concerted practice under the Chapter 1 prohibition.

- The CAT held that where competitors meet face to face and the issue of pricing is raised, it is sufficient for one participant at the meeting to reveal its pricing intentions to the other parties for a concerted practice to exist, whether or not the other parties reciprocate. To rebut this presumption, a party present at the meeting would have to withdraw immediately, informing the other parties (with written evidence) that it will no longer participate in the discussions.

- The CAT also held that if information about pricing is transmitted through an intermediary (in this case, the supplier), the indirect contact still amounts to concerted practice, where the information is used to influence market conditions (as in this case, by placing pressure on another competitor to limit its competitive activities). Disclosure of pricing information is only acceptable in the form of historical information, and for legitimate purposes not related to competition.

Chapter 1 exemptions

1.13 An arrangement which would otherwise fall within the scope of the prohibition may be exempted if it satisfies certain criteria. There are three types of exemption.

- **Individual exemption**. This may be granted for individual arrangement and must be applied for.

- **Block exemption**. This applies automatically to certain categories of arrangement.

- **Parallel exemptions**. These apply where an agreement is covered by an EC individual or block exemption under Article 81(3) of the EC Treaty, or would be covered by an EC block exemption if the agreement had an effect on trade between member states of the EU.

1.14 Agreements falling under the Chapter 1 prohibition are more frequent than those falling under the Chapter 2 prohibition.

Chapter 2 prohibition

1.15 The Chapter 2 prohibition covers the abuse by one or more undertakings of a dominant position in a market. There is a two-stage test to this prohibition: first, the undertakings must be in a dominant position, which will be largely determined by the extent to which they can act independently of their competitors and customers; and, second, they must be abusing that position.

1.16 In determining whether or not an undertaking is in a dominant position, the OFT will look first at its market share. Although it will vary from case to case, as a general rule an undertaking is unlikely to be considered dominant if it has a market share of less than 40 per cent. But this does not exclude the possibility that an undertaking with a lower market share may be considered dominant if, for example, the structure of the market enables it to act independently of its competitors. In looking at market structure the OFT will consider the number and size of existing competitors as well as the potential for new competitors to enter the market.

1.17 The Act gives examples of specific types of conduct that are particularly likely to be considered as abuse of a dominant position. These include:

- imposing unfair purchase or selling prices.

- limiting production, markets or technical development to the prejudice of consumers.

- applying different trading conditions to equivalent transactions, thereby placing certain parties at a competitive disadvantage.

- attaching unrelated supplementary conditions to contracts.

Exclusions

1.18 Certain categories of agreement and conduct are specifically excluded from the scope of the Act. They include agreements covered by a direction under section 21 (2) of the Restrictive Trade Practices Act 1976, and agreements and conduct that give rise to merger situations under the merger provisions of the Fair Trading Act 1973.

1.19 It is intended that most 'vertical' agreements (those between undertakings at different levels of the supply chain) will receive special treatment under the Act so that the Chapter 1 prohibition will not apply. This treatment will not apply to vertical agreements to fix prices. The Chapter 1 prohibition is more likely to apply to 'horizontal' agreements (those at the same level in a supply market – eg cartels).

Consequences of infringement

Enforcement

1.20 Where an undertaking is found to have breached either prohibition, the Director General may order it to terminate or amend the offending agreement or cease the offending conduct.

1.21 Further, the Director General has the power to order interim measures which require an undertaking to refrain from engaging in suspected illegal activity while he investigates the matter. But he will exercise this power only when he considers it necessary to take urgent action to protect third parties from suffering serious, irreparable damage, or to protect the wider public interest.

1.22 The Competition Commission was set up under the Competition Act 1998 to investigate breaches of the prohibitions. It also hears appeals against decisions made by the OFT. The Competition Commission replaced the body previously responsible for this area of regulation: the Monopolies and Mergers Commission or MMC. You may occasionally come across references to the earlier body.

Financial penalties

1.23 Undertakings found to have infringed either prohibition may be liable to a financial penalty of up to 10 per cent of their turnover in the UK.

1.24 Undertakings of a size below certain thresholds will be immune from financial penalties unless they are involved in price fixing. The immunity can be withdrawn in certain circumstances and does not prevent third parties from making a claim for damages.

1.25 Those parts of any agreement which are found to infringe the Chapter 1 prohibition are null and void and therefore cannot be enforced. In addition, third parties who consider they have been harmed as a result of any unlawful practice or conduct may have a claim for damages in the courts.

The Fair Trading Act 1973

1.26 The FTA 1973 gives wide powers to the Office of Fair Trading to regulate monopolies and mergers. A monopoly is defined as a situation where one company, or a group of companies acting together (a cartel), supplies or purchases 25 per cent or more of all the goods or services of a particular type in the UK, or in a part of the UK.

1.27 Note that a monopolist may be either a seller or a buyer under this definition. Either has power, potentially, to dictate the price or quality of goods on the market.

1.28 If the OFT finds evidence indicating that such a position may exist it may seek assurances from the company or companies that they will alter their business practices. Alternatively, it may refer the matter to the Competition Commission. Once it has investigated a report is submitted to the Secretary of State with recommendations for action. The Secretary of State may then directly or through the OFT take the appropriate remedial action.

1.29 The OFT also exercises some control over mergers. Under the Enterprise Act 2002, a merger is liable to investigation if the turnover of the company to be taken over exceeds a defined monetary amount, or if the merger will result in a monopoly situation. If the OFT concludes that a merger will result in a substantial lessening of competition it can advise the Secretary of State to refer the case to the Competition Commission for more detailed investigation.

1.30 Notice that there is nothing automatically undesirable about a monopoly or merger. Each situation must be examined in the light of public interest, and only if that is endangered will action be necessary. When evaluating this point the Competition Commission must consider all relevant factors, including the maintenance and promotion of effective competition, promoting the interests of consumers with regard to price and quality, reducing costs, developing new techniques and products, maintaining and promoting a balanced distribution of industry and employment, and maintaining and promoting competitive activity by UK businesses in export markets.

1.31 Notice also the possibility of a 'local monopoly'. The 25 per cent rule may apply to a geographical area within the UK, rather than to the whole of the UK. For example, in the case of **South Yorkshire Transport Ltd v MMC** (1993) it was held that this rule was applicable to the merger of certain bus companies which would have enjoyed a local monopoly, even though their share of the total UK market would have been tiny.

1.32 Provisions contained in the Competition Act 1998 have become the main enforcement powers in this area of the law, although the Fair Trading Act, as amended, remains in force.

1.33 As well as consumer protection measures, which we saw in an earlier chapter, the Enterprise Act 2002 also affects competition law.

- It allows a maximum penalty of five years' imprisonment for individuals dishonestly operating 'hardcore cartels'.

- It gives the OFT power to ask the courts to disqualify directors from acting as company directors for up to five years, for competition offences.

- It sets up a Competition Appeals Tribunal to hear cases brought by third parties alleging that companies have infringed competition law.

- It allows consumer bodies to bring to the OFT 'supercomplaints' about markets that are not working well for consumers.

2   EU rules on free competition

Article 81 of the EC Treaty (restrictive agreements)

2.1   Under Articles 81 and 82 of the EC Treaty all agreements which operate to prevent or restrict competition in the European Union are void. In very broad terms Article 81 addresses anti-competitive agreements affecting trade between member states in the EU market, while Article 82 deals with the abuse of dominant position affecting trade between member states in the EU market: the division that we have seen in Section 1 of this chapter with regard to UK law in the UK market.

2.2   Article 81 of the EC Treaty and the regulations made under it prohibit various agreements which might impede free competition in manufactured goods in the EC area. Such agreements might cover price fixing, restrictions on production and market sharing. Despite the general prohibition, exemptions may be granted in relation to individual agreements as well as block exemptions in relation to certain categories of agreement. The effects of such agreements must be assessed in the context in which they occur. Thus, where an agreement may combine with other agreements to have a cumulative effect on competition, it may be invalid: **Brasserie de Haecht v Wilkin** (1967).

2.3   An agreement covered by Article 81 is prohibited and automatically void. Such agreements might include any or all of the following.

- Directly or indirectly fixing buying or selling prices, or other trading conditions

- Limiting or controlling production, markets, technical developments or investment

- Sharing markets or sources of supply

- Applying dissimilar conditions to equivalent transactions with other trading parties, thereby placing them at a competitive disadvantage

- Making the conclusion of contracts subject to acceptance by the other parties of supplementary obligations which, by their nature or according to commercial usage, have no connection with the subject of such contracts

2.4   Article 81 is concerned with agreements which may have the effect of restricting competition. It follows that action may be taken to avoid any abuse occurring: it is not necessary to wait until it has actually occurred.

2.5   Article 81 is concerned with agreements that affect trade between member states. An agreement that affects trade in one member state, but has no impact elsewhere, is subject to national legislation and is not caught by Article 81: **Hugin Kassregister v Commission** (1979) (a case which concerned the supply of spare parts for cash registers in the London area only, where Article 81 was held not to apply, but which would now be caught by the Chapter 1 prohibition of the Competition Act 1998, which regulates the UK market).

Article 82 of the EC Treaty (abuse of monopoly position)

2.6   This article prohibits the abuse of a monopoly position by an organisation within the European Union. Abuses might include any or all of the following.

-    Directly or indirectly imposing unfair buying or selling prices, or other unfair trading conditions

-    Limiting production, markets or technical development to the prejudice of consumers

-    Applying dissimilar conditions to equivalent transactions with other trading parties, thereby placing them at a competitive disadvantage

-    Making the conclusion of contracts subject to acceptance by the other parties of supplementary obligations which, by their nature or according to commercial usage, have no connection with the subject of such contracts

2.7   Article 82 does not attempt to define a monopoly position in terms of a percentage market share. Instead, it considers the relative economic strength of the companies concerned. It is founded on the view that what matters is ability to act without taking account of competitors' actions, and the percentage market share needed to do this will vary from one situation to another. In the case of **United Brands v Commission** (1978) it was held that a dominant position was 'a position of economic strength enjoyed by an undertaking which enables it to prevent effective competition being maintained in the relevant market by giving it the power to behave to an appreciable extent independently of its competitors, customers and ultimately of its consumers'.

Mergers

2.8   Mergers are regulated by EC law just as they are under UK legislation. A merger will come within the ambit of the Merger Control Regulation if the aggregate worldwide turnover of the merged companies exceeds a defined threshold, and at least two of the parties have an EU turnover in excess of a defined threshold, unless each of the companies makes more than two thirds of its turnover in the same member state. In this last situation, the law of the relevant member state will apply.

2.9   Mergers caught by these provisions must be notified to the European Commission. If the Commission concludes that the merger will significantly impede effective competition in the whole or part of the European Union, the merger will be blocked. The Commission has the power to require any infringement to be remedied, and to impose financial penalties.

A note on WTO

2.10   The WTO is the organisation that replaced GATT (the General Agreement on Tariffs and Trade) in 1995. GATT was founded in 1948 and originally consisted of 23 nations. The objectives it sought to achieve were:

-    to eliminate quota restrictions in international trade
-    to reduce tariffs as a barrier to international trade
-    to remove restrictive non-tariff barriers to international trade
-    to ensure that measures applied to one country are applied to all
-    to ensure that any remaining protective measures are transparent to all.

2.11   Exhaustive negotiations over the years eventually brought significant progress towards these objectives.

2.12   Though the objectives of WTO are widely commended, a criticism of the body is that no enforcement powers exist, and everything depends on consensus between the member states.

Chapter summary

- Competition may be restricted or distorted by abuse of a dominant position or by the use of anti-competitive agreements. These situations are regulated by UK legislation (Competition Act 1998) and EC legislation (Articles 81 and 82), in the UK market and in trade between EU member states respectively.

- The Competition Act 1998 has two prohibitions affecting UK trades: prohibition of anti-competitive agreements (Chapter 1 prohibition – similar to Article 81) and prohibition of abuse of dominant position (Chapter 2 prohibition – similar to Article 82).

- The Competition Commission regulates mergers and hears appeals against decisions made by the Director General of Fair Trading.

Self-test questions

Numbers in brackets refer to the paragraphs above where your answers can be checked.

1   In the Competition Act 1998, what is the Chapter 1 prohibition? (1.6, 1.7)

2   What was decided in the case of **South Yorkshire Transport Ltd v MMC**? (1.31)

3   Broadly, what is regulated by Articles 81 and 82 of the EC Treaty? (2.2, 2.6)

4   How does Article 82 define a monopoly position? (2.7)

5   What are the objectives of the WTO? (2.10)

CHAPTER 21

The Law of Intellectual Property

Learning objectives and indicative content

4.1   Analyse the statutory provisions applicable to a range of intellectual property rights (IPR).

- •   Patents
- •   Trade marks
- •   Design rights
- •   Copyright
- •   IPR protection through contractual clauses

4.2   Examine the common law rules relating to confidentiality and the protection of trade secrets in English law and analyse their importance in purchasing and supply.

- •   Tort of passing-off
- •   Breach of confidence

Chapter headings

1   Patents

2   Design rights

3   Trade marks

4   Copyright

5   Confidential information and trade secrets

6   Intellectual property protection through contractual clauses

Introduction

Businesses often expend considerable time and money developing ideas, processes, designs and other intangible assets that will enable them to generate profits. Once they have done so, they are naturally concerned to ensure that they reap the benefits without disturbance from others. The law assists them in this by providing a range of measures to protect such 'intellectual property'. These laws derive from both common law and statute.

Technological inventions may be protected by the law relating to patents. Products carrying a distinctive design may be protected by the law relating to registered designs. The goodwill attaching to a particular mark or logo used by a business may be protected by the law of trade marks and service marks. Other protection is afforded by the law of copyright. Much of the protection is statutory – contained especially in the Copyright, Designs and Patents Act 1988 (the 1988 Act) – but common law rules also have a role to play.

1   *Patents*

The scope of patent law

1.1   An individual or organisation that has invented a new device, or a new process, may apply for a patent to be granted. The word 'invented' here is important: patent law does not apply to discovery of something that already exists. For example, you cannot patent oxygen, because that has existed in the atmosphere for billions of years. However, if you invent a new chemical process to exploit oxygen commercially you could apply for a patent covering the process.

1.2   To qualify for patent protection, your bright idea must satisfy certain criteria.

- It must not be in one of the categories excluded under the Patents Act 1977. Such categories include discoveries such as those discussed above, and certain specific items such as computer software. While computer software may be protected by copyright, pressure is growing from the European Union to grant patent status to computer programs. The United Kingdom Intellectual Property Office is currently preparing a response to a consultation paper inviting its views on the subject. In the United States it is already possible to patent computer programs.

- It must be an invention made or used in industry.

- It must be new.

- It must be something that would not be obvious to a large number of people.

1.3   It is clear that many commercial products, industrial processes and synthetic materials would fall into the category of patentable inventions.

1.4   Pursuant to the complex provisions of Directive 98/44/EC, patent protection has been extended to include biotechnological inventions. Member states are required to protect these under their national patent laws (article 1).

1.5   'Biological material' is defined as any material containing genetic information and capable of reproducing itself or of being reproduced in a biological system (article 2). For the purposes of the directive, inventions which are either new, or which involve an inventive step and which are susceptible of an industrial application shall be patentable, even if they contain biological material. Such material which is isolated from its natural environment, or produced by way of a technical process, may be the subject of an invention, even if it previously occurred in nature (article 3).

1.6   Plant and animal varieties and essentially biological processes for the production of plants and animals are expressly declared **not** to be patentable (article 4).

1.7   Inventions which are contrary to public morality or public order are declared to be unpatentable. These include processes for cloning human beings, the use of human embryos for industrial or commercial purposes, processes for modifying the genetic identity of human beings and processes for modifying the genetic identity of animals which are likely to cause them suffering without substantial medical benefits to humans or animals (article 6).

1.8   Member states were required to amend their domestic law to accord with the directive by 30 July 2000 (article 19).

1.9   It is clear that many commercial products, industrial processes or synthetic materials would fall into the category of patentable inventions.

1.10   What happens if an employee, such as a member of the research and development department, finds a new invention while working for his employer? The answer is that such an invention belongs to his employer, but there are provisions to ensure that the employee is compensated if the invention is of outstanding benefit to the employer. Any attempt in the employee's contract of employment to limit this right is unenforceable.

1.11   If the employee finds the invention during his spare time, it belongs to himself alone.

1.12   To decide whether an invention really contains something new – something which is an addition to the previous state of the art – searches are undertaken by the Intellectual Property Office (see below).

Registration of a patent

1.13   To secure protection for an invention, the owner applies to the Intellectual Property Office for the award of a patent. There is a register in which each patent granted is listed along with the date of the grant. This date is important in settling disputes over priority of invention.

1.14   A patent lasts for 20 years. Each year a fee is payable to prevent the patent from lapsing. The amount of the fee rises as the patent grows older.

1.15   The right given by the patent is that of control over the use of the invention. The patent holder is in effect given monopoly rights in the commercial exploitation of the invention. He may of course choose to grant others a licence to participate in such exploitation if he is not able, or does not wish, to manage the whole process himself.

1.16   A UK patent is just what it says: it affords protection within the UK. Thus if a competitor company without permission manufactures a product patented by your company, and does so in the UK, he infringes your patent. However, an overseas competitor could manufacture the product without restriction, except that he could not export it to the UK. To protect themselves against this, it is open to inventors to apply for a patent in other countries as well as their home country. In particular, it is common to seek a patent from the European Patent Office affording protection in all member states of the European Union.

1.17   If a patent is infringed, a civil action may be brought to seek an injunction to prevent further abuse, as well as damages or an account of profits. A person infringes a patent if he does any of the following things without the consent of the owner of the patent.

- He makes, disposes of, uses or imports a product covered by the patent.
- He uses a process covered by the patent, or offers it for use, when he knows, or a reasonable person would know, that its use would be an infringement.
- He disposes of, offers to dispose of, uses or imports any product obtained by means of the process or keeps any such product for disposal or otherwise.

The Patents Act 2004

1.18   The Patents Act 2004 was designed to update, modernise and improve UK patent law and bring it into line with the revised European Patent Convention. The Act is being brought into force by a series of Commencement Orders. The second of these Orders came into force on 1 January 2005.

1.19　One change has been made to the current compensation provisions. Whereas previously, an employee's compensation claim could be based only on the benefit the employer derived from the patent, now account can also be taken of the benefit derived from the invention. It will no longer be necessary to decide whether the benefit is from the patent or from the invention.

1.20　The existing provisions were often thought to be unduly restrictive for patent owners. The changes clarify the situations in which allegations of infringement can be made without fear of falling foul of the unjustified threats provisions.

1.21　It will no longer be necessary to seek permission to file abroad unless the application relates to military technology or contains information, the publication of which might be prejudicial to national security or the safety of the public.

1.22　The financial circumstances of the parties will now be a relevant factor in the assessment of costs in patent infringement litigation. This should provide some reassurance to individuals or small businesses involved in infringement proceedings.

2　*Design rights*

Registered and unregistered designs

2.1　The term 'design' refers to the features of shape, pattern or ornament applied to an article by an industrial process. In the case of registered designs (though not in the case of unregistered designs) these features must be such as to appeal to, and to be judged by, the eye; they do not include features that are purely functional.

2.2　For example, a company manufacturing a distinctive article of leisure wear, such as a sweatshirt, might be concerned to ensure that competitors do not copy their design.

2.3　Such a design may be registered at the UK Intellectual Property Office. If this is done, the owner of the design will enjoy protection for five years, and this can be extended in five-year periods to a maximum of 25 years.

2.4　Even if the design is unregistered, an automatic design right ('unregistered design right') attaches for a period of ten years from the end of the year when the article is first marketed, or 15 years after it was first designed, whichever period expires sooner. During the last five years of this period anyone may obtain a licence to make the article by paying a royalty to the owner. The rate of such royalty is fixed by the Intellectual Property Office unless agreed between the parties.

2.5　Unregistered design right does not attach to items which 'must fit' or 'must match' some larger item. For example, a motor manufacturer enjoys the right in relation to the overall design of his car, but not to a body panel which 'must fit' a particular model of car. If the right extended this far, motor manufacturers would in effect enjoy a monopoly in respect of the spare parts required for their cars, and this would restrict competition. This is the rule established in the famous case of **British Leyland v Armstrong Patents** (1986).

2.6　If a design right is infringed, whether registered or unregistered, the remedies are an injunction, plus damages or an account of profits.

3 Trade marks

Unregistered trade marks

3.1 Businesses make extensive use of trade marks to distinguish their products and services from those of other businesses. There is value to the business in maintaining the loyalty of customers who have tried their products and wish to come back for more. Abuse of such a trade mark (or service mark) by a party not entitled to it can cost the business lost sales.

3.2 To remedy this the law provides safeguards for both registered and unregistered trade marks. A trade mark is defined in the Trade Marks Act 1994 as any sign which is capable of being represented graphically and which is capable of distinguishing goods or services of one undertaking from those of other undertakings. It includes the shape of goods or of their packaging. (This overturns the decision **in Coca Cola Trade Marks** (1986) in which it was held that a Coca Cola bottle could not be registered as a trade mark. The statute thus remedies an anomaly in the case law, because it was held in **Smith, Kline & French v Sterling-Winthrop Group** (1975) that the entire surface of a two-colour pill could be registered.)

3.3 Marks which are devoid of any distinctive character or consist exclusively of signs or indications which describe the character or quality of goods or which have become customary in current language on in the *bona fide* and established practices of a trade may not be registered.

Passing off

3.4 In the case of an unregistered mark, the main recourse for the business is to bring an action for the tort of 'passing off'. The term refers to the action of a person or organisation that deceives the public by deliberately causing confusion with another (usually much better known) person or organisation. This might happen for example if the person used wrappings or other identifications similar to those of the better known person. For example, in **Reckitt and Colman v Borden** (1990) the defendants were not allowed to use packaging that closely resembled that of the claimant.

3.5 The case of **Hodgkinson & Corby v Wards Mobility Services** (1994) establishes that there must be an element of deception to justify an action for passing off. The court held that copying a product *per se* is not unlawful. Passing off could only be established where the public would be deceived into believing that they were buying from one source, when in fact they were buying from another.

3.6 It must be shown that the public are not simply concerned with the appearance of the article, but also with its trade origin. Nor is it an offence if a trader uses his own name, even if his name happens also to be that of a better known company: **Wright, Layman & Umney Ltd v Wright** (1949).

3.7 To succeed in a passing off action it is necessary to show that the goods you seek to protect are known to the public. It is not necessary to show that the defendant used an identical mark; it is enough if it was similar enough to cause public confusion. The remedies are an injunction, plus damages or an account of profits. The plaintiff may also secure an order for obliteration of the offending mark.

3.8   A key recent case in this area is **The World Wildlife Fund v World Wrestling Association** (2002). The WWF (a private environmental conservation organisation) sued over use of the name World Wrestling Federation (also known as 'WWF'). The court agreed that the Federation had violated a 1994 agreement with Titan Sports Inc which had limited the permissible use of the WWF initials overseas, particularly in merchandising. In 2002, the company announced an official name change from World Wrestling Federation to World Wrestling Entertainment (WWE). It was also ordered by the court to stop using the WWF initials in some logo forms, as it no longer owned the trademark to the initials WWF in 'specified circumstances': it may use the full 'World Wrestling Federation' name.

Registered trade marks

3.9   A registered trade mark is one which has been registered with the Registrar. The register used to consist of Part A and Part B, the former providing the stronger protection, but also being more difficult to obtain. The Trade Marks Act 1994 abolishes this distinction: there is now only one category of trade mark.

3.10   It is obviously an infringement of a trade mark if the same mark is used on goods or services identical to those covered by a registration. However, the protection goes further than this. A mark need only be similar to the registered mark, and need only be used on goods similar to those covered by the registered mark (so as to arouse a possibility of public confusion). Even if the goods on which the offending mark is used are dissimilar there may still be an infringement if the owner of the registered mark has a reputation in the UK in respect of that mark.

3.11   However, where the use of identical or similar marks on **dissimilar** goods arises, it has been held that, for infringement to take place, there must be the likelihood of confusion. In **Baywatch Production Co Ltd v The Home Video Channel** (1997) it was held that 'adult' television broadcasts and video tapes were dissimilar products so that the use of 'Babewatch' on video tapes was not likely to cause confusion with 'Baywatch' on television. The case was lost.

3.12   The definition of a trade mark (see above) is a wide one. It means that the shape of goods (subject to certain limitations) or their packaging may be registered, as may sounds or smells if they meet the requirement of distinctiveness and are capable of being represented graphically.

3.13   It is now possible to apply for a Community trade mark, which offers Community-wide protection. Application is made to the Office for Harmonization of the Internal Market at Alicante, Spain. The processing of applications commenced in April 1996, and this protection is much in demand.

4   *Copyright*

The scope of copyright

4.1   The 1988 Act gives protection to any original literary, dramatic, musical and artistic work that has not previously been published. Computer programs, rather surprisingly, come under this definition. So too does graphic work, including drawings, charts or plans. Product catalogues and advertising literature would also fit the bill.

4.2   Copyright of the work is in the first instance vested in its author, though in some cases the person paying the author may make it a condition of the contract that copyright is to belong to himself. This is normal practice in cases where an employee is the author: in such cases the employer will normally own the copyright.

4.3   There are no formalities such as registration. The right to protection arises automatically. It used to endure for 50 years from the end of the calendar year in which the author died. However, the duration of many copyrights was extended at the end of 1995 as part of the programme of harmonisation within the European Community. For literary, dramatic, musical and artistic works, copyright now expires 70 years from the end of the calendar year in which the author dies.

4.4   Infringement of copyright usually means that someone has copied a work created by someone else, or made an adaptation of it. Merely copying ideas is not a breach of copyright, but if the words, illustrations, examples etc are copied an action may be brought.

4.5   As usual, the remedies are an injunction, plus damages or an account of profits.

5   *Confidential information and trade secrets*

5.1   Certain information is protected as confidential if it has: 'the necessary quality of confidence about it, namely, it must not be something which is public property and public knowledge' (**Saltman Engineering Co Ltd v Campbell Engineering Co Ltd** (1963)). It should be of some gravity, and not mere 'tittle-tattle'. It is protected by the common law, equity and breach of contract.

5.2   Examples of confidential information are personal secrets (now protected to a degree by the European Convention on Human Rights), commercial records, trade secrets, government secrets and ideas: **Ackroyds (London) Ltd v Islington Plastics Ltd** (1962).

Ackroyds took its own design for a novel item to the plastics company to see if it could be manufactured. The plastics company produced copies of the design and sold them.

Held: this was clearly a breach of confidentiality irrespective of the fact that the contract between the companies was silent on the matter.

5.3   Even if a person already knows the information, he is obliged to keep it to himself if he knows it to be confidential. In addition, it should still be kept confidential even after it has been published, to avoid damage through repetition.

5.4   With regard to prototypes and ideas, for a claim of breach of confidence to be successful the claimant must prove a number of things: **De Maudsley v Palumbo and others** (1996).

The claimant raised his ideas for a unique new nightclub at a dinner party. Afterwards the defendants opened the Ministry of Sound club, which the claimant said was based on his ideas.

Held: There was no claim for breach of confidence. For this to be successful, the claimant had to show that the idea:

•   Contains some significant element of originality

•   Is clearly identifiable as the claimant's idea

- Is of potential commercial attractiveness
- Is sufficiently well developed as to be capable of actual realisation

5.5 An employee owes a duty of faithful service to his employer, and the employer may rely on that duty to protect trade secrets: **Robb v Green** (1895).

An employee on leaving his employment took with him a copy of his employer's customer list. He then set up in competition, making use of the list to solicit business from his former employer's customers.

Held: The employee's conduct was a breach of the common law duty of good faith, and the employer was entitled to an injunction and damages.

5.6 Note that this right is quite independent of the restrictions that might appear specifically in the employment contract, as in a restraint of trade clause.

5.7 To succeed in an action of this kind, the aggrieved employer must show that the information abused by the employee was confidential, that it was given to him in a situation suggesting confidentiality and that there has been either an actual disclosure or a threatened disclosure.

5.8 Important tests were laid down in the leading case of **Thomas Marshall v Guinle** (1978). Four factors were identified as suggesting that information ranked as confidential.

- The information must be such that the owner believes its release would be injurious to him or of advantage to his rivals or others.
- The owner must believe the information is confidential or secret, ie not already in the public domain.
- The owner's belief under the two previous headings must be reasonable.
- The information must be judged in the light of the usages and practices of the particular industry concerned.

5.9 The law draws a distinction between confidential information (which is protected) and general knowledge and skills acquired by the employee in the course of his employment. The courts will not uphold any effort to prevent the defendant from using such knowledge and skills.

5.10 A leading case in this area is that of **Faccenda Chicken v Fowler** (1986), in which the following factors were held to be relevant in deciding whether the information was confidential.

- Whether the defendant was regularly exposed in his employment to confidential information, so that he should have been aware that it was confidential.
- Whether the information was truly confidential, ie in the nature of a trade secret.
- Whether its confidential nature was brought sufficiently to the attention of the employee.

5.11 An action for breach of confidential information will generally be to seek damages for loss suffered as a result of the breach. If the confidential information can be identified with precision then an injunction may be granted. But this will not be granted in the case of non-deliberate use of confidential information: **Seager v Copydex** (1967).

6 *Intellectual property protection through contractual clauses*

6.1 There will be many contracts where ownership of intellectual property is an issue, such as licensing and technology contracts, or when a manufacturer of goods first develops and manufactures them with guidance from the buyer. It will then be necessary for a provision relating to the ownership, use and other matters relating to those intellectual property rights to be included as a clause in the contract documentation.

6.2 The model clause set out below firstly defines what the parties mean by the term 'intellectual property rights'. The clause then establishes where the ownership of the intellectual property is to lie. Finally, the clause goes on to grant the other party a licence to use the intellectual property.

6.3 Intellectual property rights – model clause

'Intellectual property' means all rights in patents, registered and unregistered designs, copyright, trade marks, know-how and all other forms of intellectual property wherever in the world enforceable.

All intellectual property rights used in or produced from or arising as a result of the performance of this contract shall, so far as not already so vested, become the absolute property of the Client, and the Supplier will do all that is reasonably necessary to ensure that such rights vest in the Client (as, without prejudice to the foregoing) by the execution of appropriate instruments, or the making of agreements with third parties.

At the Client's discretion, it shall grant the Supplier a licence to use such intellectual property on such terms as to time, extent and royalty, and other appropriate matters, as the Client deems appropriate.'

Chapter summary

* Patent protection is available for new inventions made or used in industry.

* Design rights attach to features of shape, pattern or ornament applied to an article by an industrial process.

* Trade mark protection arises in common law for the tort of passing off, and also arises under the Trade Marks Act 1994 for registered marks.

* Copyright applies to original literary, dramatic, musical and artistic work that has not previously been published.

* Confidential information is protected by the common law duty of good faith owed by an employee to his employer. Damages or an injunction may be awarded for breach of confidence.

* Intellectual property rights may be protected through contractual clauses.

Self-test questions

Numbers in brackets refer to the paragraphs above where your answers can be checked.

1   What criteria must be satisfied before a product or process may be patented? (1.2)

2   What happens if an employee finds a new invention in the course of his employment? (1.10)

3   How long does patent protection last for? (1.14)

4   What is meant by the term 'design'? (2.1)

5   What is meant by the 'must fit' or 'must match' exemption? (2.5)

6   What was established in the case of **Hodgkinson & Corby v Wards Mobility Services**? (3.5)

7   How long does copyright last? (4.3)

8   Define confidential information. (5.1)

9   What were the facts in **Robb v Green**? (5.5)

10 What factors were identified as important in the case of **Thomas Marshall v Guinle**? (5.8)

CHAPTER 22

Mock Exam

This exam is adapted from the May 2003 Legal Aspects paper.

Instructions

You should attempt to simulate exam conditions as far as possible in attempting this CIPS paper. When you have read the instructions below, turn the page and attempt the paper.

- **Section A**. Attempt both questions. You should spend approximately 90 minutes on this section. This section carries 50 marks.

- **Section B**. Attempt *two* questions. You should spend approximately 45 minutes on each question attempted. This section carries 50 marks; each question carries 25 marks.

- Time allowed: *three hours*.

Section A

Read the following case study information before attempting all the tasks.

Aquarius Ltd (AL) is a major company which holds a dominant position in the UK market in the manufacture of a particular genetic disorder treatment. It has a subsidiary in Germany that manufactures the treatment. It also licenses a Swiss company to manufacture limited amounts of the treatment.

AL does not hold a dominant market position within the European Single Market in medical products generally, but it does in relation to this treatment.

AL wants to replace all its computers in its UK offices with a new comprehensive system. It invites tenders for the provision and installation of the equipment from various computer companies with which it has dealt before. The letter inviting the tenders includes the collateral obligation statement: 'if the offer made by you is the lowest offer received by us, we bind ourselves to accept such offer'.

In response to the letter, Tiger Computers Ltd (TCL) bids £400,000, while Cheeta Ltd (CL) bids £325,000 or £5,000 less than any lower bid.

AL awards the contract to TCL. AL then places the order, stating that the contract was to be on the basis of its standard terms and conditions. TCL accepts, but the acceptance is on its contract form which comprises its own standard terms which include a price-variation clause.

Within the contract to replace all the computers at AL, TCL agrees to service the computers. TCL intends to outsource the servicing of the computers to Lyons Maintenance Systems (LMS). LMS has insufficient staff but within the service contract it agrees to a transfer of 20 of TCL's staff.

1	Evaluate AL's position with regard to competition law.	**(25 marks)**

2(a)	Explain the tendering process and what effect the insertion of the collateral obligation statement has in this case. What is Cheeta Ltd's position?	**(13 marks)**
2(b)	Discuss the relevant employment implications created by the outsourced activity in the case.	**(12 marks)**

(Total 25 marks)

Section B

Answer two questions.

3   Alpha plc contracts to sell 200 tables to Omega plc. The tables designed for Omega plc were stolen on their journey to Omega plc and sold to Xeron plc. Explain the *nemo dat* rule and describe whether the exceptions will apply in this case.   **(25 marks)**

4   Outline the main alternatives to litigation for settling a commercial dispute.   **(25 marks)**

5   Discuss the remedies available for misrepresentation with reference to case law and appropriate legislation. Consider whether the law provides an adequate solution where a **person is induced to enter into a contract by misrepresentation**.

(25 marks)

6   'Once an agent has brought their principal and third party into a contractual relationship, the agent drops out and has no rights or liabilities.'

Evaluate this statement, including a consideration of the exceptions that may apply.

(25 marks)

CHAPTER 23

Mock Exam: Suggested Solutions

From the optional questions we have selected Questions 3 and 6. For Question 4 you should refer to Chapter 10, and for Question 5 you should refer to Chapter 7 of your Course Book.

1   The Competition Act 1998 outlaws any agreements concluded in the course of business practice, formal or informal, oral or in writing, which have a damaging effect on competition in the UK. It applies to all types and sizes of business including sole traders.

The effects of non-compliance include the following:

- investigation by the Office of Fair Trading;
- financial penalty of up to 10 per cent of UK turnover;
- agreements made will be void and unenforceable;
- adverse publicity;
- possibility of being sued by those affected by unlawful agreement.

The Enterprise Act 2002 has made significant reforms and removed certain exemptions from the effect of existing competition legislation and has strengthened enforcement measures in the UK, including possible imprisonment for five years and disqualification as a director. The new provisions work alongside the Competition Act 1998. The OFT is now a corporate body replacing the Director-general of Fair Trading. The OFT applies and enforces the new competition measures alongside a Competition Commission and the Competition Appeal Tribunal.

Is AL engaged in anti-competitive agreements? Has AL contravened the Competition Act 1998 Chapter 1? This affects, *inter alia*, contracts agreeing to:

- fix purchase or selling prices or other trading conditions;
- limit or control production markets, technical development or investment;
- share markets or supply sources;
- make contracts subject to unrelated conditions;
- apply different trading conditions on equivalent transactions thereby placing some parties at a competitive disadvantage.

Is AL's conduct an abuse of a dominant market position? The Competition Act 1998 Chapter 2, which mirrors EC Article 82, shows a dominant market position to be demonstrated by, *inter alia*:

- imposing unfair purchase or selling price;
- limiting production markets or technical development to the prejudice of consumers;

- applying different trade conditions to equivalent transactions thereby placing certain persons at competitive disadvantage;

- attaching unrelated supplementary conditions to contracts.

When considering the impact of the agreements it is worth noting that Germany is in the EU, but Switzerland is not.

2   (a)   [*This is essentially a bookwork question. See Chapter 18.*]

How should a tender be arranged and managed? What are the rules and procedures? Are they fair and equitable to all parties?

A key recent case in respect of the tendering process and a case which is regularly discussed in the CIPS paper is *Blackpool & Fylde Aero Club v Blackpool Borough Council* (1990). See also *R v The National Lottery Commission (ex parte Camelot plc)* (2000). If a referential bid system is to be adopted, all parties should be made aware of this: *Harvela Royal Investments Ltd v Royal Bank of Canada* (1986).

Cheeta's bid is referential and will not be considered, since we are not told that all parties were informed that this was an option.

(b)   Transfer of undertakings and outsourcing involves buying in expertise from an outside body in replacement of an internal department. TUPE Transfer of Undertakings (Protection Of Employment) Regulations 1981, amended by the EC Acquired Rights Directive 1988 and the Employment Act 2002, are at issue here.

You must explain:

- what is a transfer of undertakings?

- is this a relevant transfer?

- has there been a proper consultation process with appropriate representatives?

- what is outsourcing – another name for redundancy?

- if this is not legitimate, is it unfair dismissal?

- five fair and five automatically unfair reasons for dismissal.

- an unfair procedure for dismissal may lead to reinstatement, re-engagement and damages of various types (identical to redundancy but for the enhanced awards arising from dismissal as a result of race and/or sex discrimination).

[*See Chapters 18 and 19.*]

3   [*See Chapters 11–13.*]

Sale of Goods Act 1979 ss 21–25 states that a sale of goods contract requires the successful transfer of risk and title. A owns tables; A sells to O; the goods are stolen; title remains with A and the tables are sold to X. We presume that an unknown third party sold to X. Good title remains with A and X must return goods to A unless X falls within one of the exceptions of the *nemo dat* rule. The *nemo dat quod non habet* rule states that a person cannot give what he does not possess. Therefore if the seller of the goods (in this case, tables) does not have good title, and the buyer (in this case X) cannot acquire a better title to the tables than the unknown seller had, the title and ownership remain with the person from whom the goods have been stolen.

The *nemo dat* rule must be explained followed by the exceptions to the rule [see Chapter 12]:

• estoppel

• sale under voidable title

• sale by a seller in possession

• sale by a buyer in possession

• sale by a mercantile agent

• sale of a motor vehicle under hire purchase

• sale under special powers

Explain the nature of the exceptions – eg what is a sale by a buyer in possession, etc, and apply each one to the scenario. Do any of the exceptions apply?

You should conclude that Xeron Ltd did not have good title to the consignment.

6 Agents may be divided into two categories – general or special – and further subdivided between factor, broker, and commercial and *del credere* agents. Agency is the relationship between agent and principal, and arises in a variety of ways – for one task or for a number of years; expressly, impliedly, by ratification, by estoppel, or by necessity. To complete the contextual introduction it will also be important to outline the nature and extent of the agent's authority, whether it is actual authority, express, implied, or apparent authority. It will also be important to outline the nature of the agency relationship with third parties if there is a disclosed or an undisclosed principal.

The examination question says 'once an agent has brought their principal and third party into a contractual relationship the agent drops out and has no rights or liabilities'.

This is largely true, as the majority of contracts derived from agency relationships will have very clear boundaries and authority and the liabilities will cease at the time the contract is signed. But there are several points to bear in mind.

• There may be reasons why the agent's liability will continue, and this could be as a result of contractual negotiations which will be upheld so long as the terms do not fall foul of the Unfair Contracts Terms Act 1977.

• In certain trades it is normal in the course of trade or business that the agent retains liability, and this will be provided for in the contract between agent and principal.

• If an agent acts outside his actual authority the principal will not be bound, although the principal could decide to ratify the contract. [*See Chapter 17.*] If the principal has allowed third parties to believe that the agent has had, and continues to have, unbounded authority, then the principal will still be liable [see *Watteau v Fenwick* (1891); Chapter 17].

• An agent will be liable if there is an undisclosed agency: *Humble v Hunter* (1948).

• An agent will be liable if he declares there is an agency and it does not exist: *UK Mutual SS Assurance Association v Nevill* (1987).

Index of Legal Cases

Subject Index